# Commercial Agreements and Social Dynamics in Medieval Genoa

*Commercial Agreements and Social Dynamics in Medieval Genoa* is an empirical study of medieval long-distance trade agreements and the surrounding social dynamics that transformed the feudal organization of men-of-arms into the world of Renaissance merchants. Making use of 20,000 notarial records, the book traces the commercial partnerships of thousands of people in Genoa from 1150 to 1435 and reports social activity, on a scale that is unprecedented for such an early period of history anywhere.

In combining a detailed historical reading with network modeling to analyze the change in the long-distance trade relationships, Quentin Van Doosselaere challenges the prevailing Western-centric view of development by demonstrating that the history of the three main medieval economic frameworks that brought about European capitalism – equity, credit, and insurance – was not driven by strategic merchants' economic optimizations but rather by a change in partners' selections that reflected the dynamic of the social structure as a whole.

Dr. Quentin Van Doosselaere is a Research Fellow at Nuffield College. He combines training in sociology and business administration to focus on the emergence of capitalism at the end of the medieval period. Adding formal network analysis tools to detailed archival research, Dr. Van Doosselaere has studied the social foundations underpinning the economic changes that initiated the Western dominance in global economic exchange. The multidisciplinary nature of his research has resulted in invitations to present his work to Business, Economics, History, and Sociology Departments in both Europe and the United States.

# Commercial Agreements and Social Dynamics in Medieval Genoa

## QUENTIN VAN DOOSSELAERE

*Nuffield College, Oxford University*

CAMBRIDGE
UNIVERSITY PRESS

CAMBRIDGE UNIVERSITY PRESS
Cambridge, New York, Melbourne, Madrid, Cape Town, Singapore, São Paulo, Delhi

Cambridge University Press
32 Avenue of the Americas, New York, NY 10013-2473, USA

www.cambridge.org
Information on this title: www.cambridge.org/9780521897921

First published 2009

Printed in the United States of America

A catalog record for this publication is available from the British Library.

Library of Congress Cataloging in Publication data
Van Doosselaere, Quentin, 1961–
    Commercial agreements and social dynamics in medieval
    Genoa / Quentin van Doosselaere.
        p.   cm.
    Includes bibliographical references and index.
    ISBN 978-0-521-89792-1 (hardback)
        1. Genoa (Italy) – Commerce – History.   2. Commerce – History –
    Medieval, 500–1500.   3. Merchants – Italy – Genoa – History.
    4. Genoa (Italy) – Social life and customs.   I. Title.
    HF3590.G4V36 2009
    382'.94518210902–dc22          2008035715

ISBN 978-0-521-89792-1 hardback

*To my Risë. May she overcome the odds.*

# Contents

# List of Figures

# List of Tables

# Abbreviations

## Currency

£       Genoese pound
FL     Genoese florin

## Unpublished Primary Sources

BA     Balard, Michel. Unpublished transcripts of notarial records. References in Balard, Michel. 1978. *La Romanie Génoise: XIIème-début du XVème siècle*. Rome: École française de Rome, pp. 678–82.

JE     Jehel, Georges. Unpublished transcripts of notarial records. References in Jehel, Georges. 1993. *Les Génois en Méditerranée occidentale (fin XIème – début XIVème siècle): ébauche d'une stratégie pour un empire*. Amiens: Centre d'histoire des sociétés Université de Picardie, pp. 480–2.

## Published Primary Sources

Annales    Airaldi, Gabriella. 2002. *Gli annali di Caffaro: 1099–1163*. Genoa: Fratelli Frilli

BO¹     Eierman, Joyce E., Hilmar C. Kruger, and Robert L. Reynolds (Eds.). 1939. *Bonvillano*. Turin: S. Lattes.

---

¹ The number that follows each abbreviation in the text refers the number of a specific notarial record and the date when (month and year) the record was minuted. For example, the abbreviation BO#224/December 1198 refers to the notarial record number 224 minuted in December 1198 by the notary Bonvillano as it was classified by Eierman, Kruger, and Reynolds (1939).

CA          Hall, Margaret, Hilmar C. Kruger, Renert G. Ruth, and
            Robert L. Reynolds (Eds.). 1938. *Guglielmo Cassinese*. Turin:
            S. Lattes.

CD          Imperiale di Sant' Angelo, Cesare, and Genoa (Republic).
            1936, 1938, and 1942. *Codice diplomatico della republica di
            Genova, I–III*. Rome: Tipografia del Senato.

DO          Doehaerd, Renée. 1941. *Les Relations commerciales entre
            Gênes, la Belgique et l'Outremont, d'après les archives
            notariales génoises aux XIIIème et XIVème siècles*. Brussels:
            Academica Belgica.

GI          Hall-Cole, Margaret, Hilmar C. Kruger, Ruth G. Renert, and
            Robert L. Reynolds (Eds.). 1939. *Giovanni di Guiberto*.
            Turin: S. Lattes.

KE          Doehaerd, Renée, and Charles Kerremans. 1952. *Les
            Relations commerciales entre Gênes, la Belgique et
            l'Outremont, d'après les archives notariales génoises,
            1400–1440*. Brussels: Academica Belgica.

LA          Krueger, Hilmar C., and Robert L. Reynolds (Eds.). 1951–53.
            *Lanfranco*. Genoa: Societa Ligure di Storia Patria.

LO          Lopez, Roberts. 1953. "L'attività economica di Genova nel
            Marzo 1253 secondo li atti notarili del tempo." *ASLI* 54:
            163–270.

OB1         Bach, Erik. 1955. "Mercato Oberto Scriba de." In *La cité de
            Gênes au XIIème siècle*, pp.150–76. Copenhagen:
            Gyldendalske boghandel.

OB2         Chiaudano, Mario, and R. M. della Rocca (Eds.). 1940.
            *Oberto Scriba de Mercato, 1186*. Turin: S. Lattes.

OB3         Chiaudano, Mario, and R. M. della Rocca (Eds.). 1938.
            *Oberto Scriba de Mercato, 1190*. Turin: S. Lattes.

S           Chiaudano, Mario, and Mattia Moresco (Eds.). 1935. *Il
            cartolare di Giovanni Scriba*. Rome: S. Lattes.

STU         Liagre De Sturler, Léone, and Archivio di Stato di Genova.
            1969. *Les relations commerciales entre Gênes, la Belgique et
            l'Outremont, d'après les archives notariales génoises, 1320–
            1400*. Brussels, Rome: Institut historique belge de Rome
            Galerie Ravenstein 78; Academia Belgica.

# Acknowledgments

Peter Bearman, Charles Tilly, and Harrison White were the three people who most shaped my sociological practice while I was at Columbia University.

I adopted Peter Bearman's commitment to theory and empirical testing. His interest in history matched my own, and his creative and crisp observations got me back on track more than once. For his part, the late Charles Tilly's ability to strip down issues to their core and his prodigious bibliographical knowledge helped me to connect my findings to a variety of historical and sociological studies. Coming from someone as prolific as he was, his quick responsiveness to my queries was, I thought, an endorsement.

Harrison White's influence was more diffuse, but his creative intelligence was in the back of my mind when I was trying to make sense of 900-year-old social ties. Aside from his scholarly inspiration, his unwavering enthusiasm for my work and the warmth of his support were a welcome boost during the lonely hours of number crunching.

I also had the good fortune to work with Martha Howell, who introduced me to historians' rigorous handling of evidence and convinced me to polish up my high school Latin in order to read medieval notarial records. Long discussions with Max Likin sharpened my thoughts about the relations between history and sociology and helped me to find a style appropriate for both fields of study. In that regard, I am also thankful to Karen Barkey for comments at various stages of my research.

Balazs Vedres helped me in the early phase of my network analysis. His input during a few working weekends in his hometown of Budapest was key to unlocking several methodological problems. In New York,

I had the chance to count on Eric Vanden Eijnden, whose eclectic mind and mathematical excellence were instrumental when analyzing the Genoese insurance network.

While a Research Fellow at Nuffield College, the serene environment of Oxford University was a perfect setting in which to finish and then revise my manuscript. In particular, participation in various seminars as well as conversations with Peter Hedström and Meredith Rolfe reassured me that I was on the right path.

I am indebted to George Jehel and Michel Balard, two leading historians of medieval Genoa, who very graciously allowed me to consult their respective private collections of transcripts, which account for years of research on the Genoese archives.

The translation and encoding of thousands of notarial contracts was a long and grinding process. At various times, Anna Rockwell, Thomas Van Doosselaere, and Paule Maillet assisted me with portions of the project. Jennine Lanouette and Russell Hahn helped me clean up my prose. At Cambridge University Press, Lewis Bateman and Emily Spangler guided me through the editing process.

Finally, I could have not written this book without the love and emotional support of friends and family. My children, Lola, Mathilde, and Theo, balanced my obsessive scientific pursuit with their wonderful desire to share their own discovery of the world. Michel, Cecile, and Ellen continued to cheer their son on. Xavier, Denis, and Thierry provided brotherly encouragement. During a period when my family needed it the most, I was extraordinarily fortunate that Allen Sperry, Karyn Zieve-Cohen, Billy Shebar, Katie Geissinger, Marc Osten, Colleen Manning, John Shelton, Didier Brassine, Tomasine Dolan, Whitney Dow, Natalie Marshall, Andreas Kaubisch, Nancy Isenberg, Loic Gosselin, Pierre Dupont, France Passaro, Isabelle and Jim de Melor, Hans Witteveen, Klaartje Quirijns, Bill Montgomery, Elisabeth Glazer, Joe Rinaldi, Mulan Ashwin, Sarah Besso, Philippa Edgar, and Martha Petersen offered their sustained friendship and tangible help.

And to Risë, my life companion and friend to whom this book is dedicated.

I

# From Sword into Capital

At the turn of the first millennium, as is true today, the Mediterranean straddled distinct and very different communities. However, while contemporary economic power lies in the West, the reverse was true prior to the revival of medieval long-distance trade.

From the time of antique trading, commerce in the West had slowed down nearly to a halt; the European economy had shrunk, and the decrease in population levels had sharply reduced the size of urban centers. Even the largest Italian ports were nothing more than villages when compared to bustling and sophisticated eastern cities such as Constantinople, Baghdad, and Cairo. In the overall context of the subsistence economy of the early medieval West, urban centers had in some ways offered fewer economic opportunities than the countryside. Whatever degree of importance the medieval cities had managed to maintain was often not because of their role as commercial meeting points but, rather, because of the military protection they could provide against the regular marauding of pirates and other invaders.

As the millennium approached, the balance of power changed and European communities, which had been in decline for hundreds of years, were able once again to challenge the military supremacy of the East and eventually gain economic dominance. It is from that period until the mid fifteenth century that Italian cities, Venice and Genoa in particular, controlled the Mediterranean Sea and served as anchors for the economic expansion that subsequently led to Western domination of the rest of the world.

Historians have examined the commerce that underpinned the Western ascendancy. Italian Renaissance cities are the object of classic social historiography, and a few studies have described the emergence of innovative commercial methods that were to shape the modern economy. However, none have systematically focused on how the mercantile social organization came into being. In this book, therefore, I analyze the rise of the three main forms of medieval long-distance trade agreements – equity, credit, and insurance – while also tracing the underlying long-term social changes that in many parts of Europe, including Genoa, transformed, the preexisting social structure, organized around men-of-arms, into the new world of men-of-capital initiated by Renaissance merchants.

To do this, I coded thousands of medieval Genoese notarial records and consulted a variety of other primary sources to build a unique data set. Starting more than 900 years ago, the data set records more than 20,000 commercial relationships between individuals who, by joining their resources, gave rise to what is commonly called the medieval commercial revolution. Modeling their ventures over a 300-year period, I followed the transformation of the structure of social ties by analyzing the link between commercial agreements and social process. I was thus able to consider commercial innovations as social patterns. The critical influence of these patterns not only conditioned economic growth but also molded the rules that governed the transformation of social ties during the period, resulting in the emergence of a mercantile oligarchy within the feudal world of medieval Italy. As such, a broad objective of this book is to demonstrate the social foundation of the economic development that brought about the rise of the modern capitalist economy by studying the interplay between institutions and social interactions.

Genoa's history is a perfect arena for this type of study for several reasons. First, while history will never offer perfect laboratory conditions in which to test theories about social dynamics, for our purposes Genoa is a solid empirical site because of its shift from feudal organization to a mercantile republic, a shift that was as pronounced there as anywhere in Europe. Indeed, from a small, fortified town dominated by warriors who went to kill and plunder throughout the seas, one that lagged behind its counterparts in the early long-distance trade growth, Genoa became an economic archetype among the city-states of the Renaissance.

Second, many key medieval innovations in financial technology – the bill of exchange, double-entry bookkeeping, third-party insurance, and public finance – either originated in, or were widely disseminated from, Genoa.

Third, Genoa's records are unique in Europe in terms of their precocity, continuity, and quantity. This meant that I was able to make unprecedented use of extensive data showing relationships between individuals and groups in order to reconstruct a long-term medieval social dynamic. As such, the quantitative method presented in this book contrasts with the approaches used by previous researchers, who have had to use a thin body of evidence that is more likely to be subjectively handpicked.

Fourth, in the absence of a large routinized mercantile class, a large proportion of Genoese directly participated in the expansion of trade that occurred in the twelfth- and thirteenth-centuries. As a result, medieval commercial records include a wide variety of men and women: princes, servants, oarsmen, dozens of different kinds of artisans, bishops, lower clergymen, doctors, and schoolteachers. Because of this they provide us with remarkably deep insight into the nature of early social activity, on a scale that is simply unattainable for other European cities.

Using the resources just described, I study the institutional framework of early European long-distance trade and document the rise of occupational categories associated with it. In doing so, I identify and measure the social mechanisms that gave rise to the concentration of capital in the maritime state's dominant class and to the emergence of the Renaissance oligarchy.

By tracing the feudal[1] origin of the Genoese Commune around the time of the First Crusade (1097–99), I show that, at first, the commenda contracts (temporary equity partnerships that organized most early trading ventures) fostered heterogeneous ties with respect to status and wealth. Eventually, the expansion of trade – in a pre-market society – and the cumulative nature of its profits decoupled the feudal domination from the economy, and a quantitative change became qualitative, so much so that commoners were eventually able to compete effectively for formal control of the city.

Over time, the Genoese elite increasingly switched to commerce and credit, a framework for routinized traders, when defining their relational ties. By the middle of the fifteenth century, along with many of the noble

---

[1] The term "feudal" should always be used with caution. No medieval social system exactly conforms to the ideal-type feudal system described by Marc Bloch (1961). Still, tenth- and eleventh-century documents and various historical pieces of evidence confirm many elements of a feudal organization. Broadly speaking, in early twelfth-century Genoa, the patrimonial social system: 1) was based on service tenement (i.e., the fief); 2) was ruled by a class of specialized warriors who benefited from classic personal privileges and feudal incident not limited to the countryside; and 3) had a fragmentary judicial, political, and military authority in the city organized around topodemographic affiliation and lordships.

clans a few commoner families completed the oligarchy, and insurance ties became one of the tools used to manage its control operations. The urban patriciate had transformed its traditional resources into commercial activities tailored to a small number of clans and was completing its mutation from a medieval feudal authority to a mercantile ruling class of the Renaissance. Conversely, the feudal transitive social order characterized by its division of centralized and hierarchical local clusters was reshaped into intense social activity inside a single homogenous and cohesive elite network that was increasingly segregated from the rest of the population.

The remainder of this chapter is divided into three parts. I start by placing this book in the context of the body of scholarship that formed the background of my research and make clear where this book contrasts with it and how it contributes. I then explain some elements of the data collection and indicate the scope condition used to interpret the coded information. Finally, I describe the organization of the book and explain the chronological signification of each chapter.

MEDIEVAL SOCIAL AND ECONOMIC DEVELOPMENT

This book draws upon a wide range of social science disciplines. First, I consider the literature on the transition from feudalism to capitalism and examine, through analysis of my data set, how it confirms my findings on the false dichotomy between markets and feudalism. Indeed, contrary to the classic Marxist theory exemplified by Dobb (1947) and Holton (1985), the Genoese dominant class did not use all its power to maintain the particular mode of production that underpinned its authority. Instead, it shows that the feudal elite used new commercial institutions to control the polity and actively participated in the sustained accumulation of capital (which is Marx's precondition to capitalism). Similarly, the same empirical evidence completes more recent transition theory, such as Lachmann's elite conflict theory (2000). Lachmann, studying a slightly later period, rightly points out that the conflicts among the existing elite left sufficient room for a commercial class to grow. However, as this book shows, the elite's participation in the dynamic of commercial innovation, coupled with the multivalence of their activity, indicates the existence of shifting alliances and more flexibility of economic interest than Lachmann's elegant model can accommodate.

My work also confirms that the Italian case does not fit easily into a Weberian conception of history. In Genoa, the routinization of commerce and the pursuit of repetitive gains preceded the emergence of a bureau-cratic legal framework and did not necessarily coincide with the Weberian cultural transition from a traditional to a mean rational attitude. Indeed, twelfth- and thirteenth-century medieval trade was not strategic but opportunistic in nature, and the pursuit of financial wealth was often initiated as a by-product of military undertakings. Over time, it is the cumulative nature of profits – which contrasted with the more discrete and often dichotomic social stratification characteristics of feudal Europe – that engendered the competition for control of the polity and locked in the never-ending capitalist process of accumulation.

## Social Foundation of Economic Development

By demonstrating, over a long period, the social foundation of commer-cial arrangements, this book reaffirms the importance of social relation-ships in economic exchange. For example, the analysis of empirical evidence shows that the institutions that define the price-regulated market follow the rise of the merchant oligarchy so characteristic of the Italian Renaissance. Here, economic institutions provide the boundaries between social networks: They are a formalization of existing practices. Thus, this finding challenges directly the theories of economists such as Douglas North (1973, 1990) and Avner Greif (1998, 2006), who rely on rational choice and human motives to explain the emergence of the mercantile domination.

For North, institutional dynamics are driven by economic efficiencies. In particular, he feels that the motor of European medieval economic development is the institution of private property, which ultimately guarantees the healthy functioning of (modern) markets. According to his modernization theory, rising medieval merchants decided on clever arrangements enforced by assertive state policy on the basis of their superior economic efficiency. Others have already noted North's anach-ronistic assessment of the ability of political institutions to enforce market contracts.[2] In addition, the analysis of scalable long-distance trade net-work parameters presented in this book demonstrates that the organi-zation of trade evolved in ways that had to do with more than just strict economic dynamics.

Underlying North's conception of history, as well as that of other economic institutionalists, is the idea that economic dynamics are

---

[2] See, for example, S. R. Epstein (2000, p. 6).

powered by the rational choice of single actors under certain constraints. Numerous criticisms of the application of this outlook to historical behavior have been formulated. To summarize this debate once more is probably not necessary. Therefore, in the context of this study on partnerships and social dynamics, I will limit myself to recapitulating the most topical objections. First, individuals do not act in a social vacuum. Instead, as Harrison White notes, they intrinsically "come out of relations, out of skills in relations" (2008, p. 135). Second, individual goals, and therefore preference ordering, are dependent on social context and the social values that are constructed with others – often in asymmetric relations. In particular, to assign an economic utility function to encapsulate the role of a medieval actor is out of historical order. Even more than today, with an economic sphere unsegregated for the larger net of sociability, goals were multifarious and defied single-track strategies.

Economists relying on game theory are particularly vulnerable to this criticism, since the equilibrium of the models they use to support their views of institutions requires a form of a priori knowledge of optimal economic arrangement, without which their explanations would present the usual circularity of functionalism. It is, indeed, ahistorical to work back from an identifiable institutional role in order to define a "usefulness" that eliminates "failed" historical alternatives.

Greif (1998, 2006) is one of those scholars who apply modern economic models when analyzing history. Studying the institutional conditions under which merchants could trust distant agents, he directly addresses the fact that commercial relationships between medieval long-distance operators were changing. In contrast to many of his colleagues, Greif is very attentive to the historical setting, and his work effectively bridges history, sociology, and political science. He recognizes that norms, culture, belief, and, to some extent, social stratification are key elements to understanding economic dynamics. In *Institutions and the Path to the Modern Economy: Lessons from Medieval Trade* (2006), Greif endeavors to establish a general theory of institutions by linking a small sample of case studies drawn from medieval history. However, while this major undertaking provides an interesting and comprehensive framework in which to study the history of institutions, Greif faces important obstacles. First, his institutions remain the incentive structures of a system in which transaction costs have to be minimized. This is a problem especially for medieval history because those costs are hard to measure and are not uniform with respect to social settings. As a result, "transaction costs" constitutes a shaky notion on which to build falsifiable theories that are portable in time and space. Second, Greif relies on game theory models that might be well designed to demonstrate how equilibrium is achieved but are inadequate for uncovering the sources of a changing context over the *longue durée*, as each iteration can only be a static answer to the continuous process of development.

Greif's solution to these two problems is to consider the particular historical setting of each case study in order to include as many features as possible of the specific social dilemmas to be resolved. While a sensible idea in concept, it compromises the precision and parsimony of the econometric models that sustain the analytical legitimacy of his project. This is not only because of the recrudescence of unmeasurable – and often interacting – variables that must be considered, but also because of the numerous potential solutions to his query.

Readers familiar with Greif's work may see parallels in our research endeavors, especially considering that one of his case studies involves medieval Genoa. However, for the most part our enterprises proceed differently. The first difference is in scope and focus. While Greif focuses on enforcement mechanisms and coordination,[3] my interest in the rise of commercial institutions is wider and deals with the specifics of equity partnerships, credit, and insurance agreements. Why, how, when, and which Genoese made certain arrangements are key questions that this book strives to answer. The second difference is methodological. Whereas Greif proceeds with analytical narratives that interpret historical details as evidence of a set of rational choice equilibriums, this book provides systematic quantitative data drawn from primary sources. In addition, my analysis is not based on any individual mean-ends approach and does not privilege commercial goals in the motives and behaviors of actors. As a result, the reader will learn that, in contrast to Greif's – and North's – assumption, it was not economic optimization that drove the key

---

[3] The questions of enforcement and citywide coordination, while certainly interesting, do not seem to me as central to the city's economic success as Greif seems to indicate. Indeed, the number of commercial disputes (or their settlements) reported in the notarial record is low, and other available primary sources do not mention such disputes as the origin of factionalist crises regardless of the presence or absence of Greif's enforcing mechanism. Some traders surely cheated (or tried to), but most did not because of a combination of belief, internalized norms, fear of the law – or of the power of the counterparty – and their embeddedness in the community. In addition, while peace is conducive to economic development, its importance for medieval commerce should not be overstated. For example, according to S. A. Epstein's review of Genoese primary sources during the thirteenth century – the century of highest commercial growth – only 32 years can be considered as peaceful "at least in comparison to others" (1988, p. 117).

medieval commercial innovation "life cycle." Rather, it was a change in partner selection, which reflected the dynamic of the Genoese social structure as a whole. Indeed, the network analysis clearly shows that the change in the type of agreements by which merchants were linked follows the demands of social survival and the lure of the opportunities for wealth that resulted from political change.

In addition, my study also brings to light the relative chronological dissociation between the emergence of modern market instruments and the medieval economic expansion. The network analysis presented in this book demonstrates that the period of highest growth in Genoa's medieval commerce was supported by custom-based commercial agreements (commendae) forming the nodes of a trade network that was the least hierarchical and least connected of the period covered in the study (Chapter 3). It was, thus, not formalization and organization that prevailed but instead multivalent social positions. This allows one to reflect on the paradoxical emergence of the market as an instrument for the consolidation of social hierarchies, rather than as an arena of economic and social opportunity. It also makes clear the dynamic relationship between microsocial interactions and the technological advancement of European commercial interactions. Thus, the analysis also departs from the classic view of certain scholars such as de Roover (1952) and Weber (1978), who assert that technological innovation in Western Europe[4] led to its commercial world supremacy and the concentration of capital that facilitated the modern industrial revolution.

---

[4] Double-entry bookkeeping is not covered in this research. Although Weber has branded this Western innovation as the key technological marker of the transition from a traditional to a modern social organization, rudimentary double-entry bookkeeping was rarely used in the fourteenth century, and its role in the genesis of the Renaissance social structure can only have been overstated. In addition, without denying the rhetorical aspect of formal accounting uncovered by Carruthers and Espeland (1991) and Poovey (1997), those scholars specializing in accounting history have demonstrated that, before the practices of separation of personal and business finance, better assessment of inventory of all assets and liabilities, and some rudiments of cost accounting, double-entry bookkeeping was a mnemonic aid and not a tool used to rationally control and allocate resources (Melis 1950, p. 598; Yamey 1978; Have 1986). Thus, from the fifteenth century on, double-entry accounting increasingly provided an effective means of keeping track of large volumes of financial commitments, but it was not a prerequisite for capitalist success. For example, the Fuggers built up the largest European fortune in the early sixteenth century without using a double-entry system, and many of the first large joint stock companies, such as the Dutch India Company (Glamman 1958, p. 244), relied on more traditional accounting methods.

*Opportunistic Merchant.* The study presented in this book is relevant to the tradition of social and economic history including scholarship that considers the "Commercial Revolution" and, more generally, the rise of a mercantile society. The intensity of this scholarship has decreased since the work of Sombart (1902), Pirenne (1914, 1987), Lopez (1938), and Lombard (1972); the skillful descriptions of the early Renaissance merchants provided by Sapori (1952), Lane (1944), and Renouard (1950); and the substantial synthesis of Braudel (1949, 1967). In this context, my goal is to revive and freshen up some of the classic questions of the field by applying up-to-date technologies, both in network analysis and in the management of large data sets. As a result, my analysis sometimes supplements but more often contrasts with recent publications, such as those by Dahl (1998) and Spufford (2002), as these have maintained the stereotype of the medieval merchant as a "modern" decision maker in a "traditional" medieval world. Indeed, my work shows that the strength of the Genoese long-distance commercial growth in the twelfth- and thirteenth-centuries stems from opportunistic and heterogeneous social ties, and not from the fixed structures that are associated with routinized mercantile networks. This finding dampens the importance of individual agency as business skills do not play the central role in the commercial success of the emergent Western merchant class. This outlook would not have surprised Braudel, who acknowledges commercial innovation but who argues that the success of medieval long-distance traders was essentially the result of the merchants' predatory instincts and their relentless pursuit of profits. For him, it is precisely the emergence of a world market – that is, the real possibility of exchanging goods for currency in disconnected geographical areas that often fall under different political jurisdictions – combined with the lack of fair competition that explains how long-distance trade ignited the only potential medieval accumulation of capital (1979, p. 228).

In showing that Italian merchants' commercial trajectories were driven by their social and historical settings, my book also complements the studies of Kedar (1976) and Goldthwaite (1993), who added analysis of cultural and behavioral empirical patterns to the economic motives that had dominated the classic mercantile historiography. Kedar points to the rise in faith to explain a change in business practices among fourteenth-century Renaissance merchants. According to him, merchants became more risk-adverse, which resulted in slowing social mobility. Goldthwaite also notices a more stagnant social structure in Renaissance Florence, but attributes this historical change to a shift in capital allocation. Studying consumption patterns, he notes the diversion of financial resources away from investment capital and toward expensive acquisition of art and real estate to explain the Renaissance slowdown.

*Genoa Long-Distance Trade.* Meticulous studies of the supply and demand for goods have allowed economic historians to describe the mechanisms that created the financial surplus seen in late medieval Europe. Micro studies of price, quantity, and geographical flows of goods and financial assets show how price differences in space and time had fortified the position of a merchant class. Portions of the notarial records have been used by historians to produce a series of studies about medieval Genoa[5] on specific topics, and particularly relevant in this context are those on the city's commercial activities.[6] These studies have focused on what, where, and how transactions took place, and they even sometimes function to portray some members of the emerging mercantile elite. In that context, commercial innovation helped merchants to increase their business opportunities and maximize return on investment. Several books have also built on the same model to describe the whole mercantile society of the medieval and early Renaissance periods in Genoa. In depicting various periods and aspects of the Genoese rise to economic prominence, Heers (1961), Balard (1978), and Jehel (1993) have written substantial volumes that provide much valuable quantitative information about Genoese commercial practice. As with other research in the tradition of the *Annales School,* their use of statistics is not analytical, but their careful accounts describe with precision as many elements of the social life as it is possible to deduce from the primary records. In so doing, their focus is naturally more on quantification of history than on abstraction and theory.[7]

In a more recent book, S. A. Epstein (1996) also makes use of the wealth of Genoese historical sources to present a well-documented narrative history that covers a period of 500 years. While his book includes references to trade and the economy, Epstein focuses on political and cultural history to create a picture of the mercantile atmosphere that permeated medieval Genoa. However, he does not consider the change in

---

[5] For example, S. A. Epstein's study on wills (1984) and Hughes's on family structure (1975, 1977).

[6] Among others, see Byrne (1916, 1930); Reynolds (1930); Lopez (1933, 1936, 1937); Hall-Cole (1938); Edler-de Roover (1941); (Krueger 1962); Bonds (1968); Slessarev (1967); and Face (1969).

[7] See Gould (2003, p. 241) for similar comments on the French school.

the relations of trade in order to make sense of the Genoese trajectory. As a result, despite interesting discussions on charity and slavery, he is left with the themes of individualism and endemic factionalism as the main thread of the city's history. In adopting the classic topics that had been developed before him by specialists of medieval Genoa such as Vitale (1956), Airaldi (1986), and Petti Baldi (1976, 1991), S. A. Epstein leaves the reader wondering how his account fits with the city's mercantile success and its ability to develop ingenious commercial arrangements.

By sometimes using the same historical sources as the Genoese specialists, my analysis often runs parallel to their studies, but at the same time differs in focus. To date no work has considered the social structure[8] of commercial partnerships, despite the fact that these partnerships usually lasted several months and were crucial for early capitalist activity in medieval Europe. Indeed, although every aforementioned study recognizes the importance of commerce in the city history, none focuses on the city trade dynamics – that is, on the ongoing change in the set of social ties that dealt with the production, transportation, and distribution of goods. This is an unsatisfying approach because the record shows that despite the reputation of the Genoese people for individualism, medieval long-distance ventures usually involved multiple parties.

For this book's analysis, I did not resort to any cultural assumptions or any actor role theories. The Genoese might or might not have been more individualistic than their contemporaries, but they definitely worked and invested together. Moreover, and without contesting the reality of continual infighting (which also occurred in most other Italian city-states), the record shows a series of close associations demonstrating that when it came to long-distance trade, boundaries between factions were a lot less sharp than what the historiography portrays. Direct and indirect ties between members of opposite factions are not rare in the data set. Furthermore, when their common interests were threatened, the Genoese deployed the military might of the entire community, which, as I explain at the end of Chapter 2, was key to their economic ascension. These facts attest to a social life that accommodated many more compromises than the city historiography often represents. We forget that, between the historical events that we compress into single time lines for heuristic reasons, there is real social time giving people many opportunities to find common ground. In medieval Genoa, the appeal of military bounty and, later, of profit from long-distance trade was surely facilitating the erosion

---

[8] Jehel is the closest (1993, pp. 157–223).

of individual antagonistic memories. In building my analysis on the change in the trade network, it is certainly my aim to capture the continuous character of history with its protagonists involved in ongoing human interaction.

*Dynamic of Social Ties.* This book's focus on social ties in the emergence of the mercantile organization in medieval Europe contributes to the body of literature that, following Polanyi (1957), has shown the social nature of economic exchange. In particular, my research aims to put in historical motion the findings of sociologists such as Granovetter and H. C. White, who have statically demonstrated the social construction of markets. It does this by showing that the history of economic institutional frameworks was as much a condition for economic growth as it was the carrier of the rules that organized the transformation of ties that gave rise to a merchant class.

In showing that markets were not merely price-mechanism institutions, Polanyi has opened a line of research demonstrating that various forms of markets can operate simultaneously and not necessarily in chronological sequence. For example, Zelizer's (1985) cultural study on the development of life insurance in the United States points out the importance of social norms in economic exchange. For their part, the economic historians Hoffmann, Postel-Vinay, and Rosenthal's (2000) analysis of the central role of notaries in seventeenth- to nineteenth-century Parisian credit transactions shows that markets can strive even under conditions of asymmetric and compartmentalized information. Similarly, in medieval Genoa, the feudal social order with its traditions of birth order and mutual obligations coexisted with the commercial sphere, and its emerging calculative business competence.

This book is historical in that I unfold details of medieval social ties. Similarly, my account of the intricacies of commercial agreements improves our understanding of how such formal contracts took hold in medieval Europe. However, my objective is not simply descriptive. Instead, in this book social ties form the empirical trials that are used to construct theories about human interactions and how they congeal into relationship dynamics. The aim is not simply to understand the structure of social relations. Crucially, I also intend to show how those structures evolved through time. Thus, this book directly engages the field of historical sociology, an area of study that, following Tilly's *The Vendée* (1964), has produced a body of research that is rich in theory and methodological advances. Although this work is not tied to any single methodological approach, graph theoretic network methods are a key facet of the analytical techniques I use. While the works of network structural theorists[9] have guided some of my methodological choices, the monographs of Bearman (1991, 1993), Gould (1991, 1995), Barkey and van Rossen (1997), Padgett (2001), and Erikson and Bearman (2006), among others, have provided me with examples of the systematic examination of historical relational data. This said, despite my commitment to algebraic methods, the fact remains that, whenever possible, I made sure to test my results by using other analytical resources to make sense of historical events.

The *longue durée* is another key element of the analysis presented here, and it addresses a major quandary of social history: how to capture the intrinsic continuity of social life. A common strategy is to read a crystallized form of social structure into the institutional history, where the constantly renegotiated rules of social encounters are expressed. However, unless the duration of a study is long enough to include an institutional dynamic, it is often impossible to dissociate the rules of the institutions from the social dynamic itself. For example, to infer the early Renaissance Florentine elite organization from accounting ledgers presents a crucial problem: the data production and organization already contains the rules of the mercantile domination and cannot account for the genesis of the Renaissance social structure. In other words, studies often use information that already expresses the social structure they aim to analyze. In particular, understanding the origin of the mercantile domination through the repertoire[10] of the mercantile classes has a tautological feel to it. In this book, commercial institutions are not taken for granted. Instead, the analysis relies on an extensive collection of data to focus on the long-run historical dynamic that brought about the emergence of credit, temporary equity, and insurance relationships in medieval Europe.

## MEDIEVAL DATA

The historical evidence available for medieval societies is a lot sparser than that available for the modern period, and this is especially true of quantitative information. In this light, this book is original in that it uses

---

[9] Among others: H. C. White et al. (1976); Bonachich (1987); Krankhart (1990); H. C. White (2008); Faust and Wasserman (1994); Burt (1995); and Moody and D. White (2003).

[10] I define "repertoire" as the repetition of familiar and established behavior that gains social meaning across settings.

what is, comparatively, a very large data set to study medieval social dynamics. The bulk of the data was obtained by compiling more than 11,000 commercial agreements harvested from the 20,000 notarial records I examined.

In addition to contracts drawn up by more than 135 different notaries, I have also used a variety of other primary sources to collect supplementary information about the parties, building a data set containing more than 18,500 ties covering a period of 280 years. It includes roughly 9,700 individuals from 4,000 different families. I coded not only details about the transactions at hand, but also, when available, a variety of information about the parties as well. This included information such as occupation, gender, formal status, geographic origins, and kinship ties.

During my research, I have identified ten types of commercial agreements,[11] each having very regular features. The largest number of entries in the data base (almost 9,000) refers to temporary equity partnerships, which are concentrated in the early phase of the commercial expansion (1150–1250). Credit agreements (more than 7,300 ties organized by 6 different legal types) display the most stable temporal distribution in the data set, whereas the insurance relationships recorded (about 2,600) cover the shortest period (1350–1440).

## Notarial Records

*Notarii publici* (notaries)[12] were a typical element of urban life in medieval Italy. They were vested with the public authority of the emperor[13] and are, thus, one of the links between the feudal tradition and the written contractual system that emerged as a way of organizing new social relationships (Clanchy 1979). They are omnipresent in Genoa's daily life. We can find them writing wills at deathbeds, drawing up marriage agreements in the houses of patrician families, and authenticating commercial documents in town squares and churches.[14] Each Italian city collected its

---

[11] Commendae, *societas maris*, exchange contracts, sea loans, sea exchange contracts, local loans, promissory notes, credit guarantees, mandates, and insurance agreements. I also coded real estate transactions in order to track down the origins of the capital invested in long-distance trade.

[12] Unless otherwise indicated, all translations in the book are mine.

[13] On November 12, 1191, the Emperor Enrico VI appointed *in palatio archiepioscopi* (in the palace of the archbishop), *Bonum Ionannem scribam consulum consular* (consular notary) and *Bonus Vassalum* on November 17 (CA #1323 and #1338).

[14] Costamagna (1970) offers a thorough description of their activity.

notaries' documents and preserved them in the public archives. In Genoa, more complete and earlier cartularies – the large books in which the notary recorded legal documents – have been saved than anywhere else in Europe.

Reading the notaries' cartularies presents enormous paleographic difficulties for anyone who has not specialized in medieval writing. Luckily, over the last 130 years, several scholars[15] have published transcriptions, in the original Latin, of almost 15,000 of the surviving records.

I have coded all these transcripts but still could not build a continuous time series past the mid thirteenth century.[16] By good fortune, however, I was able to consult the private collections of two leading historians on medieval Genoa, Georges Jehel and Michel Balard, each of whom has independently, and very graciously, allowed me the use of his private collection of transcripts, documents that account for years of research on the Genoese archives. Their combined 4,800+ records fill the temporal gap in the published sources at least until the first quarter of the fourteenth century. In addition, the geographical focus of their respective researches (western Mediterranean trade in Jehel's case and eastern Mediterranean trade in Balard's), added to the extensive published sources regarding the northern trade,[17] provide a diverse and reliable sample.

Access to private transcripts has also increased to 135 names the pool of individual notaries I coded from, and has thus further reduced the risk of sample bias resulting from any specialization in the notaries' clientele. Indeed, published transcripts account for at least 90 individual notaries,[18] while the contracts I analyzed in Balard and Jehel's private notes were gathered from 86 notaries, about half of whom do not appear in any published records. For the unpublished names, both scholars catalogued their research according to the Genoese archival recording system, which attributes a single notary's name to cartularies that may contain the work of several. In that light, the number 135 is a conservative estimate. In any

[15] Bratianu (1929); Chiaudano (1940); Chiaudano and Moresco (1935); Chiaudano and della Rocca (1938); Doehaerd (1941); Doehaerd and Kerremans (1952); Eierman, Krueger, and Reynolds (1939); Hall, Krueger, Renert, and Reynolds (1938); Hall-Cole, Krueger, Renert, and Reynolds (1939); Krueger and Reynolds (1951–53); Lopez (1953); and Liagre-De Sturler (1969).

[16] The proportion of documents that have been transcribed is much higher for the earlier periods (1154–1226).

[17] Doehaerd (1941); Doehaerd and Kerremans (1952); and Liagre-De Sturler (1969).

[18] This includes, for example, the archives of thirty-four notaries solely from the Doehaerd transcripts published in 1941.

case, I can safely assert that I coded contracts from at least fourteen individual notaries for the period 1154–1210, forty-one for the period 1211–50, forty-nine for 1251–1300, thirty-eight for 1301–50, twenty-nine for 1351–1400, and nineteen for 1401–40.[19]

Among the notarial records, I selected for coding all commercial contracts that pertained directly or indirectly to long-distance trade and that had a duration attached to them (which eliminated a small set of cash transactions). I ended up with more than 11,000 contracts for which I recorded the following information: 1) the year, month, and day of the agreement; 2) the names and roles of the participants – usually a pair, but sometimes up to five for equity partnerships and up to sixteen for insurance agreements; 3) the size of the transaction – ranging from a partnership in 1203 between a priest and an occasional traveler for a venture to Acre (in today's Israel)[20] involving a single pound to a £6,500 investment to Sicily among three members of the powerful Spinola and Cibo clans in 1377;[21] and 4) the legal type of the commercial agreement (a loan, insurance, exchange contract, commenda, etc.). In addition, different types of agreements contained specific details that enriched my analysis. For example, the exchange contracts indicate a currency rate, while the promissory loans specify payment schedules, and the insurance agreements name the captain of the ship.[22]

In addition to the documents involving commercial ties, I have also consulted, in the same cartularies, civil records such as wills and dowries. These I used to tackle the difficult problem of sorting out and identifying kinship and people's professions. This was particularly crucial because aside from the members of a small number of families, first names are often followed by filiations only, usually the father, and/or a topographic qualification. In certain cases, people are also identified by a profession or a word suggesting a professional activity, such as *Wilielmus peliparius* (William "the pelter").[23] A first comment is that, in the thousands of

---

[19] The total of these figures exceeds 135 due to overlaps.

[20] GI# 579.

[21] STU#358. Both Spinola and Cibo were consular families in the first part of the twelfth century.

[22] All contracts also contain the names of witnesses. Although at first I thought I would record this information, I ended up deciding against it because it was impossible to differentiate between socially meaningful witness participation and witnesses who had little to do with the identity of the signing parties. Indeed, very often the presence of a given witness in the record seems to be strictly a function of the time of the day or the location of the redaction of the documents. See S. A. Epstein (1994) for a similar finding.

[23] OBA #426/September 1186.

documents that I analyzed dating from before 1250, I almost never encountered a word that evoked a strictly commercial activity, other than a few mentions of *bancherius* (banker).

The quantity of these records, unique in medieval Europe, should not hide the fact that any surviving medieval documents are rare jewels for us. It is, therefore, very difficult to establish a measure of the selectivity bias on our samples, and the precision of very sophisticated statistical measures should not be mistaken for veracity. First, despite the large number of notaries represented in the data set, the surviving documents are the work of a portion of the pool of notaries at work at the time. Second, the records do not constitute a continuous or uniform time series, and my temporal comparison should be viewed with caution. Third, the practice of using notaries declined toward the beginning of the fourteenth century – because of the development of literacy and the increased use of bilateral agreements. As a result, private contracts became progressively more common, eventually gaining legal power. These caveats aside, the data set is large and diverse enough to allow us to be reasonably confident that it is representative of the nature of early commercial activity. It is just that we do not have, as we do with random samples, enough information to quantify the degree of reliability.

***Other Primary Sources.*** The remaining primary sources that complete the empirical foundation of my research fall into four categories. First, the *Annales Januences* (the Genoese chronicle) presents the official version of the Commune's history from 1099 onward. Despite the bias inherent in any official account of that period, the text offers a detailed background that can be used, with confidence, to assess other official documents. Second, a collection of administrative documents as well as ecclesiastic registers provides an insight into Genoese medieval politics. In particular, the *Liber Jurium*, a thirteenth-century compilation of a large number of official documents, provides a few lists of citizens who participated in various official functions or who voted on important communal issues. Third, financial records, such as fragments of public bank records and the partial fiscal lists for 1414 and 1440,[24] provide supplementary information about the financial dealings of specific clans. Finally, the oldest surviving Genoese customs records, the earliest extant Italian registers, supply precise information about importers for the years 1376 and 1377. Such records, meticulously transcribed by John Day (1963), provide the

---

[24] See Sieveking 1898 and 1906.

custom dues of all Genoese importers, and thus exhaustive quantitative information on the mercantile activities of hundreds of individuals.

*Scope, Periodicity, Monetary Scale, and Profits.* Before I conclude this first chapter with a succinct description of the way in which this book has been organized, I need to make four brief notes about scope, periodicity, monetary scale, and long-distance trade profits.

First, regarding scope: political and cultural histories provide crucial insights into the emergence of new modes of social organization during the Renaissance. Without denying the validity of such studies, the present research focuses on the interplay of commercial institutions and social dynamics. In the interest of maintaining a credible scope of study, I borrow only sporadically from other sources for the purposes of my analytical inquiries. This being said, I do rely on a wide range of evidence (such as records of feudal vassalage ties, political appointments, and tax records) to best define the dynamics of the elite families, as well as to specify elements of social mobility.

By the same token, geographical comparison is not a central element of this research, as no chronologically corresponding records in Europe survived. Because the strength of this study rests on linking micro social processes with larger classical sociological questions, the absence of comparable data for other cases limits the usefulness of extensive comparison. However, when relevant and possible, I position the Genoese social processes in the broader context of medieval Europe.

Second, regarding periodicity: picking the starting point for a continuous social process is clearly impossible. As Woloch (1994) and before him Tocqueville (1952) have demonstrated, even such a monumental historical event as the French Revolution cannot always be thought of as bounded within a specific historical period. With this in mind, the period covered by the formal analysis was dictated by the oldest surviving notarial cartulary, which was minuted in 1154 by Giovanni Scriba, and by a wish to include enough data pertaining to fifteenth-century social relationships to capture both the whole transition that brought about the early modern social organization and the changes in the formal agreements that organized commercial encounters. This said, it was not my purpose to restrict my study to even this long a period, as I bring forth evidence from the tenth and eleventh centuries to confirm the feudal origin of the Genoese Commune, and as I refer to the clans' political positions in the early sixteenth-century to assess the relationship between commercial dynamics and the formal status of the elite.

Social dynamics – that is, the study of changes in social organizations over time – is a central concept of this book. My objective is to describe not only the trajectories but also the mechanisms that explain the relationship between the changes in the structure of social ties and the "life cycle" of commercial institutions. In this light, the emphasis on continuity inherent in my research defies the concept of thresholds between periods, and the reader should not attach too much meaning to the words *medieval* and *Renaissance,* as I use them more as linguistic conveniences than as expressions of epochal difference. Still, I do object to the use of the term "medieval Italian trade" by historians who produce evidence dating almost exclusively from the second half of the fourteenth to the end of the fifteenth century. It is with this in mind, and notwithstanding the usual controversy, that I assume that, chronologically speaking, the Italian urban Renaissance began sometime between 1325 and 1375. There is nothing original in picking these dates. For most scholars, the markers of the epochal change are cultural. For example, the medieval Dante and Giotto died in 1321 and 1337, respectively, whereas the Renaissance Boccaccio wrote the *Decameron* in 1353, and Donatello's *David* dates from 1408.[25] My signposts regard social interactions. Thus, as the reader will learn, the dates 1325 to 1375 roughly designate a period during which social mobility declined and the distinctions among occupational categories became clearer, all bound by more rigid social ties among the elite.

Third, regarding monetary scale: this study covers three centuries of commercial ties, and I provide historical evidence that is expressed in monetary units. Examples include income and wealth measures, taxes and public debt levels, trade volumes, real estate prices, and payments for the transfer of feudal rights. Throughout the book, unless specified otherwise, I consistently use Genoese pounds (£) as the currency of reference. This means that I have converted records expressed in a foreign currency into pounds, using an exchange rate computed from exchange contracts or, when available, from those published in the secondary literature. However, consistent use of a currency of reference does not solve two thorny issues when dealing with money over a long period of time: the depreciation of money and the variation in purchasing power across time.

The value of currencies changes over time, and a comparison between epochs is hard. The usual solution is to pick a baseline date and then use inflation indices to discount the monetary value back to that time. This is

---

[25] The bronze version dates from circa 1430.

impossible in the context of this book, however, as no reliable or representative inflation indices are available for the medieval period in Genoa. Another key problem is that inflation indices only relate to average prices. They therefore do not reflect price structure dynamics and are not helpful when one is working to understand various social group consumption patterns. Thus, even if a reliable Genoese medieval price index were available, the wide disparity in marginal income would exacerbate the problems associated with using a "constant" currency level. I thus elected to use then-current prices throughout. By and large, this should not pose a big problem because changes in relative values such as capital allocation, wealth distribution, and transaction amount standard deviation are more topical to this work than are straight comparisons of monetary value over time.

With little knowledge of medieval price structure, another problem about monetary units becomes obvious: it is almost impossible for the reader to understand or even "feel" what a galley oarsman could purchase in the 1150s with the £4 he earned annually. Historians sometimes specify the price of precious commodities in order to establish a baseline, but knowing that £6 could purchase 10 grams of pepper or 7 grams of gold offers limited help to the unspecialized reader. It is probably more indicative to know that during that period, a slave could be bought for between £5 and £10; a servant earned £2 to £3 a year; a storefront could be rented for £3 to £4 per year; the price of a mule was £5 to £8; and sufficient food to feed an adult could cost about £3 a year.

Although this kind of information does not solve the problem associated with assessing relative purchasing power in medieval Genoa, at least it provides the minimum information to figure out roughly the value of the Genoese pound at the time. This is why the reader will, when relevant, find in the text prices of goods and services. In addition, the reader can consult Appendix A, which lists a few prices – drawn from primary and secondary sources – that refer to a variety of goods and services available in medieval Genoa.

Fourth, regarding long-distance trade investment return: economic historians agree that medieval long-distance trade was very profitable. If goods arrived at their destination, a hefty profit could be expected. Unfortunately, we have very little data with which to systematically quantify the return on investments. In particular, the notarial records rarely contain figures showing the outcome of a given venture. A further problem is the lack of information about speed of capital turnover. For example, it is generally presumed that commendae to Sicily or to the

North African coast were less profitable than those to the eastern Mediterranean. However, this is debatable because voyages to the former destinations were much shorter, and the capital turnover could therefore be twice as fast. At the same time, this logical line of thought exemplifies the danger of applying modern economic measures when thinking about medieval profits. Indeed, ships did not necessarily sail direct routes (see Chapter 3); travelers were not always in a hurry to come back home; and the risks of travel varied according to political and military settings. In addition, upon returning to Genoa, long-distance participants might not be able – or willing – to reinvest their venture's proceeds as quickly as modern strategic investors would.

Fortunately, even though the change in capital structure is one of the elements needed to explain the Genoese social organization dynamic, precise information about return on investment is not necessary to support the analysis presented in this book. Still, the scant information about proceeds provides some sense of the magnitude of profits. For instance, a documented series of three ventures for the years 1156–58 shows return of 36%, 96%, and 59%,[26] while a small sample of thirteenth-century commendae shows between 20% and 110% profit. Keeping in mind the anecdotal character of these numbers, the range of profits does not seem to be connected to the identity of the parties or to the nature – other than destination – of the transaction at hand.

Another way to assess profitability is by examining long-distance credit rates. Obviously, the medieval borrower must have been fairly confident that his return would exceed the 40% to 100% rate applied to sea loans (which included coverage of the transportation risk; see Chapter 4) to the Levant, or the 25% to 45% rate applied to the less distant western Mediterranean ventures. Similarly, an analysis of the exchange contracts at the Champagne Fairs, which were usually payable within less than three months, indicates an implicit interest rate that varied between 12% and 20% (thus an annual compound rate between 57% and 107%).

## ORGANIZATION OF THE BOOK

The rest of this book is divided into four chapters and a conclusion. The second chapter establishes an early twelfth-century baseline from which to study the development of medieval Genoa throughout the next three centuries, when social encounters were being increasingly defined by

---

[26] See Edler-de Roover (1941, pp. 90–1).

commercial agreements. In the first section of that chapter, I begin by placing the development of Genoa in the context of early medieval Mediterranean history and by tracing the formal origins of the Genoese Commune to the feudal base of its social organization. I then review the importance of the Crusades in the context of Genoa's development and show how the warrior class actively participated in the long-distance trade expansion. In the second section, I review early medieval commerce both in continental Europe and in the more advanced eastern community. This is done to familiarize the reader with the trading practices that existed before Genoa rose to commercial prominence from the mid thirteenth century on. I show that Genoa benefited from the multivalence of its commercial operators, who, unlike members of preexisting trade networks, could draw on the financial capital and the military support of the whole city to take over the growing long-distance trade. In many ways, it is precisely because the Italians were not specialized merchants that their commerce flourished during the early phase of the commercial expansion.

Each of the three chapters that follow addresses one of three main types of commercial ties: temporary equity partnerships, credit, and insurance. While the subjects of these three chapters are not considered in a chronological manner per se, the chapters nevertheless overlap to provide complete coverage of the period 1150 to 1450, highlighting the "life cycle" of each of the three institutional frameworks. As such, the three chapters bring to light the close association between social dynamics and economic history, by showing what kinds of social structure was historically associated with what kinds of formal economic arrangements.

These chapters are each divided into three sections preceded by a brief historical introduction to the period being considered. Each includes 1) a detailed account of the legal and economic background of the commercial framework that is the focus of the chapter, 2) a description of the social characteristics of the network's main protagonists, and 3) an analysis of the network dynamic as well as an explanation of the partner selection pattern.

Chapter 3 deals with the commenda and *societas maris*, the two well-defined medieval forms of equity association contracts that organized most social pairings during the emergence of Genoa's long-distance trade. I show that these two institutions, which originated in the eastern Mediterranean, were perfectly adapted to the opportunistic nature of trade and the heterogeneity of commercial ties that characterized the growth period of the Genoese long-distance trade. As a result, the analysis of the database provides insight into various social categories, including those into which women, artisans, and professionals fall. Building a series of networks that cover the period from 1154 to 1315, I show that, over time, status and occupational categories became salient features of partner selection, and that this in turn precipitated the decline of the temporary partnership paradigm. Thus the data offer a full institutional "life cycle" because even though both *societas* and commenda partnerships were still sporadically in use in the fifteenth century, they had lost their significance toward the beginning of the fourteenth century.

Chapter 4 takes up credit-based instruments. This type of agreement spans the whole period under study, and an analysis of the data set shows that its form and social usage mutated several times. The first section of the chapter describes the functioning of medieval credit. After this, I demonstrate that, unlike temporary partnerships, credit was a commercial framework of routinized traders. Thus, the credit network is a good locus for studying the rise of merchants. The surviving records show that, in the early part of the period covered by my analysis, credit instruments – especially promissory notes – were overwhelmingly contracted by foreign itinerant merchants, often when trading with the northern fairs. From the mid thirteenth century on, however, the Genoese elite increasingly used credit when defining their relational ties. When the Genoese opened the maritime road to the North Sea around 1280, the records show that they intensified the use of credit and currency-related instruments to supplant the traditional itinerant merchant of the northern fair.

Unlike commendae and *societas maris*, credit-based contracts were important not because they were a revolutionary social institution, but because their use consolidated commercial identities during the period. For example, the typical credit innovation of the medieval period, the exchange contract (which is the ancestor of the letter of credit coupled with a currency transaction) was never an instrument of social heterogeneity. However, it became a prevalent institution, and as such it provided a social arena that stabilized social ties and promoted symmetric relationships, which in turn induced homogeneity.

Chapter 5 examines the early use of the insurance contract from its inception, around 1350, to the middle of the fifteenth century. Although Genoa's decline is amplified by the historiography, this period does nevertheless mark the end of the city's rapid territorial and economic growth. It was also during this period that the city's public finances were reorganized to consolidate the control of the dominant families – a process that culminated with the establishment of the Bank of San Giorgio in

1407 – and my data analysis confirms the slowdown of the relative social mobility of the thirteenth century.

In this fifth chapter, I sample more than 2,400 insurance ties to identify the core oligarchic families of the period. I then formulate a probabilistic model of commercial partner selection. The nature of these relationships is very different from that of the ties of the commercial network of the commenda period. Here, the names of almost all of the elite families appear continuously. These point to domination by a group, whose members also control the city's public finances and occupy various political positions. My calculations show that the network of Genoa's elite is dense and highly cohesive, and that it cannot be partitioned. No important clan (or *alberghi*, as they were known in Genoa) is excluded, and my model indicates that each family had a propensity to spread its business between peer families. Thus, the insurance contract helped to consolidate and to define the social boundaries of the elite.

In the conclusion of the book, I consider the ways in which the data I gathered allows us to improve our understanding of the complex processes by which social relations suitable for the expansion and ultimate domination of modern capitalism arose. Specifically, while expansion in trade volumes, increased monetization, and capital accumulation are certainly markers of the transition to capitalism, historical continuity is to be found in the ongoing development of complex social relationships and of the institutions that contain the constantly renegotiated rules of their interactions.

# 2

# Genoa at the Dawn of the Commercial Expansion

Commercial ties did not appear suddenly and did not change Genoa's social organizations instantaneously. Thus, exact periodicity as such is not critical, but the proper concatenation of Genoa's historical dynamics is crucial in order to understand the transition from a medieval feudal organization to a Renaissance mercantile social structure. This chapter serves as an historical introduction both to the city-state of Genoa and to medieval commerce up until the mid twelfth century, when the Genoese created the oldest surviving notarial cartularies in Europe (Giovanni Scriba, 1155–64). The objective here is not to look for an illusive origin or starting point, but rather to establish a twelfth-century baseline from which to study the development of Genoa throughout the following three centuries, when social encounters became increasingly defined by commercial agreements.

The first section of the chapter traces the beginning of the Genoese Commune at around the time of the First Crusade (1097–99) and confirms the feudal base of its origin (Sieveking 1906; Bach 1955). The purpose is to highlight in the historiography of the city[1] those elements that provide an understanding of its social order as trade began to expand in the twelfth century. I use several primary sources and some of the early notarial records to highlight the role of the feudal elite, and I point to its financial transactions with the young Commune. I also review the importance of the Crusades for Genoa's development, and I indicate how the feudal elite, with its military tradition, did not need to break its social

---

[1] For the city historiography, see, in particular, Vitale (1955) and Imperiale (2004).

pattern as its repertoire could be usefully activated in the long-distance trade.

The second section reviews early medieval commerce in order to familiarize the reader with existing trading practices before Genoa rose to commercial prominence. Here, I explain that Genoa was primarily a military power and a relatively late entrant into the long-distance trade.

Then, in a short third section, I show how the lack of a specialized merchant network actually provided Genoa with an advantage over preexisting trade networks. The entrenched organizational practices of early medieval commercial networks such as those of Frisans, Jews, or Magribi traders tended to constrain those organizations' ability to take advantage of the growing Mediterranean commerce. It was the multivalence of the Genoese and the ability to draw on resources from the whole population through flexible equity partnerships (Chapter 3) that facilitated the city's emergence.

## 2.1. THE FEUDAL COMMUNE

The Romans used to call the Mediterranean "Our Sea," whereas for Muslim traders of the ninth and tenth centuries it was simply "The Sea." The sense of geographic unity of the Mediterranean was reinforced by the limitations of navigational practices; captains still steered by landmarks, and long journeys included multiple stopovers. For those sailing along the western coast of Italy or the southern shore of France, the welcoming cove of Genoa, almost at the northernmost point of their route, must have offered a stark contrast to the mountains that seem to rise straight out of the water. Coming from the Muslim Almeria in the southwest, travelers had successively to pass Valencia, Barcelona, Perpignan, Marseilles, and Nice. If sailing from Sicily in the southeast, they might have stopped in Palermo, Amalfi, Salerno, Naples, and Pisa.

Although Genoa could boast of a deep natural harbor, the city itself, situated almost midway into the Ligurian region extending from Monaco to Portovenere, was not very different from nearby ports. Typical of neighboring towns, Genoa is surrounded by mountains, precluding extensive hinterland growth and leaving the Genoese no choice but to turn to seaward expansion via the Mediterranean lying to the south.

If the Mediterranean was first a geographic unit, it was also a social space. The early medieval Muslim traders divided that space into three distinct regions: the "East," composed of Egypt and the Muslim countries of southwestern Asia; the "West," composed of North Africa, Sicily, and

Andalus (today's Spain); [2] and "the Land of the Romans" (*Al-Rum* by its Muslim name), which included Byzantium and most of Europe. The Christian vision of the Mediterranean also included three regions, but in a slightly different apportionment: On the east lay the Byzantine territory that extended as far as Venice; on the west, from the eastern shore of Italy to the Pyrennes, was the Frankish land that extended up to the North Sea; and the Mediterranean region to the south, from Egypt to Spain, was Muslim territory.

## Origin

Archeological research has established the antique origin of Genoa, an administrative center (*municipium*) in the Roman Empire. The city grew at the intersection of two main roads, the *vie Postumia* (from Piacenza to Genoa) and *Aurelia* (from the south of France to Rome, or to the Po Valley), and was a key node in the Roman transportation network. It is this position that gave the city an ascendancy over other Ligurian ports such as Pisa, Albenga, and Ventimilglia. As Pistarino suggests, Genoa's status as a regional center in the sixth and seventh centuries was further strengthened by the arrival sometime around 568–69 of the archbishop of Milan, who found refuge there while fleeing the invading Lombards. As a result, the city became the easternmost administrative center of the Byzantine Empire. This position would last only until the Lombard Conquest in 642. From then on, while other Italian coastal cities, such as Amalfi and Venice, remained connected to the Byzantine Empire's network, Genoa was cut off from oriental civilization. This isolation was reinforced by the degradation of the ancient road network that forced the *Genuates* or *Genuences,* as they were called, to make a strenuous journey over a rugged mountain pass controlled by hostile local lords in order to connect with the hinterland. Further relegating the city to a minor administrative and military role was the new northern rulers' strategic outlook. Unlike the Byzantines, the Lombards based their strength on land rather than on sea and considered maintaining control of the mountain pass to Milan preferable to defending the Ligurian coastline.

Despite such difficulties confining Genoese economic activity to local trade and a subsistence economy, the city was still large enough to warrant the presence of a bishopric and rich enough to be a repeated target of

---

[2] By 771 A. D., the Muslim armies had crossed the Strait of Gibraltar and taken nearly all of Visigothic Spain.

Saracen raids. In 935, the city was completely sacked, by which time, in a fashion similar to the emergence of many medieval social structures,[3] Genoa maintained its importance not so much because of its place in a larger political unit, but rather because it provided a local response to external threats. Indeed, the city's fortified walls became a refuge for the inhabitants of the countryside (Bach 1955, p. 36), also called *contado*,[4] and this fact contributed to the primarily military foundation of Genoa's social organization.

As with so many smaller feudal political units of the time, Genoa was, nevertheless, loosely part of a larger administrative unit. The city was, indeed, under the feudal control of the Marquis Obertenghi, a fief of the Frankish emperor.

Although we do not know much about the city before the twelfth century, we can surmise from a few documents that its social organization was isomorphic to the upstream feudal arrangement. Indeed, a charter of July 958, from the Lombard Kings Berenger and Albert to "*Omnibus nostris fidelibus et habitatoribus in civitata Januensi*" confirms the presence of vassalage ties and a hierarchical structure in the city's organization (CD I, p. 1). *Fidelis* refers to the men who have given *homagium* (homage), and the distinction between *habitatoribus*, or inhabitant, and *fidelis* leaves no doubt about the feudal origin of the city social system.

*Dynamics of Social Organization.* Even as the foundation of Genoese social organization continued to be the traditional land-based feudal economy and the reciprocal bond of its social and military organization, three important documents over a period of two hundred years offer insight into how the city's commercial interests were slowly emerging.

The first document is the charter of 958 (CD I, pp. 3–4), by which Kings Berenger and Albert formalized existing Genoese real estate practices and confirmed ownership of land, mills, vineyards, and woods acquired (against traditional feudal arrangements) through inheritance and custom.[5]

---

[3] See Bloch (1961) for a full discussion of this process.

[4] The etymology of *contado* is the *comitatus*, the administrative district of the Carolingian era.

[5] The king, who was exercising a tenuous control over northern Italy, was reaching down the feudal ladder to keep his own direct vassals in check. Ultimately, this type of alliance would often be beneficial to Genoa. For example, in the twelfth century, Frederic II asked the Genoese for support in case of war with Marseilles. Genoa agreed to submit to the feudal authority of the emperor, but received in exchange the right to strengthen its

The charter of 958 confirms the Genoese's exclusive concern with real estate. As in other parts of Europe, ownership of land provided not only the necessary foodstuffs but also the retinue required to maintain credible military status. Indeed, there are no references in the charter of 958 that suggest trading activities, such as taxes on imports or roadways. This ubiquity of agriculture is, in fact, confirmed by the Ligurian sources that recount Saracen incursions. There is never a mention of commercial loss – such as that resulting from the plunder of warehouses; rather, there is always the expression of a deep distress over agricultural destruction.

The second document that shows the shift in Genoese priorities dates from 1056 (CD I, pp. 7–9), some forty years before the establishment of the permanent Commune. That year, the Genoese signed a treaty with their overlord, the Marquis Obertenghi, by which the overlord swore to abide by the internal rules of the city. The focus of this document is again on feudal privilege related to landholding. The Genoese wanted to make sure that their overlord validated and respected the sale and alienation of land among the Genoese themselves. This does not mean that the Genoese intended to modify the feudal character of the landholding. Quite the opposite, several details of the agreement pertained to all feudal rights of the properties transacted (for example, the number of serfs). However, although this treaty makes no mention of commerce per se, the very idea of a liquid land market prefigured the transactional culture that would permeate Genoa's commercial institutions in later centuries.

The third document that illustrates the shift of economic focus in Genoa refers to an oath of 1157 by which the citizens swore to defend the city's commercial interests against other trading powers. This time, the document (CD I, p. 350) makes no mention of landholdings and focuses on the same overseas trading practices that I encountered in the notarial records of Giovanni Scriba. The administering of an oath was the typical feudal way to assert reciprocal social obligations. By swearing to defend the commercial interests of the city, the Genoese adapted that traditional institution. The 1157 document does not refer to a protectionist policy, but is the military commitment of a feudal social organization to defend its space.

The shift illustrated by these three documents was not the result of the emergence of a new controlling group. The recipients of the charter of 958 and the signatories in 1157 belonged, by and large, to the same

military defense along the Ligurian coast, including the construction of a castle *(castrum)* in Monaco.

families. This group had simply adapted its repertoire to new opportunities presented by the reemergence of the long-distance trade in the
twelfth century. Indeed, the notarial records of Giovanni Scriba (1154–
64) and a document related to the sack of the Genoese quarter in Constantinople in 1162[6] both confirm the strong presence of the viscountal
aristocracy and of the Church vassals in mid twelfth-century long-distance
trade. On the other hand, the notarial records also show the participation
of lesser citizens, especially in the nearer commercial opportunities such as
Sicily and the North African coast.

## Military Ventures

During the period from 950 to 1100, occasional momentary alliances
between Genoa and other Italian cities – Pisa, in particular[7] – modified the
Mediterranean Sea's military balance of power and transformed Genoa
from a defensive organization behind the city walls to an offensive maritime power. For example, in 1016, with the support of Pope Benedict
VIII, Pisa and Genoa chased the Saracens out of Sardinia (Sieveking 1898,
p. 11), and, in 1088, the two cities, along with Amalfi and Salerno, and
under the guidance of another pope, Victor III, successfully attacked the
emir of Mahdiyya on the African coast of the Mediterranean. If these
wars might at first have been defensive, the incentive for later military
operations was the spoils of conquest. For example, it is said that in return
for giving al-Mahdiyya back, the Christian troops received some 300,000
gold coins.[8]

Military expeditions would continue throughout the next three centuries, providing the Genoese Commune with a steady stream of income
as well as an endeavor that activated, solidified, and maintained the city's
unity. Among the military ventures, the Crusades, of course, come to
mind. The Crusades were the largest operations in both scope and scale,
but for the purpose of this research, it is not their size that commands
our attention, but their multiple consequences for the expansion of the
Genoese economy and the feudal nobility's participation in commercial
activities.

---

[6] This 1171 document is a reparation demand for the sack of the Byzantine Genoese quarter
in 1162 (Bertolotto 1896).
[7] For details, see Schaube (1906, pp. 63–4).
[8] See Manfroni (1899, p. 62). Although that number may seem high, even with the reality
being much lower, it is nevertheless certainly a very significant amount.

*Crusades.* The military expeditions preceding the Crusades, such as the intense involvement of the Genoese fleet in battles against the Muslims in the eleventhth century, might not have had the direct explicit religious connotation of the crusades, but the rhetoric of the Church was already behind the war efforts (Jehel 1995; Balard 2001a, p. 190). It is thus as part of the city's ongoing involvement in military operations against Islam that we must consider the Crusades.

A participation in the large debates as to whether the crusaders' motivation was cultural or material is not central in the context of this research.[9] The economic benefits of the Crusades are well documented and can easily be assessed, but so can Genoese piety.[10] Sharing in the spoils was certainly in the minds of the Genoese, but a theory of action built on long-term commercial goals is difficult to attribute to a city that was dominated by men-of-arms who acted with the same ferocity as the other Frankish conquerors when they participated in the carnage of Jerusalem and Antioch. In any case, the official chronicles, which reflect (probably from grossly exaggerated evidence) the focus of the time, do not even once mention commercial motives or consequences. The narrative describes only the religious fervor of the warriors, the division of the spoils, and the bravery of their military action. Moreover, as Balard argues, Italian commercial interests might have dictated a different history (2001a, p. 90). As we will see in the next section of this chapter, Italians had started commercial relations with the Muslims[11] and could have been worried about the Crusades' negative consequences, as affected by hordes of people of northern states, upon the Italians' slowly acquired relationships with the eastern Mediterranean markets. Thus, it seems that the Crusades were conceived for multiple reasons, each containing its own dynamic and playing out in different ways for different social networks. It is also clear that micro dynamics that were not ideological in nature amplified the crusader movement. For example, Genoa, as a main transportation hub and arguably already one of the very largest shipbuilding centers, witnessed the masses of pilgrims and crusaders crossing their town. In a tight community of warriors, not participating could well have meant the loss of one's identity and was never a matter of choice.

[9] For a sample of opinions on the controversy, see Pavoni (1992, p. 249).
[10] See, for example, Kedar (1976) and S. A. Epstein (1996).
[11] Goitein's (1967) analysis of the Geniza paper recovered in an old synagogue in Cairo provides precise information about Middle Eastern social life in the ninth, tenth and eleventh centuries and establishes the presence of Italians in the eastern Mediterranean.

Many Genoese families had firsthand experience of the Crusades. Even discounting the usual embellishment of the chronicler, it is likely that thousands of Genoese, led by members of the elite families, participated in the Crusades from the turn of the twelfth century onward. While the motives for joining the Crusades are difficult to assess with precision, the Crusades' multiple economic consequences shaped the Genoese social activity of the later centuries.

First, and most directly, as with other military expeditions, a share of the bounty was to be distributed and, as Brunetti and Lopez argue,[12] could thus serve as seed money for commercial activities. For example, each soldier who participated in the conquest of Caesarea in 1101 (perhaps as many as 8,000 Ligurian men)[13] received two pounds of pepper and forty-eight *sous de Provins*.[14] In many cases, the individual bounty was spent and not invested, but some money found its way into the Genoese economy when the crusaders returned home (Bach 1955, p. 60).

Second, every Crusade until the last one in 1270 provided income from the transportation of men and supplies. For example, a surviving contract of 1189 between the French King Philippe Augustus and the Genoese exemplified the kind of service provided by the Commune.[15] First, the signature and the oath of all ten consuls and thirty-six advisers to honor the terms of the contract are a clear indication of the city's total commitment to providing "*our*" men and "*our*" ships. This was not a private affair, but a communal one. Second, the service included not only the transportation of 650 knights, 1,300 squires, and their 2,000 horses, but also food for men and animals. For eight months, the Genoese were to provide food and, for only four months, wine.[16] Thus, it was an integrated range of defense industry services that Genoa could offer. In turn, the transportation fee, service contracts, and even financing facilities – as attested, for example, by a loan to the king of Jerusalem in June 1161[17] – provided Genoa with a diversified income stream. Additionally, aside from the large deals negotiated by the Commune, private entrepreneurs close to the political power also provided military service contracts. This was the case in August 1190 when Frankish crusaders hired Ansaldo

[12] See Lopez (1937).
[13] See Pistarino (1988).
[14] For details see Gies (1972, p. 42). The *sous de Provins* was the currency of Champagne, thus that of merchants who frequented the fairs.
[15] See G. and S. Jehel (2000).
[16] The payment 5,850 marks from Champagne (*argent de Troye*) was a huge sum.
[17] S#842.

Mallone and Lanfranco Malusfiliaster to carry horses and warriors' retinue to the Levant.[18]

Third, the transportation of warriors from all over Europe strengthened Genoa's position as a central link between northern Europe and the Orient. It enhanced the reputation of the Genoese shipbuilding and military machine-making capabilities. The export of Genoese poliorcetic skill is illustrated by the transformation of Genoese galleys into siege machines by Primo de Castello and Guglielmo Embriaco during the First Crusade, and again by a treaty of 1146 between the king of Castile and the city of Genoa that stipulated the payment of 10,000 marabotins for Genoese military machines (Jehel 1993, p. 35). In addition, the strong transportation industry[19] solidified relationships between the great Frankish lords and the city. For example, Godfrey of Bouillon, the first Christian ruler of Jerusalem, and his retainers took Genoese ships back and forth, and, in 1189, both Richard the Lionheart and Philippe Augustus visited Genoa to negotiate the leasing of ships. The political benefits of the Genoese transportation capability were to continue, as is evident from the king of France's designation of Baldovino Guercio to carry his daughter Agnese to marry the future Emperor Isaac II.

Fourth, the Genoese – having helped the founders of the crusaders' kingdoms – were able to benefit from perduring relationships to build up their eastern commerce because the need for the Genoese nobility's seafaring and military skills did not end with the conquest. Indeed, the experience of the Christian Kingdom's Frankish knights was on land and not on sea, making the participation of the Italians patrolling and protecting the crusaders' ports indispensable. The continuous traveling of the warrior class in the eastern basin became a natural training ground for their subsequent long-distance trading activity. In addition, the large presence of Genoese aristocratic families in the Orient facilitated the coordination of long-distance commercial activity (Day 1988, pp.108–9).

A fifth positive economic outcome of military operations was the preferential custom rates granted to Genoese traders. While this is the widespread argument advanced by social scientists as they unsuitably apply modern economic theory to medieval exchange, it is also the weakest. Indeed, too much emphasis has been put on trade concessions as the main commercial outcome of the military victories. In light of the huge profits that commercial ventures were bringing, treaties such as the

---

[18] OB3#599.
[19] See, for multiple examples, Balard (2001a, pp. 192–3).

one between the Genoese and Abd-el-Mumim, the first king of the Almohade dynasty, providing the Genoese with a preferential 8% toll (as opposed to 10% for the rival Pisans),[20] did not make a meaningful difference. Additionally, the notion "preferential tariff" was relative. In many ports, several maritime urban centers from the north Mediterranean would benefit from a "special" custom rate (Ashtor 1986, p. 20 and p. 41). The return on investment for medieval long-distance trade shows that securing capital and exchanging goods that were safely transported would yield very high profits. Under these conditions, a real commercial payoff of military expeditions such as the Crusades was the establishment of a permanent presence in foreign markets, usually materialized by the ability to build a *fondaco*, quarters where the Genoese built their social network as well as where they eventually warehoused their goods. This was the case in 1098, when Genoa received a concession in Antioch of a *fondaco con pozzo* (with a well) and thirty houses, along with the right to establish its own jurisdiction (CD I, p. 11), and, in 1104, when Baldwin of Jerusalem gave the Genoese similar privileges in Jerusalem and Acre (*Historia Patria Monumenta*, vol. VII: col. 16). However, the flip side of this permanent presence was that the *fondaco* also allowed the local authority to control the foreign merchants (Jacoby 2001, p. 379).

### The Commune's Foundation[21]

The timing of the Crusades is highly relevant to understanding the city's social and political organization. Historians agree that the Genoese Commune was formally created around the last decade of the eleventh century. The Compagna and its elected consul seem to have been a voluntary alliance of men giving an oath (Vitale 1956, pp. 16–17) that was certainly solidified by the experience of the First Crusade during the last two or three years of the eleventh century. This is not to say that an urban association would not have developed had it not been for the Oriental campaigns, but the timing reinforced the warrior and aristocratic nature of the association, which was at first a naval association.[22] As a contrast, the timing of the formation of subsequent urban associations in many other parts of Europe was associated with later commercial developments

---

[20] See Mas Latrie (1866, p. 89).

[21] For the general historiography of the emergence of the commune in medieval Europe, see Pirenne (1938); Lestocquoy (1952); Mundy and Riesenberg (1958); Sestan (1960); and S. R. Epstein (2000).

[22] See *Annales*, pp. 63–7; Sieveking (1898), p. 15; and Bach (1955), p. 42.

and, therefore, with a variety of social circumstances, each of which molded the social dynamic in a different manner. As Sieveking puts it, "the guild consisted of merchants, the Commune of warriors."[23]

There is little doubt that pre-Crusade military ventures probably produced temporary formal political organizations in the city (Vitale 1956), but their shorter duration did not translate into the lasting institutions that were cemented by the Genoese's long-term commitment in Syria during the twelfth century. Further strengthening the Commune was its rise as the regional political center while the Genoese's consuls represented smaller Ligurian towns in the negotiations over the spoils of the crusader conquests (Pistarino 1992, p. 34).

It is important to note that the Commune association was of "all arms-bearing men" (*Annales* I, p. 5)[24] – clearly not a commercial or occupational but a military criterion – who swore allegiance to the Compagna and its emerging institutions. It is a modern interpretation to believe in the commercial foundation of the Commune. The image of the Commune as a capitalist society, described by Lopez (1975, p. 41) and Balard (1978, p. 15), might well describe late thirteenth-century Genoa. But as Pavoni (1992, p. 249) explains, it is difficult to agree with the interpretation that this was already the case two hundred years earlier. Indeed, to give primacy to commercial ventures does not reflect the focus of the warrior class at the turn of the eleventh century, especially considering the Genoese's relatively late start in long-distance trading in comparison to other Italian maritime towns. More likely, as S. R. Epstein demonstrates, the Communes were born from "the fragmentation of territorial rules,"[25] and their internal organizations were only later cemented by the "quickening of the pace of trade" (2000b, p. 278).

The men who swore an oath were warriors whose social position was a function of their military power and their retinues. The historian Sieveking demonstrated that the objective of the Commune was the "*stolus*," that is, the right to engage in war and especially in sea war. Accordingly, the *Annales* recount the countless military operations lead by the consuls, from the siege of Caesarea in 1099 onward (*Annales*, pp. 63–5), and it is the whole of the ruling elite that took ownership in the interventions. For

---

[23] "*Die Gilde umfasst die Kaufleute, die Compagna die Waffenfahige*" (Sieveking 1898, p. 18).

[24] Although not all Genoese men were part of the Compagna, the newly created institutions seem to have been able to engage and draw on all military power (see Pavoni 1992, p. 249).

[25] See Lachmann (2000) for similar processes.

example, a surviving document dated from 1146 of an alliance treaty between the count of Barcelona and the Genoese to participate in a military campaign in Tortosa shows that no less than 150 members of the Genoese aristocracy, representing all the leading families, solemnly swore to abide by the agreement (CD I, p. 210).

Until at least the end of the eleventh century, Genoa was still a community striving for security and subsistence rather than for economic growth.[26] As in many other parts of feudal Europe, accumulation of territories increased security, food supply channels, and independence. The Genoese warriors who sailed the Mediterranean were simply looking for a new space of activity (Airaldi 2004, p. 65). Commerce – among which was food supply from nearby Provence, Tuscany, and Sicily – was certainly burgeoning,[27] and its increasing importance was to mold Genoa's social organization, but could not already be the primary focus for these men-of-arms. Caffaro, the great Genoese statesman (the insider) and Benjamin de Tudela, a Spanish rabbi traveling around the Mediterranean (the outsider), whose separate accounts are the surviving eyewitness testimonies of Genoa before the 1160s, reported military activities but very little commerce. As Tudela writes around 1162, "The Genoese dominate the sea and construct vessels which are called galleys, and go to spoil and plunder throughout the Christian and Muslim seas, and the land of Greece as far as Sicily, and bring the spoil and booty of all places to Genoa."[28]

*Formal organization.* After the conquest of Caesarea, around 1099, four consuls were elected for a period of either three or four years. Aside from their collegially attending to Genoa's interests, the demotopographic character of the Commune is attested to by each consul's individual jurisdiction over different parts of the city. We do not know the exact voting mechanism, but it is clear that only the urban elite carried the responsibility for selecting the consuls. The Commune was not an egalitarian organization. Inhabitants of lower condition, such as craftsmen and small farmers, were excluded. Furthering their isolation from the political process was the creation of a system that included the whole elite swearing allegiance to the Commune, therefore reducing the possibility of alliance between the disenfranchised population and discontented elites (Pavoni 1992, p. 250).

---

[26] "Genoa's economic organization was close to a subsistence economy," notes Lopez (1937, p. 435).
[27] See S. A. Epstein (1996, p. 116).
[28] In Roth (1950).

Most political fights remained internal to the ruling class, the members of which in time of external threats always found a way to rally to defend their common interests. While the length of each political appointment and the size of the consular college varied during the first few years of the Commune, the political organization seemed to start to take a more stable form around 1122. From that time on, elections took place every January, and the four consuls[29] kept their appointments for a year. Over time, a differentiation of responsibility inside the organization signaled the increasingly broader scope of the Commune's role. After the emergence of a clerical and bureaucratic function around 1120, a reform in 1130 divided the executive as well. Aside from the four consuls *rei publicae*, who were responsible for Genoa's military, maritime, and financial administration, the assembly began electing an additional eight consuls "*de placitis*" or "*pro justitis*" (justice of the plea), who carried out justice in each of the eight *Compagna* that divided the town: *Borgo, Soziglia, Porta, Portanuova, Castello, San Lorenzo, Maccagnane, Platealunga.*[30] Over the course of the twelfth century, the emergence of several new communal offices, such as those for financial management (*clavari* or *clavigeri*) (Imperiale 2004, p. 26) and fiscal supervision (*consul maris*), signaled the growth of the Commune. Further consolidating the Commune was the city's increased sovereignty, manifested in the right to coin its own money granted by Conrad II, king of the Germans (CD I, p. 106).

The broadening of the role of the Commune and the routinization of its administrative practices did not necessarily mean, at first, a differentiation of the city's focus. Indeed, the *Breve della Compagna* (*Liber Iurium 1*), a set of surviving documents that contains the Commune's official rules and regulations, confirms the feudal foundation of the social organization. Aside from the definition of responsibilities in the communal functions, the documents include countless dispositions regarding relationships between vassals and overlords, including how to deal with potential conflicts of allegiance between obligations to the Commune and obligations to a "foreign" lord. It also reiterates the exclusive character of the Commune members, and insists on the obligation of the consul of the plea to carry out justice for all, including the plebeian population not part of the Commune (Bach 1955, p. 40). Other regulations, such as limits on

---

[29] Every now and then, the number varied slightly.
[30] Initially, the number of the consul of the plea was fourteen. It was reduced to eight from 1134 onward.

tower size and the right to bear arms in the streets, give us a clear idea of the warrior nature of the city's organization. A few dispositions regarding foreign merchants attest that commerce certainly started to emerge as a key economic activity, but Genoese social relationships were still being conducted on the basis of the hierarchical and military repertoire of a feudal social structure.

### Local Lordship

However successful the Genoese were on the sea, the Commune was still under the tutelage of local lords and, in particular, under the four lineages of the Obertenghi family (Malaspina, Pelavicini, Massa-Parodi, and Marchese d'Este) (Sieveking 1906, pp. 4–5). This changed during the period from the mid eleventh to the thirteenth century as the military nature of the city was also deployed on land, and a succession of victories by the urban forces provided increasing control over the whole of Liguria. Indeed, the official records are full of documents stating Genoa's seigniorial control over the countryside and showing the swearing of allegiance to Genoa by countless local lords and their subjects. Among others, Genoa took over Portovenere from the Verazzo lords in 1113, and the castle of Fiacone from the Marquese of Gavi and the castle of Rivarola from the count of Lavania in 1132. In some cases the city bought, often in forced sale, the feudal privileges from its overlord, as in 1138 with the purchase of land from the Barcha brothers (*Liber Iurium* I, p. 61), or as in 1148 from the Marquese of Parodi (CD I, p. 235). Similarly, in 1150, Genoese troops forced the Marquese of Gavi to renounce his *pedaggio* rights (road toll) on the Genoese (Rovere 1996).

The city's objective was not the direct administration of the land, but to establish suzerainty over local lords who would abide by the city's rules. This could mean either an oath of obedience from the original local baron, or the enfeoffment to allied urban families through political nomination, or even the sale of feudal privileges to allies (CD I, p. 234). As a result, while the Commune was progressively transforming its political institutions, the *contado* under its domination often remained under feudal control well into the fourteenth and even the fifteenth century. For example, in July 1450, the lord of Sassello, Filippo Doria, a member of one of the four leading Genoese families, signed a convention with a group of men. He promised to build a tower and to maintain a military presence, while the men swore to continue paying feudal dues (settled in kind with oats, fodder, and chestnuts) and to participate in the defense of the fief.[31]

Even in the city itself, feudal hierarchy coexisted with the communal rules, as evidenced by a notary act of 1190 that relates to Alberto Marchese Malaspina's feudal right over some urban activities.[32] In fact, the superposition of the Commune's rules over feudal organizations in the *contado* was similar in many ways to the city's internal organization. Indeed, the urban nobility, often descending from the *viscomes*, had also, over time, accumulated privileges, including the traditional fee (*introitus*) on ovens, mills, and fishing and a percentage of the toll revenue from various excises and shipping taxes (Byrne 1920, p. 201). Some of these privileges they were able to maintain well into the fifteenth century. These *viscomes* were descendants of the Carolingian officials and had represented the margraves of Liguria. Over time, what had been a tie of vassalage in return for feudal rights over the city became hereditary privileges. These dues became transformed into private rights when the urban nobility severed its allegiance to its overlords. In particular, ten of the most powerful urban families can be directly traced to the tenth-century family of Ido Vicecomes, which had exercised feudal rights over the city (Belgrano 1872). The Avvocato, Piper, de Mari, Serra, and Usodimare clans were descendants of Oberto Vicecomes. The Spinola, de Castello, Brusco, Embriaco, and della Porta can be traced to another son of Ido, Berto de Maneiano. The identification of these clans is important because the continuity of their leadership in a changing economic world is attested to in the analysis of the commercial documents. At least seven of these ten names often resurface until the middle of the fifteenth century.

*Commercialization of Feudal Privileges.* In addition to granting fief, Genoa often sold the feudal privileges of their newly conquered territories.[33] In the rest of Europe, a financial component to the acquisition of rights was not unknown, as the granting of fief, out of gratitude or

---

[31] As reported by Heers (1961, p. 525 and p. 531). He also noted that fifteenth-century documents still used the terms "enfeoffment" and "number of men" with regard to some of the changing ownership of land.

[32] See OB3# 262/March 1190.

[33] Not only in nearby Liguria (CD 1, p. 234), but also in overseas territories. The classic examples are the enfeoffing of the Mallone in Tortosa (Spain) (CD 1, p. 203) and the Embriaco in Syria (CD 1, pp.292–3). The latter clan's independence would become so pronounced that, toward the end of the twelfth century, they would refuse to pay an annual lease to Genoa or to return holdings into the hands of the Commune for reinvestiture.

friendship, was sometimes accompanied by monetary compensation to the overlord. However, in Genoa, acquired feudal rights could be subsequently bought and sold without the consent of the overlord, creating a kind of secondary market in feudal dues and in the personal rights attached to them.

Rural lords constituted the natural pool of primary suppliers to that market, as their economic status, derived from agriculture activity and various feudal incidents, was being eroded. As the wealth of the urban commercial elite grew rapidly, the country nobility's more stagnant income was often insufficient to compete, not only for the same goods but also for the same labor force. The country-dwelling nobility's difficulties were amplified because feudal dues and agricultural revenues (often in-kind), although more regular than commerce, were not geared to building up the wealth necessary to participate in the emerging capital market. As a result, the records I analyzed contain several sales by financially pressed lords – who had not been involved in commercial activities – of their feudal hereditary rights to the commercial urban nobility.[34] The latter had the ability to pay upfront the stream of future cash flow and to provide the seller with disposable capital. This was the case for Opitzo, Marchese di Malaspina, who, in 1182, sold his hereditary feudal rights to the road toll of Torregio, as well as the revenue and incident associated with the castle, for £230 – a substantial amount considering that two and a half pounds was probably enough to feed an adult for one year (Byrne 1920, p. 198) or that the average sale of real estate for that period was £7 – to Simone Vento, a member of a consular family that was very active in the long-distance trade. The agreement specifically calls for the typical enfeoffment "by the glove" (*investimus te inde proprio guanto*). Once in the secondary markets, feudal rights such as the one bought by Simone Vento could then be resold or even divided among other members of the urban elites (*carrati*).

Similarly, the lease of seigniorial privileges by country-dwelling lords or by urban investors also contributed to complicating the classic, feudal, vertically latticed social organization. Indeed, I have found many notarial records involving payment by the urban nobility of an upfront fee for the future stream of feudal dues, such as for the right to operate a mill for a limited time.[35] However, although I have found no formal rules regarding

---

[34] Examples include: OB3#257 and #264/March 1190; GI#1872/April 1206 and #2037/ July 1211.

[35] See, for example, OB3#592 and #648 in August 1190.

status restrictions for the purchase of feudal rights, ownership change did not seem to be a mechanism of status mobility. Almost all the buyers I found in the twelfth century were part of the urban nobility who retained, as such, the political authority associated with feudal rights.

*Church.* The Church, represented by a bishop who controlled, organized, and delegated a large agriculture activity, was the other authority. The enforcement of its power came from the bishop's hierarchical seigniorial control over the local aristocratic elite. A list of thirty families registered as the vassals of the bishop *"de nobilibus huius civitatis qui fidelitarem Domino Archiepiscopo facere debent"* can be found in a surviving record (*Registrum Curiae* I, pp. 24–30). The typical reciprocal tie between the Church and the vassals included the latter's obligation to provide armed men when the bishop traveled in exchange for receiving the Church's land usufruct. Additionally, according to the *registrae*, the bishop collected the customary tax on the harvest, as well as a tax on the import and export of cereals. This is an indication not so much of the size of trading at the beginning of the eleventh century as of the natural seigniorial origin of taxes on movable goods.[36] The list of the bishop's vassals includes the descendant of Ido Vicecomes mentioned here earlier, as well as several others lords whom Belgrano[37] calls *"signori interni,"* or internal lords, such as della Volta, Pedecola, Rufo, de Caschifeloni, Caffaro, Bellamuto, and Canella.

Although most of the elite families are on the list, the strength of the vassalic tie between the Church and the Genoese aristocracies should not be overestimated. Unlike those in other parts of Europe, the Church seigneurial rights in Genoa were limited. In the documents regarding the political history of Genoa that have been published in the *Codice Diplomatico*, I have found little mention of participation by the bishop or his representatives in political decisions. Similarly, while international treaties still systematically pay formal deference to the bishop in the mid twelfth century, this becomes less the case later as the holders of the Commune's institutions take hold of the city's international representation. As the

---

[36] This is not special for Genoa. The seigniorial granting of commercial rights to the Church applies to other Italian cities as well. For example, Otto I granted to the bishop of Bergamo the revenues from the fairs frequented by the merchants from Venice, Comacchio and Ferrara (Doehaerd 1978).

[37] Belgrano has published extensive genealogical research into the founding family of Genoa.

Genoese specialist Pistarino notes, "The bishop, not invested with powers
by the king as in other fields, and therefore without control on political
matters, maintained a high moral rank, yet only exerted judiciary power on
ecclesiastical matters."[38] Additionally, the documents in the *Registrae*
show that, with minor exceptions, the Church's income was similar to that
of ecclesiastic authorities in other parts of Europe. Various taxes and
revenues from land ownership – often in kind and not money – constituted
a solid financial base in the agrarian economy, but could not easily be
transformed into financial capital with which to participate in the emerging
profitable long-distance trade.

A further complication in the transition to a market economy might also
be related to the Church's uneasiness with financial reward on loans and
even on equity investments. As a result, while our data set contains the
names of several members[39] of the clergy participating in the long-distance
trade, either as sedentary investors or as regular long-distance travelers
carrying commercial goods as a side occupation, the small number of
transactions in which they were involved,[40] the mention of kinship ties
with co-participants in several contracts,[41] and the lack of repeat transactions that could otherwise have pointed to an agency relationship, seem
to indicate that all acted as private citizens rather than as representatives of
the Church. By contrast, the data set contains countless real estate transactions involving the clergy – buying, selling, renting – which confirm that
land remained the Church's primary economic activity.[42]

In the Church, medieval cities often found the organization that they
were lacking before the institutionalization of communes.[43] However, in
Genoa's case, as the political institutional practices became more routinized and widely accepted, the organizational relevance of the Church
receded. Further undermining the Church's influence was the Commune's

---

[38] "*Il vescovo, non investito di delega di poteri da parte sovrana, come invece in altri luoghi,
e quindi privo di dominio in forme signorili, gode sí di alto prestigio morale, ma esercita
competenza guidiziaria unicamente in sede ecclesiatica*" (Pistarino 1993, p. 41).

[39] For example, S#865/July 1161, CA#858/April 1191, GI#1371/June 1205, and BA
#57/April 1257.

[40] From the portion of the data set that regards trade from 1154 to 1250 involving at least
one member of the clergy, the average transaction is £36 versus £70 for the whole
sample.

[41] See, for example, S#814/March 1163.

[42] For example, I counted 7 transactions in a three-month period (April to June 1203) in the
sole notarial cartulary "Lanfranco" (LA #221, 227, 243, 279, 312, 353, and 369).

[43] For a discussion of the institutional role of the Church in the rise of small political units in
medieval Europe, see S. R. Epstein (2000).

increasing international recognition. The bishop was an ally of the Genoese founders during their early struggle with the emperor and the local lords,[44] but the Church, whose economic relevance waned with the decreasing proportion of agriculture in the total Genoese economic output, lost its political relevance as the Commune strengthened. Even changes in the marriage law seemingly took place without the Church's direct intervention.[45]

## Public Office and Public Debt

As Gino Luzzatto writes, "There is no doubt that the urban commune was a creation of feudal society. It came into existence with the transfer of certain public rights from feudal lord to a group of vassals associated for the purpose" (1961, p. 69). If, at the onset, the basis of this new political organization was not commercial, it would slowly shift to reflect the growing importance of commercial ties. Later chapters in this book will show the role of commercial institutions in that process. However, an analysis of the first few decades of the Commune already shows a crucial change in the ruling elite's repertoire of control, a change that was not directly associated with commerce.

First, by equally engaging all members of the community to protect the commercial interests of the Commune, the new association supplemented the fragmented military feudal organization and rationalized the expense associated with defense. Thus, even though the distribution of the economic surplus became increasingly unequal, the public policy reinforced the process by protecting the return on capital of the leading families at a lower cost.

Second, the financing of the public policy – a policy that was so beneficial to the elite willing to participate in the growing commerce – provided a second tool of control. Not only – as was the case in other European fiscal entities – would Genoa's tax farming guarantee a high return for the tax farmer who could advance capital to the public authority,[46] the growth of the municipal debt also offered the ruling elites a new instrument through which to concentrate their financial resources

---

[44] See, for detail, Airaldi (2004, p. 84). The Church also played a role in the early territorial expansion as Rome was steadily enlarging the area of authority of Genoa's archbishop (Pavoni 1992, p. 252).

[45] See S. A. Epstein (1996, p. 45).

[46] Tax farming discharged the public authority with the operational problem of collecting. In addition, the lending operation by the tax farmer was often crucial for chronically indebted public authorities.

by transferring public taxes paid by all into interest paid to the holder of the debt.

The public-policy financing for the private benefit of the leading Genoese families is best illustrated by consulting the list of the purchasers of a variety of communal revenues sold to clear the municipal debt (CD1, pp. 240–2, 254–5, 257–8). For example, surviving documents show that the minting operations, the city banking rights, and customs revenues were mortgaged to a group of the consular elites in *maxima necessitate communis* (CD 1, pp. 130–9). Often, as in 1149, when the four consuls Guglielmo Piccamiglio, Ansaldo Doria, Guglielmo de Nigro, and Otto Leccavella took part in an important tax consortium (CD 1, p. 240), the members of the political elite bought the public income stream that they were selling on behalf of the community. The commercial records indicate that several commoners had enough resources to lend to the Commune, but, with one minor exception, all of the purchasers belonged to the consular nobility close to the political power. One could argue that the lack of interest of lay citizens in investing in the sale of public assets could be purely financial. However, this is unlikely. The terms of the 1149 agreement were so egregiously in favor of the investors that it contains a split payout over a cap. If the consortium's return on investment exceeded 25% a year, it had to share a portion of the extra income with the Commune.[47] The Chronicler liked to present the consortium members as Genoa's saviors. However, self-interest seems to be more at play than civic feelings: The external debt of the city, some £8,000 (Imperiale 2004), was fairly high, but certainly very manageable. A fraction of the yearly income from foreign trade around that period,[48] or of the spoils of the conquest of late 1140 that involved most of the consortium families, could easily have covered that sum.

The command of public finance would continue well into the fifteenth century and was a key social control mechanism for the ruling elite. In the end, as I will show in the next chapters, the nobility who did not participate in the commercial opportunities or in the emergence of public

---

[47] This is a sophisticated conditional payout that is not representative of other, more plain transactions.
[48] Although a precise estimate of annual long-distance trade in the mid twelfth century is difficult to assess, Slessarev (1969) provides an educated guess of around £200,000. While his number seems a little high in regard to more reliable records of the early thirteenth century, even if trade amounted to only half that amount, and considering a very conservative 33% return on equity, the £8,000 was a large sum, but it could easily be financed by the long-distance operators or by an exceptional levy on commerce.

finance were progressively eliminated, with a few exceptions, such as the powerful Fieschi family, whose feudal territories were large enough and threatening enough to extract revenues from the city and who, at the end of the thirteenth century, succeeded in catching up with other elite commercial clans.

## 2.2. GENOA AND MEDIEVAL TRADE TO 1150

In this second section, I review key elements of the early medieval long-distance trade in order to help the reader position Genoa in the context of the commercial expansion that began after the first millennium. In a first part, I review the dynamic of medieval trade before the commercial revolution. Then, I compare the more advanced trading practices and commercial networks in the eastern basin of the Mediterranean with those more rudimentary ones of Christian Europe. I show that, among the maritime cities that increasingly provided a bridge between those two civilizations, Genoa was, during the tenth, eleventh, and even twelfth centuries, commercially less advanced than urban centers such as Venice, Amalfi, Salerno, and Pisa. In addition, more than these competitors, men-of-arms controlled Genoa when the city expanded its commercial activity and rose to preeminence in the thirteenth century.

It is well to remember that, concerning early medieval economic activity, that is, commerce and trade in Europe before the twelfth century, the reader cannot simply transpose modern analytic concepts. Economic activity today often means profit maximization, and commerce is about margins. In medieval times, by contrast, goods were often sold and bought or exchanged out of necessity, with no other intention than subsistence. Second, gifts – simple exchanges between Church dignitaries, princes, and members of the ruling elites – constituted a large portion of the luxury goods markets behind the long-distance trade. Third, when goods were sold for money, the extreme fragmentation of the markets and high transportation costs made for a pricing system that was not a mechanism for adjusting between supply and demand. As a result, the inelasticity of the supply, faced with an undiscriminating demand, created opportunities for very high returns for those merchants who could simply provide something (Grierson 1959). The situation was different in the much larger and liquid Middle Eastern market. There the records show bargaining about attributes, such as color or quality of textile. Demand was also more price-sensitive, and thus merchants' profit margins were lower than in the West.

## Early Medieval Trade

The fall of the Roman Empire began a period of decline in international trade in continental Europe that was then amplified by the decrease in the Mediterranean trade attributed to the seventh-century Arab conquest. So large was the decline that the theory of the economic historian Pirenne (1987) (i.e., that the Arab conquest drew a curtain that blocked all exchanges between East and West) was the preponderant academic view for decades and the key point of reference of any discussion of medieval trade.[49]

One of the first to challenge Pirenne and to offer a competing global vision was Lombard (1948). In a reversal of Pirenne's hypothesis, he suggested that the economic expansion of the Arab world gave the impetus for European commercial growth. In addition, Lombard noted that the Muslim conquest had cut Byzantium off from its traditional food providers and had forced the city to look west, especially to the Po Valley, for new suppliers.[50]

In particular, Lombard showed that the Arabs' demand for raw materials – and, in particular, for lumber, which was almost nonexistent in African countries north of the Sahara, but abundant along the northern shore of the Mediterranean – stimulated the Mediterranean trade and, as a byproduct, activated the whole continental trade in Europe from the south up. Since Lombard's article, the uncovering of new evidence has confirmed the historical continuity and then the renewal of trade development between the Middle East and Europe through the northern Mediterranean ports.

First, while Pirenne might have been right in noticing the disappearance of Syrian traders in the sixth century, new evidence has now established that other eastern merchants, among whom the Jews were well represented, replaced them in the seventh and eighth centuries. Those merchants (collectively known as "*mercatores syrici*" regardless of their place of origin, which does not facilitate the work of historians), belonged to communities whose networks spanned both Europe and the Middle

---

[49] For a general comment about Pirenne's thesis and its influence on the debate, see Havighurst (1958). During the major conference of medieval economic historians in Spoleto in 1993, almost all presenters mentioned Pirenne's thesis.

[50] Dietrich Claude has offered another alternative to the Pirenne theory. In a decisive article, he shows that the decline of commercial activity in the early medieval era was not due to exogenous factors. According to Claude, the diminution of commercial activity after the seventh century could be attributed to the increased role of the Church and its distribution system, which by-passed the use of professional merchants (1985).

East and continued throughout the medieval period to supply a small European market with luxury goods from the East (Citarella 1971).

Second, demand for European products in the eastern basin of the Mediterranean throughout the early medieval period has, since then, been confirmed.[51] Aside from wood, slaves, furs, and arms, which certainly constituted the bulk of European export in the early Middle Ages (Lombard 1972, p. 40), records from the old Cairo's Geniza have brought to light the existence of numerous European imports into Egypt – and, thus, most likely to the rest of the eastern part of the Mediterranean. Among those, many items that could easily have been produced in Genoa were foodstuffs, such as "cheese, hides, peeled almonds and other nuts," and furniture, such as "bureaus, bed stands, jewel boxes and bridal chests, pillows, bed coverings of brocade and furs" (Goitein 1967, p. 46). This is certainly confirmed, at a couple of hundred years' distance, by some of the commercial partnerships recorded in our data set. In fact, Genoa might have provided these kinds of goods much earlier, but because it was a latecomer in the Mediterranean trade, these goods more likely came from cities with less contentious relationships with the Islamic world. This was the case of Amalfi, the inhabitants of which were the only western people whom the Arabs knew by their true name, rather than by the generic term *Rum,* and who entertained such close relationships with the Arabs that the ruling Fatimides even requested their military help in 969 (Jacoby 2001).[52]

Third, a renewed focus on the Byzantine trade has confirmed that trade between Frankish Europe and Constantinople never came to a standstill. The record shows that precious goods such as silk and pepper[53] made their way to European courts, but progress was slow. Part of the problem was the discrepancy between some of the luxury goods and the feudal way of life that is illustrated in an anecdote reported in the chronicle of the monk of Saint Gall: when Charlemagne saw his vassals dressed in oriental silk clothing bought in Pavia, he forced them on the spot to a

---

[51] For example, direct and indirect sources confirm the existence among Arabs of strategic needs for lumber and, in particular, for big planks and trunks for naval and military construction (Citarella 1993).

[52] Amalfi entertained regular commercial contacts with the caliphate of Cordoba as early as 942 (Pavoni 1992).

[53] Demand for spices dropped, probably as culinary consumption changed, but started to increase along with the new interest in spices as medicines, showing thereby the new influence of the more advanced Arab pharmacology (McCormick 2001, p. 791).

cavalcade in the woods and meadows in bad weather. They came back beaten up and with the cloth in shambles (Sabbe 1935).

Still, commerce picked up in the ninth century (McCormick 2001, p. 791). In 812, practice also became more formalized when Charlemagne and the Emperor Michael of Byzantium signed a treaty that gave Venice's merchants the protection of the Carolingian kings of Italy. Then, in 840, the expansion of trade toward the central and northern parts of the Carolingian empire was further facilitated by a treaty, called the *pactum Lothari*, that exempted the Venetians from certain taxes and tolls throughout the Frankish territory (Violante 1974, pp. 6–10). Venice, which straddled the middle line between the European Franks and the Byzantine Empire and succeeded in escaping the control of both of them, had always maintained some relations with the Islamic bloc.[54] Thus, Venice's political independence, which expressed itself in its multivocal possibilities, explains the city's centrality in the Mediterranean commercial network, especially in the trade of precious textiles, jewels, and spices (Heydt 1886, pp. 108–11). In some ways, Amalfi's emergence as the other main European trading port during that period can also be explained by its political multivocality, although in a more restricted sense because it lacked a Frankish link. Amalfi had long remained in the Byzantine Empire while, at the same time, maintaining privileged relationships with the Muslim world. However, unlike Venice, Amalfi's expansion was interrupted by the Norman conquest of Sicily. As Citarella (1968, p. 543) states, the conquest "robbed Amalfi of her political autonomy and set limits to her freedom of trade by dictating the direction of her commercial enterprises from political rather than economic considerations."

*Genoa in Early Medieval Mediterranean Trade.* The regularity of records showing Italian vessels in Arabic ports certainly indicates a continuous trading activity throughout the Mediterranean basin, including the eastern part, which represented the gate to the more advanced civilizations of Byzantium, the Muslim world, and the Far East. However, before the eleventh century, it is highly unlikely that Genoese ships regularly ventured into the eastern Mediterranean basin. Whereas early

---

[54] As many as ten Venetian ships arrived in Cairo around 850, and we know of at least two other trips in 828 and 838 (McCormick 2001). As early as the tenth century, Venice maintained regular trading relationships with Alexandria, Constantinople, and Syria (Lestoquoy 1947, p. 6).

medieval records indicate the presence of Amalfitians, Sicilians, and Venetians well before the millennium, the first record of Genoese presence in the Levant is dated from around 1060 in a letter between two merchants in Cairo sharing information about the arrival of Italian ships. Quite evidently, the frequency of "post–First Crusade" instances of Genoese presence in the eastern Mediterranean quickly increased and soon caught up to the other Italian maritime powers. For example, Airaldi (1986) notes the presence of Genoese ships in Cairo between 1101 and 1130, and David Jacoby (2001) reports evidence confirming the Genoese presence in Alexandria in the early part on the twelfth century, that is, a shipwreck on the southwestern coast of Italy of a Genoese ship returning from Alexandria in 1131.

Genoa's relative absence in the Mediterranean trade before the Crusades can be attributed in part, on the one hand, to the successful attempts by the Byzantine Empire to boycott those regions of the Mediterranean where the sovereignty of the eastern emperor was not recognized, and, on the other, to the Genoese's adversarial relationship with the Muslims. Indeed, the city had been detached from the oriental Rome since the middle of the seventh century, and had been successively under the control of Goths, Lombards, and Franks. Being the target of Saracen raiders until at least the middle of the tenth century, and then in constant military contention with the western part of the Islamic world throughout the eleventh and the first part of the twelfth century, Genoa was in no position to provide bridges between any of the three large economic blocks. At the edge of the Frankish space, tucked in behind the Alps, Genoa had to wait until the Crusades, and the renewal of its relations with Byzantium, to transform its position from isolation to centrality in a now reshaped Mediterranean economic space.

Throughout the early phase of the commercial revolution, Genoa was almost constantly engaged in maritime warfare (Airaldi 1997, p. 270), and the city's military culture persisted throughout the Middle Ages (Pistarino 1992). Before the thirteenth century, Genoa was certainly increasingly interested in commercial growth, but that was far from the only objective, as its social organization was controlled by men whose experience and focus was on war making and the industry that depended on it. A clear evidence of this is the contrast between the ubiquitous presence of the Genoese men-of-arms in the Mediterranean military historiography[55] and the comparatively reduced evidence of their

---

[55] The Crusades, of course, but also Bugia 1136, Almeira 1137, and Spain 1146–48.

participation in the commercial exchange before the middle of the twelfth century (Goitein 1967, p. 40).

Similarly, the different focus of Genoa also explains the chronology of the establishment of Genoese *fondaco* around the Mediterranean. For example, while the Genoese helped the Christian Normans in the re-conquest of Sicily in 1072, it was not until the middle of the twelfth century – much later than all other cities participating in the liberation of Sicily – that the Genoese requested a *fondaco*.[56] Likewise, the Genoese had to wait until late 1150 to have official quarters in Constantinople (Day 1988) and were the last to have a *fondaco* in Cairo (Jacoby 2001).

### Merchant Network

The evidence of the East's economic superiority during the early medieval period is plentiful and has been well documented (Hobson 2004). Because urban development and commerce have been positively correlated,[57] it is sufficient for us to compare the sizes of the largest cities of the more advanced Byzantine, Muslim, and Far East worlds with the emerging European urban centers to illustrate the difference in economic development. Around the year 1000, Cordoba – in Europe but then under Muslim control – counted 450,000 inhabitants, Constantinople 300,000, and Cairo 250,000, while Baghdad's and Samara's populations were probably close to one million (Lombard 1972, p. 97). By comparison, the largest European cities, Paris and Venice, had no more than 30,000 to 50,000 inhabitants.

Thus, at first, most of the medieval long-distance trade consisted of exchange between unequal civilizations that relied on very different commercial dynamics. In the following paragraphs, I compare the more primitive European organization of trade with the practices of the eastern markets to inform the reader of the antecedents that made up the starting point of the commercial revolution in the twelfth century. This will provide the necessary background to this chapter's concluding discussion on how the relative lack of commercial experience and specialization among Genoese travelers provided the right mix from which they could take control of the Mediterranean trade expansion.

---

[56] "In Norman Sicily, the Genoese were last in getting a commercial quarters" (Heydt 1886, p. 123).

[57] For a short discussion on the relation between urbanization and commerce, see Tilly (1964, pp. 16–18).

*European trade network.* Before the medieval commercial expansion, the distribution of goods on the continent was, on the whole, determined by the manorial economic system. The economy was still geared toward subsistence, and most of the meager and irregular surplus was bartered locally. Additionally, whenever surplus was sold on markets, the great landowners and the Church[58] tried to manage without the costly services of intermediaries. The evidence shows, for example, that surplus craft products of monasteries were directly sold to the markets by the members of the monastic communities.[59]

Early medieval continental social organization consisted, by and large, of separated self-contained communities. Thus, those traders – as integral parts of their respective communities[60] – belonged to disjointed networks and could not, at least at first, be the connecting agents between multiple economic entities and the diversity of production surplus that they offered. These agents could not, in other words, increase the range of goods beyond what was produced in the nearby manorial organizations. For those few who also developed some activity outside the manorial control in the countryside, their role was often to supply foodstuffs to the town and to transfer the surplus from those regions that had been fortunate in their harvest to others less fortunate (Doehaerd 1978, p. 171).

It remains true, however, that throughout the early medieval period a demand for "exotic" goods by courts and ecclesiastic dignitaries drove a small traffic in luxurious foreign merchandise (Spufford 2002). Thus, along with the autarchic manorial system, which covered almost all economic activities, there coexisted a very small commercial network of long-distance traders who supplied goods not readily available in the local context and that fell outside the manorial production system.

The information about the itinerant merchants in precious goods who made up these networks is not abundant, and, unlike the case of eastern

---

[58] Pirenne also noted that various fiscal immunities would make it advantageous for the Church to deal for them (1938). Indeed, Ganshof later also noted that the direct control of trade by the Church was also the result of the attachment of the merchants to an ecclesiastic community as a way to avoid paying local fiscal dues such as the *tonlieu* (1964).

[59] See Doehaerd (1978, pp. 170–8) for further comments. One of her examples is that of the abbot of St. Philibert of Noirmoutiers, who had his men carry out trade with the product of his abbey. The tenants of the estates of the count or of the abbott sold the wine and wheat of the village markets.

[60] Among those agents, Pirenne has described the palace "*negociator.*" During the Carolingian period, the *negociator* was, first and foremost, a buyer for the local court rather than for him (Pirenne 1938). For examples of *negociatores*, see Lestoquoy (1947, p. 15).

civilizations' traders, very few details about their commercial practices, such as financing and the quality and quantity of merchandise, have survived, possibly because they were rather primitive. What we know, aside from commercial itineraries, is the place of origin of some agents of trade as they are indicated to us by surviving documents related to taxes or to protection treaties granted to merchants by powerful overlords.[61] Among those merchants, the Frisians, who frequented the mouths of the Meuse, Rhine, and Schelde (Lebecq 1983), and the Jews, who linked southern and northern Europe, constituted two of the most important groups and are certainly good examples of the kind of long-distance network that operated in early medieval Europe.[62]

The Frisian traders often steered their own ships to carry goods by sea and up the European rivers to reach Scandinavia in the north, southern Germany in the south, and the British Islands in the west (Slichter van Bath 1965). From the south Rhine region, they transported wheat, wine, wood, arms, and glass north to Scandinavia and England. From the north, they brought back skins, ivory, and amber, whereas from the British Islands they carried slaves and metal back south.

In one of the only studies specifically dedicated to a medieval merchant community, Lebecq has shown that Frisian traders were independent entrepreneurs who sometimes took part in professional associations (1983). These associations provided some form of mutual assistance, and sometimes even fostered ties that facilitated the retail distribution of their cargo. However, there are no indications that these associations developed any kind of differentiation or standardization of tasks. Frisians remained individual transporters who sold their goods themselves before loading a new cargo. Their main skill was navigation, and their ships were their biggest assets. As Lebecq shows, it is very unlikely that any financing or capital outside their own accumulation of profit leveraged their activity. Similarly, we do not have any record of any form of credit, such as promissory notes, that could have solidified or enlarged the mercantile associations.

---

[61] For example, Otto II granted his protection to the *cives cremones liberi*, who devoted themselves to the trade (Doehaerd 1978, p. 181). Also, in 1018, Frisians called on the protection of the emperor against his vassal, Count Dirk (Lebecq 1983, p. 15). For more, see also Vercauteren 1967, p.109.

[62] Other smaller networks active in the early Middle Ages included English and Breton traders who frequented the north seas, Saxons who were active in Pavia, and Venetians who sailed the Adriatic.

Unlike the Frisians', the long-distance Jewish network was composed of two different types of agents. Sedentary merchants located in key European cities provided the relay stations for those traders who traveled with the goods. Additionally, unlike the Frisians', their commerce might sometimes have extended beyond Europe, as merchandise would be transported east by oriental Jews. The *Book of Roads and Provinces*, written toward the end of the ninth century by the postmaster Ibn Khurdadhbeh, described the activities of Rhadanite Jews who acquired Frankish goods, such as cloth, bearskins, marten skins, swords, and slaves, and transported them to Mecca and Medina and even all the way to China. However, this activity seems to have been limited as the Geniza records indicate that for the most part eastern Jews were more culturally and religiously than commercially connected to European Jews (Goitein 1967).

Another difference from the Frisians was the ethnic bond between the network of Jewish merchants and the great European lords' buying agents, which probably facilitated the distribution of goods (Pounds 1974, p. 74). For example, Charlemagne's *Formulae* mentions the privileges granted to a few Jews who enjoyed the imperial protection and who served the palace to the profit of the treasury (Doehaerd 1978, p. 177). Beyond these two differences, the European Jewish network, like the Frisians', relied on rudimentary commercial techniques that rarely included using capital outside each merchant's own wealth.

*Eastern Commercial Network.* As a contrast to the primitive European commerce, the exchange economy in the eastern and southern part of the Mediterranean was, during the early medieval period, more developed and the organization of trade more sophisticated. In the Islamic and African urban centers, the market was a central institution of social life, and, as Geertz has suggested, the bazaar was representative of the whole social organization. For him, the ubiquity of the bazaar was a distinctive characteristic of the Islamic way of life (1979, p. 123). Even though it has now been demonstrated that the bazaar within the city walls preceded the Muslim expansion of the mid seventh century (Kennedy 1985), it remains that the Islamic world then provided very good conditions under which to further commercial growth.

First, Islam conferred on the merchants an honorable place in society (Muhammad himself had been involved in commercial dealing). As Lieber puts it, "The fact that the merchant republic of Mecca was the cradle of Islam pervaded all institutions and, from the beginning, secured for the merchant a great deal of influence on the affairs of state" (1968, p. 230). As a result, Lieber and other scholars[63] have deemed the political and legal framework of the medieval Muslim world as usually liberal from an economic point of view.[64] Further facilitating exchange was the state's placing very little restriction on the circulation of goods and people regardless of their places of origin. Even when the custom called for extra taxes applied to foreigners, they weren't necessarily collected (Gointein 1967, p. 81). Second, pilgrimage was already widespread in Islamic religious practice. The flow of pilgrims carrying local goods to sell on their way to faraway holy cities, and who later returned home with merchandise purchased in large cities such as Mecca, facilitated the dissemination and exchange of goods and information (Simon 1989). Third, the Islamic world formed a more or less single political and economic space extending from Arabia all the way to the south of Spain, which contrasted with the fragmented political entities of the European continent.

Finally, as mentioned earlier, the sheer size of places such as Cordoba and Baghdad signaled an increased social differentiation and the emergence of a division of labor that fostered the intensification of trade. While commerce certainly consisted mainly of craftsmen selling their own products, the long-distance trade was based not only on exporting local production, but also on taking advantage of the differences in price among distant markets, thus enhancing the overall liquidity of supply. This constituted another difference between the eastern and European commercial systems that brought about very different practices. While the eastern commercial activity grew at least partly because of price differences for similar goods accross different geographic locations, the European long-distance commercial network was providing goods that could not be produced locally. In the East, the market was more uniform and liquid. Commerce was about competition in price and quality.[65] Access to supply networks in the eastern markets was also important, but it appears to have been more a matter of organization than uncertainty. As a result, it was not as important for Middle Eastern merchants to travel with their goods as it was for the Europeans, and, when merchants traveled, they would sometimes settle in faraway places for extended periods to serve as

---

[63] For example, see Lewis (1951); Goitein (1967); and Hobson (2004).

[64] This certainly contrasted with Byzantium, which placed strict controls on commerce and maintained the old Roman exclusion of merchants from political appointments.

[65] As Greif puts it: "The trade within each trade center was free and competitive, with many buyers and sellers interacting in bazaars and storehouses, where they negotiated and competed over prices using brokers, open bid auctions, and direct negotiations" (1989, p. 860).

overseas agents. As Goitein writes, the "division of merchants into travelers and those who stay put and send shipments with others is fully
borne out by the testimony of the Geniza." Further facilitating the sedentary activity of the merchants was the institution of *wakil al tujar*,[66] a
merchant representative, whose functions included collecting debt,
pressing claims, and taking on a variety of commercial activities on behalf
of the absent trader.

As a contrast, long-distance trade in continental Europe was all about
transportation and was carried out by itinerant merchants who formed a
commercial network activated by incessantly moving nodes. The profit
margins on transactions were very high, but so were the risks inherent in
traveling.[67] Consequently, while the task of the early medieval European
merchant was to safely supply goods around Europe[68] and to deal, along
the way, with the numerous local authorities, each requiring their own
fiscal levy, the Easterners were much more concerned with the business
risks and with the goods themselves. The Geniza letters present us with
the image of merchants neatly packing their goods, discussing fine differences in the quality of pepper or cloth and ways to extend credit for a
few days. All these preoccupations certainly concerned the Europeans
who carried out the medieval commercial expansion, but they really
became central only in the later part of the thirteenth and in the fourteenth century. In Genoa, in particular, it is, for example, only from 1225
onward that the notarial contracts mention differences in pepper's
quality. The difference between the Easterners' and the European pre-
occupation is best illustrated by the first records we have of Genoese
merchants' buying practices in the eastern basin of the Mediterranean.
Indeed, the Geniza record contains letters written between 1060 and 1070
by a Jewish merchant in Alexandria to his cousins in Cairo relating that
the Genoese did not understand pricing systems:

They [the Genoese] bought indigo at the auction for excessive price and some
brazilwood for 120 [dinars per camel load, also an exorbitant price]. They do not
distinguish between first-class and inferior goods: for every quality they pay the

---

[66] See Goitein (1967, pp. 186–92) for a description of his role. There was no equivalent to
the *Wakil* in continental Europe.

[67] For example, groups of Saracen thieves controlled the overland access to Genoa from the
west by blocking the Alpine pass and killing travelers or holding them in ransom until at
least 983 (Lestocquoy 1947). See also Heyd (1888, p. 96).

[68] This does not imply that eastern and southern commerce was devoid of risks, but that
traveling risks were balanced by business risks.

same price. Likewise, the flax they buy the poor quality for the same price as the excellent and are not prepared to pay more for the latter.[69]

***Trust Network.*** As Greif's (1989) research into trust relationships as a way to resolve market imperfections has shown, eastern long-distance trade organizations appear to have been composed mainly of a series of disjointed clusters of traders of similar ethnicity or, even more restrictively, of the same place of origin. This personalization of commercial relations – for transactions other than cash, at least – is a remedy for the uncertain enforceability of agreements in the absence of a public authority.[70]

No doubt some partnerships between Muslims and members of other communities took place (Goitein 1967, p. 72), but, for the most part, the commercial networks appear to mirror the social organization built around ethnicity, place of origin, and kinship. For example, the Jewish Magrhibi traders, whose commercial correspondence edited by Goitein (1967) forms the basis of Greif's empirical evidence, all originated from the same place and did not mix much with other Jews in commercial dealings.[71] As Greif demonstrates, while simple repeat dealings and information sharing is the basis of cooperation, the size of a trust network is limited by the robustness of its information-transmission mechanism. In other words, Greif simply points out one of the reasons for the inverse relationship between size and the proportion of transitive ties in social networks.

As a result of the size constraint, tight communities had little to gain by including members of other ethnicities or origins in their group (Landa 1994). Greif's argument is valid, but he is quick to dismiss kinship (1989, pp. 858 and 875) and social embededness in long-distance trade so as to reinforce his claim that the long-distance trading network can be understood on the basis of economic criteria only. Indeed, Greif's contention that the trust was strictly economic is too restrictive. Although we might accept the suggestion that it was not "mutual help or altruism" that motivated the parties, it remains that, in that case – at the very least – the consequences of "economic sanctions" (the expulsion of the trade

---

[69] See Goitein (1967, p. 46).

[70] For a complete discussion, see Belshaw (1965); Dewey (1962); and Geertz (1979).

[71] Despite the close connections among the Jews of southern France, only Marseilles is mentioned as a port from which one sailed directly to Egypt (Goitein 1967, p. 40); Magrhibi traders were originating from "the Abbasid caliphate" (centered in Baghdad) (Greif 1989, p. 861) and maintained "a distinct identity" in business dealings.

network) carried a very high social cost. If noneconomic social bonds had nothing to do with cohesion, why did the traders all have the same place of origin? Why would that selection criterion provide for a more robust network than a random group of merchants all equally rationally afraid to lose their commercial relationships?

Greif points out that part of the reason that the long-distance trade network needed to be divided into cohesive and tightly knit groups stems from the relative lack of a legal framework with which to enforce contracts. While this is one reason, the clustering of commercial networks also, more simply, reflects the inherent embededness of economic activities in social life.

## 2.3. LINKING TWO WORLDS

As Mediterranean trade increased throughout the Middle Ages, two important factors in the rise of Italian maritime power were geographic position and shipbuilding capability. Still, neither of these is enough to explain why preexisting commercial networks did not simply expand their operations to meet the expansion of long-distance trade. Similarly, these factors do not explain why the much more sophisticated eastern merchants, who also benefited from a favorable geographic location, did not diversify their operations by selling their wares directly to Europe, where the returns on equity were much higher than in the eastern basin. In fact, the Italians benefited from the failed history of all of their potential competitors, facilitating the expansion of their trade during the later medieval period. In this short section, I conclude the chapter by summarizing the conditions that facilitated the emergence of Genoa as a major commercial power.

First, the growing presence, from the tenth century onward, of Italian ships in the eastern Mediterranean contrasts with the near-complete lack of Islamic and Byzantine traders along the northern shore. For Cahen, this lack of mobility was an outgrowth of the point of view shared by Fatimids and Byzantium that it was fiscally more advantageous to attract the Italians to them than to travel the distances themselves (1965). This is certainly a plausible explanation, but the profits in the long-distance trade were so high that an import tax could have been imposed on their own merchants to provide the same revenues. Another possible explanation is based on the path-dependency of economic process. Easterners thought that the markets in Europe were too small and too fragmented to warrant the long-distance travel, which, in some ways, was a correct assessment.

Merchants involved with urban centers, such as Cordoba in the West and Baghdad in the East, did not bother with towns on the scale of Pavia, Verona, or even Venice, whose populations were only a fraction of those of the great eastern cities. As Cipolla puts it:

> To the Arabs, [Western Europe] was an area of so little interest that, while their geographical knowledge continually expanded between AD 700 and 1000, their knowledge of Europe did not increase at all. If an Arabian geographer did not bother with Europe, it was not because of a hostile attitude, but rather because Europe at the time had little to offer of any interest. (1993, p. 206)

Easterners simply did not anticipate the rapid growth of European commerce. Consequently, when trade expanded, the Italians had control of transportation across the Mediterranean. By then it was too late for the Easterners to catch up.

Second, the expansion of early medieval trade organizations was limited by the insularity of the existing commercial networks. For example, not only is there no surviving record of partnerships, or even transactions, between Frisian and Jewish merchants,[72] but also, more tellingly, the goods sold by the Frisians were all produced in their sphere of operations, confirming that, by and large, each merchant was supplied directly from the producers. Similarly, it was often the case that the long-distance merchant who bought the goods from the producer sold them himself to the final retail consumer. When the economic historian Sabbe described three categories of merchants (1935), he classified them by their geographical reach and the quality and quantity of the goods they distributed. This, though, should not be confused with a modern distribution system in which a merchant's size is usually an indication of the merchant's position in a vertically integrated system.[73] Thus, as trade between East and West rose, those preexisting distribution networks were not prepared for the vertical integration and the dissociation between financing and operations that facilitated the organization of a larger trading volume.

Third, a critical consequence of the insularity of the commercial networks was the merchants' difficulty in drawing on capital outside their mercantile communities to help them keep up with the rapid commercial expansion of the thirteenth century. In many ways, the commercial relationships, organized by practices based on trust and kinship, could

---

[72] Despite the scarcity of early medieval records, the lack of records certainly constitutes at least a strong indication of the absence of commercial interactions between Frisian and Jewish merchants.

[73] Vertical integration was prevalent in the eastern commerce (Robinson 1970, p. 24).

not easily be enlarged,[74] and were certainly not geared to attract capital from outside the professional networks, as the Italian organization did. Indeed, as will be apparent in the next chapters, the Italian commercial expansion included the participation of a wide range of investors, including members of the ruling elite, who could invest capital accumulated from a variety of income streams in the long-distance trade.

Fourth, it must be kept in mind that the key to success for early Mediterranean trading ventures was the ability to safeguard goods not only while they traveled but also while they were stored in the warehouses of faraway cities. Delivering goods to a marketplace would nearly guarantee very high returns on investments. As trade grew, and each ship's cargo became increasingly large and valuable, it became crucial to protect each individual venture against piracy. This protection could be provided by either the public authority or the merchants themselves, and plenty of evidence shows that the Fatimid and Byzantine authorities were just as ready as European lords to protect merchants – foreigners and locals alike – who transacted in their territories. However, by and large, Easterners did not organize the maritime protection of their own merchant network the way the Italians did.[75] In particular, Genoese merchant vessels received regular protection from armed galleys sent by the public authorities. In Venice, ships were required to travel in convoys organized and protected by the city's military mariners. Similarly, while the members of the Italian political and military elite were directly associated with trading,[76] the early medieval commercial networks in continental Europe had been dissociated from the public authority and could not easily gain access to the military support that the expansion of their activity would necessitate. For example, Jewish and Frisian commercial networks were made up of "men from outside" (Vercauteren 1967, p. 186) who did not, and could not, participate in the exercise of power.

However, even for Italians, formal military protection was often not available, and the goods had to be protected by the Italian "merchants'" themselves. Easterners had been traders for generations, and, for those who traveled, encountering regular violence was an occupational hazard. But these men were first and foremost specialized professionals trained to

---

[74] Greif provides an explanation for the limited size of trust networks: in a system that relies heavily on information transmission and on people's conduct, the group – in Greif's terms, the coalition – cannot have the long information channels of large communities (1989, p. 879).

[75] For a similar argument, see Citarella (1971, p. 396).

[76] For evidence about Venice, see Lane (1973).

negotiate, to evaluate, to pack or even to transform goods, and their
relational ties were intimately linked to commercial activity. Fighting was
sometimes a necessity for survival but not a way of life. Italians, who were
incessantly involved in military campaigns (Airaldi 2002), were different.
Their fighting skills could usefully be deployed in the long-distance trade,
and it is no surprise to read in the chronicle that when, around the middle
of the twelfth century, a Genoese ship, returning from Egypt laden with
precious goods, was accosted by nine galleys of Saracen pirates, the
mariners, instead of surrendering, "furiously attacked the pirates with
armor and sword in hand and killed almost everyone" (*Annales*, p. 98).
During the entire expansion of medieval trade, security remained essential, and the Genoese crews always included armed sailors. A couple of
documents from the mid thirteenth century about hiring ships (*nolis*)
illustrate the continuous military character of long-distance commercial
transportation. In a notary contract of 1259, during a period of relative
peace, a group of investors chartered a vessel with a crew of fifty mariners,
of whom forty were armored and ten were *balistierii* (crossbowmen).
That same year, in another contract, a galley was hired with 116 crewmen
on board; 30 of them were armored, and 10 others were crossbowmen.[77]

Genoese involved in trade early on were, by and large, regular citizens
who leveraged the multiplicity of their skills and their noncommercial
network in the long-distance trade. It is this multivalence – the ability of
these men to transform themselves successfully into artisans, sailors, men-
of-arms, or farmers – coupled with the possibility of drawing on the
financial capital and the military support of the whole city that proved
crucial to the rise of the Italian maritime commercial powers. It is precisely because Italians were not specialized merchants that they were
successful during the early phase of the commercial expansion. In the next
chapter, I proceed by analyzing the commercial ties that link the multivalent Genoese to each other as they build a long-distance trade network
throughout the twelfth- and thirteenth-century expansion.

---

[77] This was standard practice. Almost all the *nolis* agreements of the time specify the
number of armed sailors. Another example is given by Canale (1860, p. 342): *Bonflillius*
hired a ship with a crew of twenty-five sailors, ten of whom were armored, and six
crossbowmen armed with three bows made out of wood and three made out of horn.

# 3

# Equity Partnerships for Heterogeneous Ties

Around the year 1155, Genoa, reacting to the military threat of the German Emperor Barbarossa, undertook a vast renovation and consolidation of its fortified wall. The footprint of the wall provides us with a fairly precise measure of the town of 55 hectares (about 120 acres) and, thus, with a solid base from which to estimate Genoa's population at the time to be 30,000 to 40,000.[1] While the mountainous terrain surrounding Genoa[2] certainly created one of the most densely populated towns in Europe, its population was surpassed by several other Italian cities, such as Venice, Bologna, Milan, and Naples. On the Mediterranean Sea, though, Genoa was rapidly catching up with Venice to become one of two dominating Mediterranean powers. First dominating the western basin, Genoa was soon to share with Venice the eastern part as well. It was during this period that Italian cities enjoyed the rapid commercial

---

[1] Heers uses a comparison to other towns' density during later periods to get to the higher number of 52,500 inhabitants. This is rather high considering that, in medieval Europe, some of the foodstuffs were directly produced inside the city walls, thus reducing the density of the population. Most other estimates, like Chandler's (1987), are around 30,000 to 40,000 inhabitants. For a slightly later period, Day's estimate (1988) of 50,000 to 60,000 based on wheat consumption is in line with Chandlers's number. Demographic trends are especially hard to estimate because the dominion was expanding. Lopez posited that the population had grown to a realistic number of 100,000 by the mid thirteenth century (1975, p. 17).

[2] Among the fifteen largest Italian cities around that time, only Salerno and Amalfi were mountainous urban centers, like Genoa, but neither of them would match its importance in the thirteenth and fourteenth centuries (Sestan 1960, p. 83). Genoa is probably the only large Renaissance city that had no easy hinterland connections by way of water or land.

expansion that set the stage for Western economic supremacy during the Renaissance and, ultimately, the rise of capitalism.

From 1150 to 1300, Genoa's trade grew steadily, so that, by the beginning of the fourteenth century, Genoa might well have been the wealthiest city in the wealthiest part of Europe, with its power extending from its commercial dealings in Bruges to its colonial dominion in the Black Sea. One indication, among others, of the Genoese relative wealth at that time is provided by the levies assigned to various Italian cities by the Emperor Henry VII (1308–13) to cover the expenses incurred by his vicar general. Genoa was to pay 40,000 gold florins per year, substantially more than Milan and Venice, which followed with 29,760 and 28,880, respectively (Hyde 1973, p. 64).

In this chapter, I analyze several thousand equity associations dating from 1154 to 1315, to demonstrate how the medieval commercial upsurge altered the organization of trade and the social dynamics of Genoa as a whole. In contrast with the northern trade, which was almost exclusively organized by credit relationships between specialized and – at first – mostly foreign traders (see the next chapter), equity associations, contracted for the duration of a single trading voyage, comprised almost all Genoese investments in the Mediterranean commerce. These agreements – called commenda – which served as the ventures' framework, followed rules that were similar to those followed in other parts of the Mediterranean. The commenda contract – by far the prevalent institution of the time – was particularly well suited to the Genoese trading association because of the simplicity of its norms-based rules, combined with the limited duration of the arrangements, which fit the occasional nature of commercial pairings.

However, as routinization and specialization settled in from the second part of the thirteenth century onward, and as the Genoese elite increasingly defined their relational ties through commerce, the commendae did not survive the long-distance trade network changes. "One-voyage" partnerships were increasingly replaced both by more permanent equity ties and by credit relationships (Chapter 4), both of which emerged to form the institutional framework that defined the Genoese commercial pairing.

This chapter is divided into three sections. First, I review the formal functioning of the equity arrangements that organized Genoese ventures. In so doing, I make use of the data set to illustrate some of the standard contract clauses, showing that certain statistics contribute to a more classic economic history about what, where, and when trade took place. The second section describes the makeup of the commenda network by analyzing successively its gender, occupation, and status distribution. Finally, in a third section, I formally review the commenda network over time to show the morphological change in the trading ties. From a series of feebly tied star-shaped clusters in the second part of the twelfth century, the network's cohesion at first decreased because of its lost hierarchy, before regaining connectedness through status and occupational ties.

Before proceeding, it is appropriate to give a word of explanation about periodicity. Unlike many historical studies, this book does not present its research in a strictly chronological manner, and each remaining chapter concerns a type of institutional dynamic that organizes the trading network. These institutions have their own temporality; as an example, this chapter refers mainly to Genoa's history from roughly 1150 to 1315, as the periodicity is dictated, on the one end, by the oldest surviving notarial cartulary minuted in 1154 by Giovanni Scriba and, on the other, by the decline and – as a result – the increasing scarcity of the commenda contract from the beginning of the fourteenth century onward. This period also roughly corresponds to the strongest growth period of Genoese long-distance commerce and to the golden age of the Champagne Fairs (Doehaerd 1941).

## 3.1 COMMENDA: A STAPLE FRAMEWORK FOR OCCASIONAL PARTNERS

It is virtually impossible to know how many Genoese traveled the Mediterranean with their own funds or their own merchandise to sell overseas. No doubt some did, but historians seem to agree that, predominantly, those who sailed away entered into joint ventures with sedentary investors. In addition, it can safely be assumed that – at least for the earlier part of the commercial revolution – most of the agreements found their way into the notarial cartularies. Indeed, an analysis of a variety of historical documents, such as the list carried by the ambassador Grimaldi in 1174 regarding the financial loss in the plunder of Genoese assets twelve years prior[3] and the custom duty of 1214, give us a strong indication that most of the Genoese exports were not financed by the travelers themselves, but by the pooling of resources among two or more partners.

For the most part, the contract followed one of several formal templates, each of which corresponded to several specific financial agreements and mutual obligations. Every year thousands of contracts were duly recorded,

[3] See Bertolotto (1896, pp. 389–97).

and even if most did not survive the passage of time, many can still be found in the Genoese archives. Out of more than 18,000 commercial ties that I have coded in my database, about 14,500 refer to the period between 1154 and 1315. Leaving aside agreements, such as promissory notes and exchange contracts, that pertain mainly to overland transactions and that will be covered in the next chapter, the database contains more than 8,400 ties organized by sea venture standard agreements.

Economic historians typically bunch two credit mediums, the sea loan and the maritime exchange, together with commenda contracts in order to study commercial flows. For the purpose of this research, I have decided to deal with the commendae separately because equity partnerships constituted an altogether different type of social tie than creditor/debtor relationships.

While we will see later in the book that credit agreements were preponderant in the northern overland commerce, maritime equity contracts formed the overwhelming majority of sea bound ventures. An analysis of the various types of agreement that bonded the participants in the maritime trade from 1154 to 1300 reveals that over 93% of all maritime commercial ties coded in the data set were organized through commenda contracts (6,764 out of 7,221). This confirms the findings of other economic historians, namely, that Genoese investments followed rules very similar to those of other maritime cities. Indeed, although commenda took various names in different cities – such as *accomendacio, collegantia*, and *societas maris* – the contracts' remarkably uniform features formed the foundation of the vast majority of investment partnerships across the western Mediterranean. As Lopez wrote, "The Mediterranean commerce strikes us by the uniformity of it norms and contracts" (1975, p. 291).

The commenda, which has been the object of several specific studies, such as those by Chiaudano (1925), Astuti (1933), and more recently Pryor (1977 and 1983), was an agreement between an investor (the *commendator*) and a traveling partner (*the tractator*, also called the *socius portat* [carrying partner]) to engage in a commercial enterprise that usually took place overseas.[4] The terms of the contract invariably included the following:

---

[4] Commenda contracts sometimes organized local industrial partnerships, but this was not frequent in Genoa. Indeed, while I recorded more than 8,400 commenda ties for overseas ventures from 1155 to 1315, commenda partnerships in local enterprise could not have amounted to more than a couple hundred. This is another piece of evidence in support of S. A. Epstein's (1988) assertion that, in contrast to the eastern Mediterranean, where

1.  The traveler acknowledged the receipt of the capital from one or more investors and swore to abide by certain instructions concerning the use of the money, such as restrictions on destinations or goods transacted. To the capital received, the traveler might also add his own capital (always to the ratio one-third traveler, two-thirds investor). In this case, the agreement was called a "bilateral commenda." In some other cases, the traveler specified that he was also carrying his own capital segregated from the commenda agreement.

2.  The agreement was for the duration of one voyage.[5] Upon the return of the traveler from his overseas venture, the partners shared the profit. After deductions for traveling expenses and restitution of the capital originally invested, the venture profits were divided as follows: In a unilateral commenda, the investor collected three-fourths of the net proceeds and bore all liability for loss, while the traveler received only one-fourth of the net and bore no capital risk. In a bilateral commenda, often called *societas* in Genoa, the equal division of profit between the traveler and the investor seems at first different from that of the unilateral version, but when taking into account the share of the traveler's return on investment, the economics behind the payout was identical.[6] In a bilateral venture, the liability for loss was proportional to the respective initial investments of the participants.[7]

---

craftsmen's partnerships were the common practice (Goitein 1967), wage labor was the predominant factor in determining the Genoese work relationships.

[5] Unlike the craftsmen's partnerships so prevalent in the east, time-based commercial associations were very rare.

[6] In the bilateral commenda, the traveler receives ¼ profit made on the ⅔ of the investors' funds, which is $¼ * ⅔ = 1/6$. In addition, he collected all of the net proceeds from his half of the investment.

[7] I have adopted Pryor's idea that unilateral and bilateral commenda are essentially the same agreement. (See Luzzatto for the same opinion: 1961, p. 119). As he noted, the only evidence of a repeated partnership, for which we have enough accounting to understand the passage of one to the other, is that of Ansaldo Baiardo and his *commendator* Ingo della Volta from 1156 to 1158 (1977, p. 9). In that investment's sequence, Ansaldo, who probably did not dispose of much capital, started off as a "unilateral" partner. After accumulating his quarter profits from two successive ventures, he entered into a *societas* with Ingo della Volta in 1158 (Edler-de Roover 1941). From that evidence, as well as from the common form of the legal statutes of both the commenda and *societas* and the perceived interchangeability of the contracts across destinations and partner pairings, Pryor concluded that the decision to enter into one form or the other was strictly based on the travelers' basic economic level. This would in turn explain the slightly higher average value per transaction of the *societas* over the commenda, and the historical concomitance of the contract form. Further contributing to Pryor's theory of the interchangeability of the two

## Equity Partnerships

The relationships within the commendae differ fundamentally from other financial ties organized through a variety of agreements, such as sea loans, promissory notes, and exchange contracts, all of which are credit instruments that are analyzed in the next chapter. Indeed, although the financial outcomes of credit agreements were simply a function of the solvency of the creditor, that is, the ability of the creditor to pay the principal (in whatever currency specified) and interest at the due date, the commendae outcome depended solely on the success of the business enterprise, and was thus akin to a one-voyage venture capital partnership. Thus, whereas the credit agreement united a creditor and debtor in a credit tie, the commenda formed a real joint venture. It comes as no surprise, therefore, that the traveler and the investor were referred as *socii* (partners) in the statutes of Genoa, Pera, Marseilles, and Pisa (Pryor 1977, p.14).

But, unlike modern venture capital agreements, and unlike some medieval credit agreements, commendae's financial terms did not vary according to market conditions until the end of the thirteenth century. Indeed, the payout of each of the partners followed a fixed rule and was virtually independent of either the business characteristics at hand or the social circumstances of the partners. In fact, in a sample of 4,860 commenda ties from 1154 to 1265, which cover ventures to dozens of long-distance destinations, with sizes ranging from less than one Genoese pound to several thousand, and which involved a wide variety of merchandise, only a handful[8] of contracts provided a payout different from

forms is a comparison of the network measures for both unilateral and multilateral forms of commenda during the 1154–64 period and the 1182–97 period, when both forms could be observed in large quantities. The bilateral form network is slightly more centralized, but exhibits a degree of integration similar to that of the unilateral commenda network. As such, network theory is not very helpful for providing additional clues as to why the *societas* disappeared in the thirteenth century, just to give further credit to Pryor's theory. While commendae and *societas* provided the same returns on investment and labor for both parties, it may well be that the commenda – which until the thirteenth century had been an "introductory" contract – became prevalent because long-distance trade growth opened opportunities for a more heterogeneous pool of participants who found in the commenda the most flexible framework in which to formalize their agreements.

[8] Throughout the western Mediterranean ports, different payouts were extremely rare for long-distance ventures. However, they were more frequent for local commercial arrangements and even for trading along the Ligurian coast. Those kinds of commerce were often contracted not for a single venture but for a time period. Another exception to the standard payout are the few commendae contracted for free (*gratis et amore*). These may have been for an exchange of favor (Doehaerd 1941, p. 125). See, for example, LA#473/August 1203.

the customary one-fourth/three-fourths payout for the unilateral commenda and the half-and-half-payout for the bilateral commenda. It is important to keep in mind that it was the payout schedule that was fixed, rather than the return on investment to the investors: commendae were not capital investments with a fixed interest, like preferred stocks, but a straight equity investment.

During the last quarter of the thirteenth century, the payout structure started to change. Although the great majority of commendae maintained the customary ratio of profit sharing, the traveler's cut became higher for very small commendae (worth usually only a few Genoese pounds) because during this period of rising prices and diminishing returns, the traveler needed enough profit to justify the trip. Nevertheless, even during the course of the fourteenth century, which saw an increased variation in the division of profit, the payout of one-fourth/three-fourths in Genoese commendae remained the rule. As such, the commenda's institutional resistance to market fluctuation, a resistance that had been an attractive feature for occasional investors, could not accommodate the biggest investors, who presumably became unwilling to share such a high proportion of their increasingly large profits. It is, thus, from both economic sides that the commenda's stable framework became obsolete beginning in the last quarter of the thirteenth century, and its inflexibility accelerated the demise of a type of agreement that could not survive the change in the social structure of the long-distance trade network.

## Origin of the Commenda

Udovitch (1962, 1970) and Pryor (1977) have been the two preeminent scholars debating the origin of the Western commenda. Both seem to agree that the commenda originated in the customary law of commerce and not in the legal sciences. The wide dispersion of a constant set of institutional practices among interconnected maritime communities from a variety of judicial traditions supports their position. While Udovitch has also argued that the preexisting Muslim commercial agreements, called *qirad,* show the most similarity to the commenda, Pryor also noticed that the Byzantine *chreokoinonia* and the Jewish *isqua* have elements that probably shaped the Western partnerships as well.

My intent in mentioning the debate on the commenda's origin is not to try to adjudicate between these two positions. For the purpose of this book, it is sufficient to know that the commenda originated in the near eastern Mediterranean (Liber 1968, p. 240) and to point out the influence of some Eastern procedures on Western practices.

My goal in doing so is to ascertain why the European commenda facilitated the pooling of capital amoung disjointed social networks in a way that the Eastern formal framework could not.

First, both the *chreokoinonia* and the *isqua* agreements suggest the idea of debt, or at least equal and joint liability, which severely restricted the pairing of participants with substantial differences in wealth. Under the *chreokoinonia* and the *isqua*, a man of humble condition could not withstand the financial risk of an association with a wealthier partner involving large amounts of capital, whereas in the western Mediterranean, any traveler could take a large amount invested by a wealthy investor on a sea venture because his loss was limited to the value of his labor.

In this regard, the Muslim *quirad* seems at first to be similar to the commenda mainly because of the limited liability of the traveler (Pryor 1977). However, this agreement presented two key variations, which also limited the involvement of the whole community. First, any proportional division of net proceeds agreed to by the partners was deemed acceptable, so much so that, as Udovitch (1970, pp. 190–6) reports, Muslim legal manuscripts considered a wide range of profit splits, from half-and-half to 1/20–19/20. In other words, the cost of capital among eastern Mediterranean long-distance participants was a function of market conditions and, of course, of one's position in the traders' network. Thus, outsiders were at a disadvantage, and it is likely that they did not benefit from the same terms of trade as the more specialized operators. Moreover, the uncertainty that accompanied the constant reset of the payout favored the formation of clusters, as partners were more likely to build on previous experience and to do away with the bargaining.

In the West, room for bargaining was very limited. No doubt experienced traders could extract marginal advantages in the negotiation of commercial ties, but, because of the absence of a liquid financial market, there was very little flexibility within the institutional framework. The stable profit split encouraged the involvement of Genoa's occasional participants, who benefited from the same commercial protections as the more regular traders. This was especially true because – in a period when economy of scale did not seem to be substantial[9]– the stable profit split

---

[9] Economy of scale did not seem to play an important role. Transportation costs did not vary with quantity, and the great variety of merchandise involved in some single

also allowed small investors to expect returns similar to those of some of those larger operators.

Thus, in many ways the Western long-distance equity agreement was a lesser market instrument than the original *quirad*. As an aside, this shows how inaccurate North was when he wrote that one prime evidence demonstrating the more efficient West was the commenda, which was – according to him – "devised" by Italian merchants (1973, p. 53). In the course of doing research, every social scientist will make errors leading to inaccurate historical claims. Although I have endeavored not to, I am convinced that I have made some myself. For the most part, though, errors of this type do not necessarily vitiate whole theories, and have little significance when confronted with the empirical regularities organizing large sets of evidence. But, in the case of North's assertion, without the luxury of quantitative data, this error is particularly emblematic. Indeed, the commenda originated, and was in use, in the eastern part of the Mediterranean centuries before it came to the western Mediterranean. It is only in the context of a different social organization in Italy that the commenda took its meaning as an engine of revolutionary growth. Thus, the historical evidence specifically inverts North's theory by placing the historical primacy on social structure, as opposed to economic optimalization.

## Goods

A second difference between the Eastern and Western equity partnerships was that, according to Muslim laws, the *quirad's* capital – unlike that of the Western commenda – could not consist of commercial merchandise or even precious metal, but only of coinage.[10]

The difference in capital formation points to a difference between the Easterners, whose commercial ties formed a tight network of merchants with access to money and credit, and the Westerners, whose principal occupation was often not commercial. In particular, the Genoese ability

---

commendae shows that the partners were not concerned with obtaining better pricing by concentrating their capital into single items. For example, on April 5, 1206, Giacomo de Bombel agreed with Guglielmo Crispino to take £100 worth of cloth, saffron, and other goods in *acciomendatione* to Ceuta (GI#1838).

[10] See Udovitch (1970, pp. 176–83). This difference might be especially significant in the formal conception of the partnerships because, as Goitein noted, commercial practice did not always follow judicial rulings. Indeed, the Geniza records show many *quirad* in which the capital consisted of commercial goods (1967, p. 173 and pp. 175–6).

to invest goods instead of money was significant in the city's initial commercial development not only because it increased the volume of capital available for investment, but also because it facilitated the participation of those citizens among the less well-off who did not necessarily have access to monetary instruments.[11] This was especially true during the initial period in which monetary instruments were not widespread, but also toward the end of the thirteenth century, when the ability to sell one's own production overseas encouraged artisans, who would not otherwise have participated in the long-distance trade, to export their product.

Unfortunately, aside from that specific case, an analysis of the notarial documents often does not yield enough information to make a meaningful assessment of the nature of the commendae's capital. Indeed, the great majority of commenda contracts do not indicate of what the capital consisted. In most cases, the contract simply mentions the value of the investment that the traveler received to conduct business abroad.[12] For example, on April 8, 1190, the notary Oberto Scriba recorded, in front of the house of Nicolaio Mallone, a typical agreement in that regard, which reads:

I *Bufarus Saragus* received in commenda from you *Ottone Mallonus* 138.5 Genoese pounds that I will take to Sicily to do business.[13]

It is possible that he was to leave Genoa with a bag full of coins, but that is not necessarily the case. Indeed, there are two other possibilities: either £138.5 represented the value of merchandise that Ottone Mallonus was entrusting to Bufarus Saragus, or Ottone had no specific requirements as to what Bufarus would carry abroad and gave him the flexibility either to carry the currency or to purchase, prior to sailing off, whatever goods made the most sense to him.[14]

---

[11] Pryor actually developed the opposite argument by stating that the fungibility of specie was actually conducive to the pooling of resources by very small investors (1983, p. 413). However, individual average investment per commenda with multiple investors was actually higher than investment per commenda with single investors. In a sample from 1210 to 1300, the average was £94 for multiple investors (n = 504) as against £73 for single investors (n = 2705). It was thus not a form of investment specifically favored by small operators.

[12] The nature of the enterprise was referred to by expressions such as *causa mercandi* (to do business), *causa vendendi* (to sell), *causa negociandi* (to negotiate), and *laboratum* (to work on). The variation in terms seems in this case to have more to do with the writing style of each notary than with the specific nature of the enterprise.

[13] OB3#368.

[14] It seems to me, for large amounts in particular, that when a commenda's total investment was not a round number, it is more likely that the traveler received capital-in-kind. Also,

The lack of thorough information about the goods exported in com-menda makes it difficult for historians to make quantitative assessments about Genoese exports. In particular, for the purposes of this research, it is impossible to systematically test for an interaction between the com-mercial pairing and the makeup of the commendae's capital. However, a look at changes in the kinds of goods exported provides an indication of what kinds of investments were put together and also, indirectly, of one of the increasing constraints – while it was not yet a barrier to entry – to participation in the long-distance commerce. During the earlier period covered by the data set (1154–99), the evidence points to Genoese exports consisting of a variety of merchandise, such as foodstuffs (wine, cheese, almonds), lead, and animal skins. Additionally, the steadily increasing proportion of cloth, in particular fustian (an inexpensive fabric produced in northern Italy from imported cotton or linen), already indicates what would become the staple Genoese export.[15] Aside from those exports, a handful of contracts mention goods from the eastern Mediterranean basin, such as pearls, silk, and dye materials (indigo, exotic wood), which were sometimes transiting through Genoa before being rerouted to the Maghreb and Muslim Spanish littoral. For example, in April 1191, Ottone Farmons traveled to the North African city of Ceuta with £12 invested in pearls.[16]

As the Genoese long-distance trade increased, so did cloth exports. In a sample of 287 entries from 1200–49 documenting commendae ties specifying the capital carried, not only were textiles the most important export, but high-quality and expensive cloths constituted more than 45% of the total value of "in-kind" commenda. For that period, the rest of the exports were varied, so that no other category of goods particularly stands out (precious metals and jewelry, 17%; cheaper cloths, 12%; commodities and foodstuffs, 10%; manufactured products, 5%; all oth-ers, 11%). The increase in the quality of cloth[17] was due not only to the increase in imports from the north, but also to the development of

in some rare cases, it is possible that the partners did not want to mention the types of goods carried because it was illegal to export them. This was probably the case when the Genoese exported wood and iron to Alexandria during a period in which it was for-bidden for Christians to provide these crucial raw materials to the Muslim weapons industry.

[15] For example, see S#678/June 1160; OB2#173/October 1186; CA#488/April 1191, #805/July 1191.

[16] CA#496.

[17] My sample for the twelfth-century textile export shows that half was made of cheaper cloth (fustian).

Genoa's own textile industry, which was geared toward enhancing basic cloth by, for example, embroidery or simply coloring basic fabrics. Thus, even if the famous Genoese gold thread (*aurum filatum*) does not appear to have been an important export, it may be that from the early thirteenth century onward, the threads were exported as ornaments for the precious northern cloth.

Aside from textile-related goods and a few isolated types of merchandise, such as knives and helmets, the data set does not include many manufactured products before the second half of the thirteenth century. From then onward, the records refer to a growing amount of goods that seem to have been the craftsmen exporters' own production.[18] In a sample of 323 in-kind commenda from 1250 to 1300, 68% of nontextile exports involved craftsmen whose occupation matches the goods exported. However, those commendae concerned much smaller ventures, in comparison not only to the overall average, but also, more specifically, to all of the "in-kind" commendae. In that light, an analysis of the changes in the standard deviation and in the average amount of capital pooled together per commenda show that, toward the second part of the thirteenth century, the long-distance trade became much more polarized with respect to size. Indeed, the average value of all the commendae sampled stood at £65 for the period 1154–99 and at £48 for 1200–50, before rising to £199 for the next period. Conversely, the ratio between these averages and the corresponding standard deviation equaled 1.22 and 1.32, respectively, before jumping to 2.71.

The changes in both the average and the standard deviation of the monetary value of commendae ties indicate that, while small operators continued to be active in the long-distance trade, the capital build-up was increasingly in the hands of a smaller group of regular long-distance traders. As such, the evidence pointing to an even larger range of "in-kind" commenda volume in the context of the steady participation of craftsmen is an indication of the growing vertical integration of business operations. Indeed, the largest Genoese traders who – beginning in the 1250s – increasingly frequented the Champagne fairs themselves, as opposed to relying on foreign merchants, directly purchased those goods that they sometimes enhanced in the Genoese artisans' shops. Conversely,

---

[18] Prior to that, there are only a handful of "nontextile" artisans exporting goods they could have manufactured themselves. While excluding textiles the manufactured products represented only 3% of the total in-kind agreements between 1200 and 1249, the proportion jumps to 20% for the 1250–1315 period.

a growing number of commendae contracts involved artisans carrying their manufactured goods themselves or sending them by way of fellow craftsmen.

## Autonomy and Improvisation

If the notarial records only seldom specified the types of goods to be carried overseas, it was more often the case that the contracts stipulated a destination that left the travelers with different degrees of autonomy, a detail that certainly informs us of the kinds of ties that existed between the travelers and the investors. Varying from a stringent clause imposing a one-stop, round-trip itinerary, the range of geographical constraints reflected the great uncertainty of medieval long-distance commerce, uncertainty caused not so much by fluctuations of supply and demand as by unpredictable traveling conditions and local political instability.[19]

Economic historians, who wish to portray medieval commerce as an embryonic modern market like to point out that supply and demand required changes in itinerary. However, if this started to be a concern for the fourteenth-century Italian merchants, during the early phase of the commercial revolution, the high return on capital driven by an inelastic demand certainly could have accommodated a short-term rise and fall in local prices – even the kinds that seem very large to a modern analyst. Strong evidence that price fluctuation was not the primary concern of the investors is the fact that, among the thousands of contracts I have analyzed dating before 1315, I have never encountered an explicit condition imposed on the travelers as to a maximum price at which goods should be purchased or at what minimum price they had to be sold.

Political and transportation-related uncertainties were of a different nature than supply and demand fluctuations, and could altogether ruin a venture – or an investor, for that matter. While the traveler was obviously exposed to changes in sailing conditions caused by weather, a ship's technical problems, or the activities of pirates, his itinerary could also be dictated simply by the captain's unilateral opportunistic decisions.

Likewise, changes in local politics were another potential hazard. The sack of the Genoese quarter in Constantinople in 1162, or that of Alexandria in 1200, are certainly some of the larger-scale consequences thereof. But even smaller changes in local politics might also be damaging

---

[19] See Pryor (1983, p. 154).

to the traveling Genoese, whose legal status was to some degree at the mercy of the local rulers.

To respond to the dangers of travel, the investor might sometimes restrict the area of the intended destination of the venture and demand the traveler's full financial responsibility in case of transgression. For example, on October 8, 1191, Pietro della Croce, Marino de Veredeto, and Fulco de Ponte de Sori formed a partnership that was to send Fulco to Catalonia and "wherever he thought best fitted" with the exclusion of Alexandria (*preter Alexandriam*).[20] Obviously, this exclusion of the Egyptian port situated almost at the opposite end of the Mediterranean from Catalonia indicates that Pietro della Croce and Marino de Veredeto were well aware that Fulco de Ponte's journey might take him all over the Mediterranean Sea, and thus left him with maximum autonomy. However, they wanted to ensure that he avoided Alexandria.

Similarly, the investors sometimes tried to control the sailing risks by forcing the traveler to make use of a specific ship. It is easy to understand why a ship's age, size, and speed, to name but a few characteristics, would have affected the investor's level of comfort. Additionally, in a city where a captain's reputation – not only for good stewardship but also for military bravura – could be part of the popular historiography, the investor might also be reassured by knowing his investments were in good hands.[21]

This said, the exclusion of stopovers and constraints on the ship and/or the captain were rather uncommon. Indeed, I have analyzed and coded the exact language organizing 2,320 commendae ties from 1154 to 1230, and I found fewer than three dozen exclusions of stopovers and fewer than 100 specifications of ship or captain. So, in the cases in which the investor tried to limit the traveling risk, the most common way was to control the intended destinations, which he usually did by simply imposing a strict round-trip journey to a specific port, requiring the traveler then to sail directly back to Genoa.[22] But this clause was often not compatible with the overseas realities. As a result, aside from this most

[20]  CA#1197/October 1191.

[21]  For example, there is the mention "*nave que vocatur Francesca*" in LA#327/June 1206. The importance of the captain's reputation and the ship's characteristics in the eyes of the investors is confirmed by the fourteenth- and fifteenth-century insurance contracts, which almost always linked the policies to both the skipper and the ship.

[22]  For example, CA#476/April 1191, which specifies that trade had to take place in Palermo and in Sicily and on all the land of the king of Sicily (*Panormi et per siciliam et per totam terram Regis Sicilie, causa negociandi*).

rigid clause, the commendae could stipulate several others that provided the travelers with ample flexibility to improvise and to make the best traveling decision as events unfolded.

Dictating narrow destination autonomy, be it of a country or a region[23] or a determined set of stopovers, was a way for the investor to maintain some restrictions. It remains that the great majority of commendae specified only an initial port[24] from which the traveler should sail, and whatever destination he deemed the most appropriate (*et indo voluero*).[25] At the open end of the spectrum, many contracts did not mention any destination at all, and each venture could take the traveler to any of the Mediterranean ports. Some historians have wanted to see in the lack of the mention of destinations in certain contracts a desire to conceal a profitable market from other traders or to avoid tip-offs to pirates by their spies. This does not sound very plausible, though. Indeed, a given ship could carry tens of traders with various cargos, and it was thus impossible to keep the intended destination secret when so many had knowledge of it.

The lack of geographical constraints did not mean that the traveling partner was making strategic decisions about the destination, or even that he was in full control of his itinerary, as sailing conditions often dictated his trading circuit. Evidence of this is the common commendae clauses "where God will let him sail"[26] or "whenever goes the ship in which he shall go." This type of formula, as well as "*vel quo sibi Deus aminis-traverit causa mercandi,*" has to be interpreted as autonomy for the traveler and not a casual habitual clause, since it sometimes precedes an interdiction, as in "*excepto in Romania.*"[27]

The great autonomy left to the traveler gives further meaning to the term "partner" in the relationship between the traveler and the investor. Even in the asymmetrical relations between a wealthy investor and a traveler of lesser means, the traveler's autonomy is further evidence of a cooperative partnership within the ties of a commenda, which differs from the emergent fourteenth- and fifteenth-century agency relationships with stricter guidelines.

---

[23] A recurrent practice was to bunch Corsica and Sardinia. See, for example, GI#680/ September 1203.

[24] This did not preclude the traveler from buying and selling goods on the way to the first destination.

[25] See, for example, S#209, #210/ June 1157.

[26] See, Jehel (2000, p. 126).

[27] See, for example, GI#779/September 1203 and GI#1222/May 1205.

*Destinations.* Researchers have used the quantitative breakdown of the commendae's first destinations as a proxy for the pattern of distribution of Genoese exports. When considering that, especially during the early part of the commercial revolution, Genoese could leave without goods but with currency, this cannot be accurate. Additionally, unless the commenda imposed a round trip on the traveler, a stipulation that became increasingly rare in the course of the thirteenth century, it is a stretch to try to break down the Genoese trading destinations by port, or even by country, when in reality the destination in the contract is only an indication of one commercial stopover of a journey that was likely to include many, and one single journey could cover the whole Mediterranean basin. For example, on October 4, 1198, Oberto Primavera carried £36 belonging to a tanner called Wilielmus. He would first sail on the ship *Dianna* to the Levant and then to Ceuta, at the opposite end of the Mediterranean, "if that was where the ship went."[28]

The objective in selectively introducing a geographical component of Genoese long-distance trade is not only for the purpose of loosely controlling for possible bias in our samples,[29] but also to check for possible geographical interactions in the unfolding of the commercial network. In light of the autonomy left to the traveler to improvise, and of the inherent uncertainty of medieval sailing, unless it is for a rare event that can be otherwise specified, it makes little sense to break down the destination beyond the three-area division usually devised by historians:[30] the Levant, the western Mediterranean, and the northern territories. Indeed, a finer clustering grouping of destinations that are in the same wide geographical area and, thus, that correspond to comparable sailing practices, and probably to more or less similar supply and demand conditions, is difficult. For example, a clustering that separates all voyages to North Africa from those to Provence and to the near Spanish coast would prove wrong[31] because common sailing routes (Udovitch 1978; Devisse 1972)

---

[28] BO#88/October 1198.

[29] In that regard, because the data set is based not only on the analysis of comprehensive notaries' cartularies over short periods, but also on the two private personal transcripts of Professors Balard and Jehel, who have respectively selected Romania and the whole western basin as the base of their research, and on the published transcript of contracts between Genoa and northern Europe (Doehaerd 1941, 1952; Liagre De Sturler 1969), the sample should be representative.

[30] Doehaerd (1941); Balard (1988); Jehel (1993); and before them Byrne (1920) and Krueger (1933).

[31] See CA#1118/October 1991 and GI#226 and 228/June 1200 for a justification of that clustering.

make it hard to distinguish trips to North Africa from those to Sicily in the east or to Spain on the western route. Likewise, Tunis is much closer geographically to Sicily than to Ceuta, which was reached after a journey that usually included a stopover in what is today Spanish Majorca, which was, until 1229, under Muslim rule.

Thus, in the context of this research, the clustering of eastern Mediterranean basin trade into one region seems to be an adequate simplification. While the cultural and political conditions varied, the frequent use of the word "Levant" to designate the whole eastern basin clearly represented a commercial reality.[32] A trip to the Syrian coast, to Egypt, or to Byzantium involved similar traveling conditions and exchanging the same range of goods. Moreover, periodic fractures in commercial relations with certain eastern destinations meant that, during several periods of time, the Genoese concentrated their commerce on only some of the potential Levant destinations. Similarly, the grouping of all northern destinations is justified by the term "Ultramontanus," indifferently used by the Genoese in the notarial records to designate all northern destinations. Before the end of the thirteenth century, that meant almost exclusively the Champagne fairs, but when the Genoese opened a sea route to Flanders and England that quickly supplanted the overland trade, the term came to include any northern European marketplace. But this not need to concern us yet because, as will be apparent in the next chapter, the medieval commerce with the north was organized not by temporary equity partnership agreements but mainly by credit relations, and is thus not central to this chapter.

An analysis of the average value of commenda contracts confirms other studies indicating that the Levants partnerships were on average larger than those involving the western basin, but the record also shows that smaller ventures were not excluded from the eastern trade.[33] A prevalent economic historians' explanation of this difference is that the higher profitability of the eastern markets attracted the largest and more routinized operators. However, while it is likely that imports from the east could provide higher margins, the increased transportation risk and the required

---

[32] Actually, even the term *Ultramare*, which is commonly narrowly interpreted as the Christian Kingdom of today's Syria, often referred to all eastern basin destinations.

[33] From 1154 to 1199, the average amount commenda per tie is 82 versus 52; from 1200 to 1249, 53 versus 37; and from 1250 to 1299, 121 versus 82. The range of amount of ventures is large for both western and eastern destinations: from 1154 to 1199, the standard deviation is 84 versus 66; from 1200 to 1249, 61 versus 46; and from 1250 to 1299, 293 versus 156.

length of the trip meant that it was not necessarily more profitable than the closer western trade, which provided a quicker capital turnover.

Likewise, another theory that links the mid twelfth century Syrian trade to the ruling elite's monopoly over the most "profitable" long-distance trade is part of the same "rational choice" anachronism that portrays the Genoese as having the ability to make strategic investments based on accurate profit forecasts. The Syrian trade was very profitable, but no more than other Levant trade. To understand the Genoese aristocracy's choice of trading destinations, it is better to look at their social familiarity with certain ports rather than at price differences. As John Day shows in his book on the Byzantine trade (1988), Genoese traders tended to sail where they could count on an established social network. In particular, dynasties of the warrior ruling elites had long fought in the eastern basin and, therefore, relied on ties throughout the crusader states and Byzantium.[34] Confirming the notion that strict economics does not go far enough to explain how investment choices were made is the fact that nobles of that period were proportionally less active in the Alexandrian trade than were the other long-distance travelers, even though commerce with Egypt was probably the most profitable of all eastern trade.[35] Similarly, the members of the Genoese nobility, who had few relations and little combat experience in northern Europe, were almost completely removed from the profitable northern trade (less than 8% of total volume before 1250, almost all sedentary). It is only when seafaring routes began to replace overland transportation that the aristocrats developed their northern trade network.

In the next section, I will further explore the activity of these men-of-arms as I describe the social fabric of the whole long-distance commercial network that grew up as Genoa built on its military might and established its preeminence in the growing medieval commerce.

## 3.2. *JANUENSIS ERGO MERCATOR*: THE MULTIVALENT GENOESE

In examining the twelfth- and thirteenth-century commendae data sets, one is immediately struck by both the large variety of people involved in

---

[34] This does not mean that the crusades were ex-ante commercial enterprises. Balard shows that the financial advantages to Italians were limited and that the growth of Italian trade with the crusaders' states lagged behind the conquest by fifty years (2001a, p. 205).

[35] The historian Eliyadu Ashtor has demonstrated that goods were cheaper in Alexandria and that the relatively small custom exemption could not have made a difference in profitability (1986, p. 25).

the long-distance trade and the occasional nature of their activity. Furthermore, the very large number of names in the surviving notarial records indicates that, during the "commercial revolution," a substantial part of the Genoese community became engaged in the Mediterranean long-distance trade.[36] As a result, the records provide a unique collection of quantitative information about a medieval urban commercial organization, and the description in this section of the social make-up of the data set offers empirical evidence with which we can begin to understand some of medieval Genoa's social dynamics.

The participants' diversity expressed itself in the variety of places of origin, occupations, status, and even of gender, as women constitute a nontrivial segment of the commendae data set. It is in this light that the ubiquitous saying *"Januensis ergo mercator"* (Genoese therefore merchant) should be understood. A great many Genoese were engaged in the Mediterranean trade, but only a very small – albeit growing – minority made commerce their primary activity. That long-distance trade was a side activity for many persons is evident in the case of all those artisans who showed up only once in our data set,[37] or in the case of those servants who took advantage of an overseas trip with their master to carry the capital of fellow Genoese overseas. This was, for example, the case for Oberto de Parma, the servant of the regular long-distance operator

---

[36] Even knowing the approximate number of notaries at work for different periods, the proportion of the population involved in long-distance trade is difficult to assess. However, for those few periods for which we have multiple cartulary access, it is tempting to extrapolate. If Lopez's estimate based on tax records of thirty notaries at work for the year 1190 is correct, we can safely assume that several thousand Genoese directly participated in overseas commerce. Indeed, based on the cartularies of two of them, over a combined twenty-three-month period from 1190 to 1192, I have counted 1,363 individuals involved in the long-distance trade. Of those, I identified approximately 450 foreigners or operators living in nearby towns. That leaves around 900 Genoese for two notaries only. Obviously, since using a given notary over another was to some extent a matter of customer's choice, it was not uncommon to record business through more than one notary, and we should not multiply 900 by 15 to assess the participation. Nor should we assume that all notaries drafted equal numbers of long-distance trade contracts. Nonetheless, it is fair to assume that over a period of a few years, several thousand Genoese were directly involved in the long-distance trade.

[37] Such as the grocer Fredericus, who, in September 1220, carried £25 to Ceuta (JE#101), or Obertus, the shoemaker who invested £3 in a commenda venture to the Levant on July 17, 1190 (OB#541).

Pelegrino de Nigro, who traveled to Constantinople on April 26, 1274, carrying a modest £6 in commenda.[38]

The sporadic nature of long-distance investment also mainfested itself among the most powerful operators. Even for the two largest and most illustrious traders in the city's commercial historiography, Ingo della Volta (1132–85) and Benedetto Zaccaria (1235–96), trading was only a small part of their activity. Ingo della Volta, the head of the ruling feudal clan for much of the mid twelfth century, administrated justice, led military operations, organized the city's foreign policy, and attended to his feudal estate in the *contado*. Considering these activities, the few yearly transactions in which he participated over a ten-year span appear to be a lucrative – maybe even crucial – side operation, but quite different from the time-consuming commercial obsessions of the Renaissance merchants. Similarly, at a distance of a century, Benedetto Zaccaria was certainly very involved in trading commodities. However, his wealth derived from a monopoly of alum mines in Phocea granted to him for his military services to the Emperor Michael, and his omnipresence in Mediterranean military history at the helm of his fleet on behalf of the republic or of other European rulers makes him much more a military commander than a trader. Benedetto Zaccaria was an admiral in the service of the house of Castille and later in the service of the French crown. The book he wrote was not about commerce. It was a treatise on naval strategy for Philip the Fair of France in view of a possible naval blockade of England.

The distribution of contracts per participant did not change much during the thirteenth century. As historians[39] have previously noted on the basis of smaller samples, for most people the long-distance trade was still a rare event. However, the variations in the basic network's measurements, presented in this chapter's last section, show that the Genoese trading network experienced a morphological change that reflects the rise of a commercial elite and a shift in its social makeup.

*Onomastic Considerations.* The bulk of the data that forms the empirical evidence for this research can be divided into two time series: a series of joined projects between persons, and a series of formal commercial

---

[38] BA#272. Note also that the propensity of servants to be part of a long chain of investors indicates that they also tagged along on their masters' investments: 66% invested with others as opposed to 11% for the population as a whole.

[39] See, in particular, Bach (1955); Krueger (1962); Jehel (1993); and Balard (1978).

agreements. We have enough documents to define the latter and to classify them by a few legal and/or economic criteria. However, the task is more challenging with regard to persons who, over 900 years ago, increasingly joined their resources and formed the nodes of the long-distance trade network owing to the fluidity and multiplicity of activities on the part of persons who escape convenient pigeonholing according to modern terms.[40]

In general, aside from the members of a small number of families whose names were rather stable, the first names of Genoese medieval documents are often followed only by filiations, usually the father, and/or a topographic qualification: for example, *Bertoloto filius quondam Alberti* (Bertolotto the son of the deceased Albert)[41] or *Obertus de Langasco* (Langasco is a town twelve miles north of Genoa).[42] More rarely, the first name preceded a word that might describe the appearance of the person, or just a nickname, such as *Boccanegra* (black mouth/face).[43] In other cases, a profession or a word suggesting a professional activity, such as *Phillipus macellarius* (Philip the butcher),[44] also helped to distinguish people. Thus, in this case, the trade names of artisans supply one means of classifying the vast majority of the Genoese population, who were slower than the elite to adopt fixed surnames. The use of qualifications other than the first name was essential in urban centers as the same given name recurred constantly. Diverse studies on the distribution of first names in Genoese documents, such as Kedar's (1973), have indicated the historical signification of the frequency of certain names. In a sample of 2,000 names from 1190–92 in our database, 19% of all male persons are called either *Wilielmus* (Guglielmo) or *Iohannes* (Giovanni), thereby underscoring the importance of surnames.

The use of surnames as a way to establish the commercial network's social stratification on the bases of onomastic consideration is certainly prone to uncertainty, but often I had a few other choices when trying to identify key characteristics of commercial actors. In particular, the use of a toponymical adjective or a place name preeceded by a preposition, such as *di* or *de,* to determine the places of origins of persons in medieval Genoa has been the object a controversy.[45] In general, I tried to look for

---

[40] See, for similar comments, Reynolds (1945); Krueger (1962); and Pistarino (1992).
[41] S#455/June 1158.
[42] OB#594/August 1190.
[43] JE#10a /March 1252; DO#780/December 1252; BA#620/August 1284.
[44] LA# 1597/October 1225.
[45] See Emery (1952); Lopez (1954); and Kedar (1973).

explicit indications of citizenship whenever possible, or I relied on context and filiations to establish the places of origins. To some extent, the remarks about toponymical adjectives also apply to identification of the trade names that sometimes follow the first names, and they have also been the object of controversy.[46] For example, *Otto Ferrario* (Otto "the iron worker") is identified by the notary Gilberto as a *draperius*,[47] and some surnames can be misleading or inconclusive. To compensate, in some cases, I had to rely on the detection of a pattern to make a deductive decision. In general, however, identification was clear. This said, in most cases I had no difficulty confirming that *Enricus draperius* was indeed a draper, because the surviving records show that between 1198 and 1211 he purchased £2,507 worth of fabrics in thirty-eight transactions from twenty-one different sellers. Still, my remarks regarding occupations and places of origins should be taken in the spirit of the medieval lack of information. As the time line of our study advanced, the stability of surnames increased, and onomastic research does not contribute significantly to social stratification analysis; but by then a larger variety of records supply additional information about the Genoese.

### Gender

On September 25, 1216, Auda "the sister of the late Obertus Boletus" gave £10 in *accomodatio* to Iohannes de Vulturi. He was to invest the capital in the eastern Mediterranean and "other places." Upon his return, after deducting his expenses, he was to keep a quarter of the venture's profit.[48] The agreement, duly recorded in front of three eyewitnesses in the church of San Lorenzo, contains all of the commendae's standard legal provisions. Although Auda, like most women in the data set, is identified by her relation to one or more males (the identifier was often the husband, but sometimes the father or the sons), nothing indicates that she did not have full authority to invest the ten pounds.[49] In fact, women's participation in long-distance ventures was commonplace and constituted a meaningful segment of the trade network.

---

[46] See Hall (1935); Sayous (1937); and Reynolds (1938).

[47] GI#1886/April 1206.

[48] See LA#1134/September 1216.

[49] That does mean that they did not benefit from their relative's network. For example, in August 1190, Boneta, "the mother of Rufus banchierus," might have profited from her son's experience when she decided to invest the large sum of £60 in a venture to the Levant (OB3 #657/August 1190).

Many records involve women investing either the nuclear family's money when the husband was traveling, or that of underage kin left under their authority.[50] In most cases, however, they simply put up their own capital. A small amount could have been saved from years of labor or could be a small inheritance, as may have been the case in September 1210, when Zibona, "the maid of Henricus de Murta," gave £5 to Iordanus "the son of the butcher Zilius," who was traveling to the Levant; but larger investments probably related to their marriage contracts.[51] Indeed, a consulary brief of 1143 (CD 1, pp. 145–6) that eliminated a woman's right to a third (*tercia*) of her husband's assets provides a clue as to how married women might, from that period onward, have had increased access to liquid funds – as opposed to tangible assets[52] – that would have been available to be invested in the Mediterranean trade. That year, the consuls – most likely intending to slow down the rate at which estates were being divided because of an increase in family size – ended the traditional women's right to the *tercia*. As a result, women lost standing in their destination families, but a larger dowry (which the husband could use during his lifetime) and the *antefactum*, a sum given by the husband to provide for the wife in widowhood, increased their liquid assets (Hughes 1975).

Historians familiar with the Genoese archives have recognized and an-alyzed women's participation in Mediterranean trade, but these studies have been based on partial records and/or on shorter time periods.[53] Al-though quantitative comparison is difficult because my unit of analysis is actual ties and not, as in previous studies, the number of contracts involving at least one woman, an analysis of the data set leads to similar general findings. For example, women's venture destinations were similar, but their partnerships concerned, on average, smaller investments (see Figure 3.1).

A more original and more interesting finding is the only slightly smaller number of ties of women, on average, in comparison to those of men (average network degree centrality). Considering that their "careers"

[50] S. A. Epstein noted that husbands did not always appoint their wives as tutors, but that this was often the case in the wills he sampled (1984).

[51] Jehel shows that unmarried women constituted a minority of the women investors (1975). Among females, the largest female commenda's investors of the early thirteenth century in the data set, Drua Streiaporco, Giardina Boleto, and Mabilia Lecavella, were all widows. See GI#26, #494, #787, #809, #850, #1087, #1141, #1407, #1408, #1611, #1853, and #1964.

[52] Women were much less likely than men to specify an "in kind" investment (24/535 against 699/5286).

[53] See Jehel (1975); Pistarino (1978); and Angelos (1994).

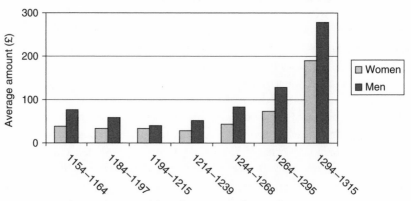

FIGURE 3.1. Average commenda value (per tie) by gender.

were shorter (unmarried women represent a very small part of the sample, and many of them started to invest only after their husband's death), this small difference is not an indication that women were less active than men; rather, it is another confirmation that the network was mainly composed of occasional participants.

More significant still in the context of this book is the historical trend of women's participation in the long-distance trade reported in Figure 3.2. Because it involves nonspecialized operators,[54] the pattern reveals the social dynamic of investment in its entirety. First, the height of women's participation, the first half of the thirteenth century, is representative of the involvement of the whole Genoese community during that period. Second, the rare involvement of women in the early segment of our data set, along with the empirical regularity of their decreased participation toward the end the thirteenth century, further confirms the finding that the period of wide and heterogeneous participation in the long-distance trade was sandwiched between two stages of more restricted involvement.

Further evidence of the decline in women's direct participation is reflected in the increase in men's investment on behalf of women. While rare in the early part of the century, from 1296 to 1315 a quarter of women's ties in the commenda network are by an agent, as opposed to other direct participants. Furthermore, those who represented women

---

[54] A notable exception to this is Eliadar, the wife of Solomon di Salerno, one of the most active women in the whole data set and the only one to have contracted a variety of standard commercial agreements, both equity and credit. For a description of her participation in the long-distance trade, see Abulafia (1977, pp. 241–53).

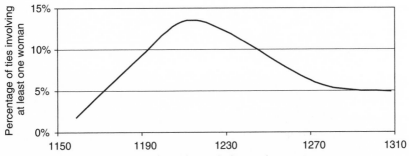

FIGURE 3.2. Percentage of commendae including at least one woman.

were generally more active and more central participants than others, pointing, thereby, to a trend toward specialization.

As historians have noted, women constituted an integral part of the medieval economic order, but their significance declined over time. For example, both Howell (1986) and Herlihy (1990), referring to slightly later periods, emphasize that the deterioration in women's positions was caused in part by their inability to access public office, coupled with the loss of their traditional role in production. The analysis of Genoese women's investment patterns also provides insight into the cause of this decline. First, in the same way that the rise of guilds drove women out of urban labor forces, the rise of a more specialized merchant group all but eliminated women from the long-distance network. Second, the trend in partner selection patterns in the long-distance trade network toward partners who were homophilic with respect to occupation and status (see the next section) further reduced women's choices. An alternative may have been for women to develop their own trade networks, but for obvious reasons, it was almost impossible for them to fill the role of traveling partner.[55] Third, the increased accent on status as a criterion in partner selection, concurrent with a rise in commercial kinship ties (see Chapter 5) and the enlargement of clans beyond the nuclear family, further reduced women's commercial role. Wives who had traditionally lent a hand in their husband's business when he was away were increasingly replaced in that task by the clan's males.

[55] There are almost no records of women being *tractator* (only five in the entire data set).

## Economy and Occupation

The previous chapter described the feudal foundation of Genoa's social organization and the elite who controlled it. These men-of-arms and Church dignitaries, who, by and large, until the end of the twelfth century, also formed the Genoese network of the economic elite, constituted a small minority of the population. In the next few paragraphs, I examine the occupations of some of the rest of the urban population.

Common people leave fewer historical traces than elites,[56] and this disproportion is amplified during periods for which we have scarce records. This is why, with the exception of a few monographs, such as *Montaillou* (Le Roy Ladurie 1975) and *The Cheese and the Worms* (Ginzburg 1980), medievalists tend by default to build their narratives around the stories of powerful people and the institutions that organized their social encounters. This conception does not necessarily make for "just-so stories" that rely on individual actions to power history; it is simply that scholars must work with whatever records have survived. In some ways, classic historiography in regard to periods before the middle of the twelfth century presents the same shortcomings in Genoa as in other parts of Europe: the histories of the local nobility left just enough records to provide an idea of the elite structure.[57] However, beginning with the continuous surviving notary records from 1154 onward, Genoese documents provide an insight into common people's occupations much earlier than in other parts of Europe (Slessarev 1967; Face 1969). One should be careful, however, in interpreting heuristic categories, because the Genoese could engage in multiple activities. Trade is no exception; as mentioned before, it remained for most a side occupation. As a result, it is very difficult to define a "merchant" category in the early phase of the commercial expansion. In particular, in the several thousand documents dated prior to 1250 that I analyzed, I have not encountered a single word

---

[56] "Elites," "patricians," and "bourgeoisie" are all terms that are sometimes interchanged, and they all refer to a social identity that is always recomposed and redefined. However, we are searching for ruling groups. In Genoa, we have to be careful: the reference can be to distinction (*discreti*), status (*nobiles*), birth origin (*gentes,*) or power (*potentes*) (Brautein 1997, p. 31). Any attempt to establish a social stratification will have to confront the several layers of the elites. For the purpose of this study, wealth and political representation form the main variables. When possible, the narrative will carry other criteria, but these two variables make sufficient explanatory values.

[57] The emergence of a multiplicity of activities renders the status of clans more ambiguous in Genoa than in most other places, but the identification is facilitated by overlapping information and the continuity of records that span multiple generations (Forcheri 1974).

that evoked a strictly[58] commercial activity other than a few mentions of *bancherius* (banker). It is thus important to keep in mind that this section is not meant to give a precise idea of Genoese economic activity, but rather to outline a few criteria and methods to present elements of stratification that are relevant to understanding the intrinsic multivalence of economic activity.

*Sailing.* Reading a list of medieval urban occupations is a challenge for the modern reader because many of those activities simply do not exist any more and refer to skills that have disappeared. The partial list of Genoese occupations established from the data set reported in Appendix B provides a clear illustration: just the modern translation of "tanner" regroups six different occupations.

However, the variety of occupations and the fine specialization of functions in certain industrial fields hide a fundamental medieval reality: most men, even artisans, would not easily fit into the modern rigid occupational classification because they were all capable of devoting themselves for extended periods to activities as diverse as agriculture, war making, and house building.

This fluidity of occupation was especially evident in Genoa because it was the sea, above all, that presented the primary economic opportunity, and sailing seasons or military ventures could at any time draw the Genoese far from their regular occupations. As is evident from the employment contracts that were almost exclusively for the duration of a single round-trip voyage, many artisans took leave from their occupation to find temporary employment on ships. For example, the names in the oarsmen's employment contracts for the 1234 Ceuta expedition are often a first name followed by a craft. Similarly, it is not surprising to see, as late as 1339, a woolworker *(lanerius)* and a gardener *(ortolanus)* taking temporary employment on a galley. In doing so, they, like thousands of Genoese before them, gained a direct taste of the overseas exchange economy, which they could then bring home to share with their kin and neighbors. For some sailors, overseas trips also provided a small

---

[58] With the possible single exception of *Fredenzione xamatarius* ("Frederick the broker" or, more precisely, "the buyer"): LA#274, 341, 154, 201, 316/March to May 1203. Grocers and drapers certainly engaged in commerce, but neither occupation was strictly commercial. For example, the medieval grocers *(speziarius)* dealt with spices, and their occupation was more akin to that of today's pharmacists. Similarly, I will show in the next chapter that drapers *(draperius)* were artisans who most often sold their own production.

opportunity for entrepreneurship, as each crew member was allowed to carry a minimal quantity of merchandise to trade upon arrival.[59]

It is difficult to estimate the size of the Genoese fleet, but Krueger's analysis (1985) from the lone surviving notarial records of 1155–66 provides a sense of it. Krueger enumerates seven galleys, fifty *navis,* and numerous smaller boats. Knowing that the largest vessels, galleys and *navis,* employed respectively 100 to 120 and 20 to 30 sailors each, and knowing that at the time a dozen notaries[60] were at work in Genoa, S. A. Epstein's estimate of several thousand Genoese men simultaneously at sea each sailing season seems fairly reasonable (1996, p. 98). Of course, when the city was at war, that number could increase considerably.

While for many Genoese sailing was not a regular occupation, conversely, the record shows that sailors often interrupted their employment to return home in time for the harvest (Byrne 1920; Krueger 1933). In this regard, they were no different from other members of the community for whom agriculture was a regular side occupation. Even those in the urban center, whose main occupation might be draper or grocer, farmed the countless parcels still situated, as in most other European towns, inside the city walls (*Castrum* and *Sancto Donati*) or just outside the gates (*Domoculta, Mortedo, Caligniano.*).

When not at war, at sea, or in the fields, some Genoese worked to supply their community with basic services. Among these occupations one can find barbers, butchers, and shoemakers, as well as a large number of servants[61] and apprentices, all providing the necessities of the city's daily life. Unlike artisans, who could export their own production and did not necessarily need access to monetary instruments, the "small service providers" were able to benefit from long-distance trade as a way to invest very small amounts of capital. (During the period 1200–50, the

---

[59] The existence of this practice, called the mariner *pacotille,* can be documented in medieval Venice, but there is little surviving evidence of it in Genoa, probably because sailors preferred to use the onboard scribe rather than the notaries to draw their contracts. However, indirect evidence is provided by ship-leasing contracts that sometimes specified the maximum load the crew could transport of their own goods (Byrne 1930, p. 66).

[60] Of course, an estimate of the fleet's size should not be the number of ships found in that lone surviving cartulary multiplied by twelve. Ships surely would have been mentioned in more than one cartulary.

[61] Throughout the medieval period, the large population of slaves also provided many of those basic services and constituted a reservoir of cheap labor. Even common people like *Gerardus barberius* (Gerald the barber), who bought a slave in August 1201, could be slave owners (GI#367). For more on the slave population in Genoa, see Delort (1966) and Verlinden (1977).

average value of a long-distance tie for the "small service providers" was less than £4). Those small-venture profits might improve living conditions, but could hardly serve to build up equity. Indeed, unlike wealthier investors, whose consumption was limited by the scarcity of goods, the less well-off could always find basic local goods they could use.

*Industry.* The next broad heuristic category of occupation includes all the artisans involved in industry. While the sea presented Genoa's primary employment prospect, it also molded the occupational landscape inside the city. The port naturally promoted the maritime and armament industries, and shipbuilding was the first among them. A variety of specialized craftsmen transformed fabrics, iron, wood, and other material into sails, anchors, nails, and rope with which to build and equip ships. This made for a growing industry as the rising long-distance trade and the increasing size of military operations required a larger fleet. Adding to the demand was the ships' short life spans – probably not exceeding an average of ten to twelve years (Krueger 1985) – not only because of natural aging, but also because wars and storms claimed many ships. The shipyard also filled a steady foreign demand for Genoese ships. Finally, aside from the building of new ships, the maritime economy also included all the men involved in the maintenance of vessels, as well as the porters who loaded and unloaded the cargoes. Armament production was the other main industry that benefited from Genoa's rising maritime power. Military vessels and commercial ships had to be armed. Thus, as the size of the fleet increased, so did the demand for local production of weapons such as shields, armor, swords, and the famous Genoese crossbow.

But the sea was also a constraining factor for the development of other crafts, for one main reason: the very high return on long-distance trade investment drew almost all the available capital. In contrast with other Mediterranean cities, especially those in the eastern basin, only a very small number of records refer to commenda investment in local handicraft. In many cases, especially in the early phase of the commercial revolution, even craftsmen themselves found it more lucrative to invest their surplus in long-distance trade than in their own activities.

Another argument concerning the impact of the sea on Genoa's lackluster industrial growth is advanced by Lopez (1942) and S. A. Epstein (1988, p. 114). Both note that imported goods from around the Mediterranean presented stiff competition for the local production, especially considering that the city, for the most part, did not impose protectionist policies. However, this line of reasoning is much weaker than that of capital allocation because in order to offset the high costs of transportation at that time, it assumes that production costs were much lower abroad. There is little empirical evidence, to support that theory. Instead, the presence of European artisans in middle eastern urban centers indicates that the reverse might have been the case. In reality, the proximity of the sea and the access to raw materials such as alum (a salt that was a critical ingredient in the textile dying process) fostered what industrial growth Genoa could build, as was the case with the export-oriented textile industry during the thirteenth century.

No matter how the industry grew, long-distance commerce is what drove Genoa's economic development. Genoese craftsmen never developed the kind of trade association based on monopolistic training that was so crucial in advancing the political success of guilds in other European towns such as Florence and Bologna. There certainly existed an association of butchers (*macelarius*) and possibly of the artisans involved in foodstuffs, such as bakers (*panettierius*), but those derived from the feudal rights associated with the occupation, and preceded the commune. Similarly, the most ancient occupational association might very well be that of the *muateri* (muleteer), but again, those are more auxiliaries than artisans in that sense (Vitale 1949).

Further weakening artisans as a group was their relative spatial dispersion, which contrasted with the concentration of certain trades in specific neighborhoods in most other urban centers. With the possible exception of drapers, who seemed to have been more or less concentrated around via del Cannetto, and the wool workers around the stream of Bisagno and Polcevera (Grossi Bianchi and Poleggi 1979), artisans set up shops everywhere (Heers 1961, p. 583).[62] This dispersion was a reflection not only of the lack of relative critical mass needed to occupy a certain space, but also of the historical legacy of the Commune establishment in 1099, which had provided association through residency in one of the seven, and later eight, districts. Districts were designed so that each had access to the sea as opposed to control of a gate, as in other urban center partitions, or to link to a specific social or occupational group. Additionally, the increase in trade partnerships that established commercial ties across professions and social categories contributed to decoupled residence and occupational activity in Genoa in a way that was different from the pattern in the rest of Europe.

---

[62] "*Les travailleurs de la soie et de l'or filè, cordonniers, tailleurs, èpiciers, sont dans tous les quartiers*" (Heers 1962, p. 583).

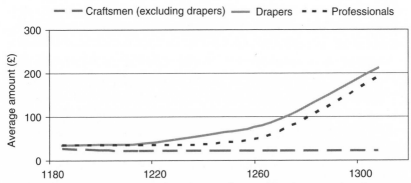

FIGURE 3.3. Average commenda value in three selected occupational groups, 1182–1315.

Also impeding and weakening the constitution of a large group of independent craftsmen was the relative absence of artisans' partnerships compared to the numerous employment and apprentice contracts in the notarial records, which confirm that wage labor was more prevalent in Genoa than other parts of the Mediterranean (Petti Baldi 1980). For example, in contrast to the situation in Genoa, the records of old Cairo indicate that artisans' partnerships and not employment was the rule in the eastern Mediterranean (Goitein 1967, p. 87). As S. A. Epstein points out, "One of the most crucial differences between the two economies was the concentration of Genoese profits in a smaller numbers of hands" (1988). This does not mean that industrial production was out of the household (Herlihy 1958, p. 136), just that a master craftsman could hire up to a dozen helpers who would all live in his house, where the factory was also usually located (Petti Balbi 1980). As Figure 3.3 suggests, this was mainly the case in the textile industry, where a few drapers succeeded in building capital that, when reinvested in the long-distance trade, further amplified the wealth difference between capital holders and others.

***Professions.*** Professions typically rely on the monopolistic mastering of esoteric knowledge to become regarded as high-status occupations, and are predicated on the idea that their practices benefit society as a whole. Defined as such, the term "profession," when referring to a medieval social organization, is, for the most part, out of the historical order. At the time, almost no occupation could claim this dual condition, and education was the privilege of clerics.[63] Furthermore, there was little room in the middle of the honor-based dichotomous social division (Weber 1978, p. 930).

However, the increased use of written documents in the fast-growing administrative and commercial practices fostered the reemergence of occupations requiring a higher level of literacy, which had all but disappeared in the early Middle Ages. Among those, the commendae records list, for example, teachers, notaries, lawyers, and scribes. As demand for these professional skills increased throughout the twelfth and thirteenth centuries, members of these occupations, along with a few others such as physicians, enhanced their positions by bringing into play their relationships with universities in order to claim exclusive access to their practices (Bullough 1969).

At first, however, a profession's emergence did not necessarily translate into higher income or enhanced status vis-à-vis manual occupations.[64] However, economic growth, and increased long-distance trade in particular, provided opportunities for upward mobility. First, professions directly involved in commercial dealings benefited from the trade expansion. This was especially the case for those whose arithmetic expertise was sought after by rising merchants' families. For others, such as physicians, the increase in disposable income and enhanced regulation (Bullough 1969) led to increased demand for their services. Second, as Figure 3.3 reports, investment in overseas ventures provided professionals with an opportunity to solidify their emerging status with increased wealth. Indeed, the increased difference in the average investment's size between the two largest urban occupational groups clearly indicates the rising material welfare of professionals, who formed a base for the emerging middle class.[65] While the disparity in investment size was, in some part, explainable by higher income,[66] this is not in itself sufficient to explain this dynamic. Indeed, although teachers' salaries and physicians' fees rose, so did the earnings of artisans. In addition, an increase in

---

[63] As Le Geoff reports: "The equations *clericus = litteratus, laicus = illiterates* are significant." (1980, p. 107).

[64] See, for more details, Gorrini (1931); Bullough (1961); and Le Geoff 1980.

[65] The term "class" might be somewhat out of historical order as well, but it aptly expresses the increased grouping of people according to their economic interest.

[66] It is difficult to measure the difference in income growth. Undoubtedly, income for some professions outperformed the average. However, this was not a guarantee: intellectual occupation could also be a competitive business. For example, the number of notaries was around thirty at the beginning of the thirteenth century and had jumped to several hundred by the middle of the fifteenth century.

professional incomes did not necessarily translate into an increase in disposable income, as the professional lifestyle was more costly. However, although the whole community was using their services, professionals catered mostly to the ruling elites, with whom they enjoyed more cultural affinity than the craftsmen did. As will be developed in the next section, when trade expanded, professionals were then able to leverage these relationships by pairing off with wealthier associates in a way that manual workers would not.

Before describing in the next paragraphs how status cut across the Genoese population in a much sharper way than occupation, it is worthwhile to mention in the context of this review of professions the presence of bankers at the middle of the twelfth century. At the onset of the commercial revolution, bankers formed a very small group of people who probably came to their positions in the economy via a craft such as silversmith (Hall 1935). More will be said about the development of their profession in Chapter 4, when those occupations most closely associated with commerce that emerged toward the second half of the thirteenth century, are discussed.

## Status and Politics

While the previous paragraphs have dealt with the burgeoning medieval economy and the rise of occupational categories, status is historians' fundamental way to ascertain a role structure for that period. In medieval Europe, formal status defined one's judicial, fiscal, military, and land ownership rights and obligations.

For the most part, the medieval aristocratic class conformed to an ideal type that takes its definition from a functionalist description of the social organization. Nobles took upon themselves political and economic control as a condition for providing military protection for the community (Weber 1978). In many ways, the Genoese men-of-arms who formed the *gente nobiles* did just that. At least until the middle of the thirteenth century, the nobles exclusively controlled the institutions[67] that organized the city's social encounters. However, the long-distance Mediterranean

---

[67] The best evidence of this control is the almost exclusive presence of the ruling clan's names in the magistrates, ecclesiastic, consular, and military nominations. In many cases the same individuals filed all the roles. For the relation between the nobility and Church, see Chapter 2, p. 41.

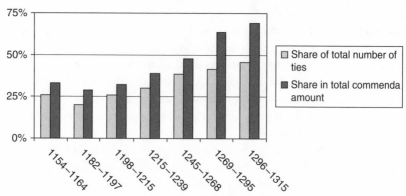

FIGURE 3.4. Aristocrats' participation in commenda networks (measured by percentage of the long-distance population and by percentage of trade volume).

trade gave them an economic opportunity that fit their fighting and sailing skills in a way that did not exist in many other parts of Europe.

Figure 3.4, which reports the proportion of aristocrats among the commenda network's participants, as well as their share of commenda investments for seven networks from 1154 to 1315, confirms earlier findings about the crucial impulse given by the aristocratic elite to the Mediterranean long-distance trade. In addition, the long-run trend points to a growing aristocratic participation in commerce, which contrasts with the classic historiography that links the development of a merchant class with the emergence of "new men." This informs a central theme of this book about the emergence of a mercantile oligarchy, not so much as an outcome of economic development, but as a consolidator of social relationships. It is thus significant to follow the commercial pattern of the nobility because, as a heuristic device, it points directly to the shift of the ruling elites from a group of families deriving their power from their position in the feudal organization of the city to an oligarchic group that united some of the old feudal urban clans, newly emigrated country-dwelling lords,[68] and a handful of lay families who rose in status because of their wealth, as opposed to their birth origin or their accomplishments in the military or public office, which had provided some social mobility during earlier periods.

---

[68] Such as the very active della Croce and de Savignone clans, who naturally maintained their formal status when emigrating to the city.

*Tracing Lineage.* The task of identifying members of the nobility in most of medieval Europe is usually straightforward. Cumulating and over-lapping information about formal titles, feudal obligations, and political rights is usually sufficient to make a distinction between commoners and the aristocratic caste. This process of identification in Italian urban centers such as Genoa works well enough. As it was in other parts of medieval Europe, participation in the city's government was contingent on formal status. Until the second part of the thirteenth century, only *gentes nobiles* had access to the consular position. Furthermore, from that point onward, the emancipation of the commoners (the *"populares"*) did not mean a democratic regime in the sense of equality of rights. Indeed, political rights and administrative appointments were allocated according to a well-defined proportion between aristocrats and others.

Statically, it is therefore easy to place families in one status group or another at any given time. However, in contrast with other, more stable medieval European social organizations, the Genoese urban nobility's composition changed over time, so that it becomes difficult to track the feudal antecedents of the growing group of aristocrats. Thus, although the eleventh- and twelfth-century classic feudal organization of the city is confirmed by the relatively consistent match between the list of names of consular appointees and a variety of aristocratic attributes – such as vassalage to the Church, military leadership,[69] and feudal possession – from the late 1100s onward, it becomes more difficult to ascertain status. This is mostly due to aristocratic immigrations, as well as – to some extent – to a social fluidity that facilitated de facto cooptation and the accession to political emancipation to a few families of *populares* origins. This explains why eminent specialists of medieval Genoa differ in their classi-fication even of some of the most influential clans. For example, the status of the greatest, thirteenth-century Genoese statesman and military commander, Benedetto Zaccaria, remains undetermined. Similarly, Balard (1978, p. 525) excludes the members of the de Nigro clan on the objective basis of their later affiliation with the *populares* clans, while most other historians do not (Scorza 1973). As a result, I have relied on several primary sources that include 1) a list of the church's vassals found in the *Registrae Curia* (pp. 24–5); 2) the consular appointments until 1270 as established by

---

[69] For example, evidence for the Platealunga, Embriaco, de Castello, Doria, Guercio, and della Volta include the following: Maurizio Platelunga was a leader during the First Crusade, and Nicolaio Embriaco, Fulcone de Castello, Simone Doria, Baldovino Guercio, and Rubeus della Volta were chieftains in the Battle of Acre in 1190.

Canale (1860); 3) the 1188 peace treaty with Pisa that listed aristocrats ahead of commoners (CD 2, pp. 321–2); and 4) the lists of the grand councils of 1380 and 1382 (Jarry 1896), which are particularly precise as they classify most of the Genoese clans according to neighborhood and status. I have then complemented these primary sources with other information about places of origin and feudal tenure contained in the secondary literature in order to establish a double codification of the data set. A first group, which I will call the "old aristocratic families," is composed of the families that can clearly be traced to Genoese feudal lineage or that belong to the consular nobility before the thirteenth century. The second group – whose composition is very similar to that used by Kedar (1976), Balard (1978), Grendi (1987), and Jehel (1993) – is much larger as I added to the first group what I call "new aristocratic families," that is, all other families belonging to the nobility at the end of the thirteenth century.

An analysis of the data set shows a steady increase in the proportion of "new" versus "old" aristocrats in the commenda networks from 1154 to 1315. Starting with just less than 8% of total trade volume, the "new" aristocrats accounted for up to 40% of the nobility's long-distance trade a century later. It is, indeed, only toward the mid thirteenth century that the growth of their participation leveled off,[70] precisely at the time when the political strength of the nobility – the older families, in particular – declined and the feudal elites switched repertoires and increased their long-distance operations. However, the distinction between the two groups does not necessarily provide an indication of status mobility, as many aristocratic families emigrated. Thus, the rise of the new nobility should be considered when thinking about social mobility inside the ruling aristocratic group and about the incidence of the long-distance trade in the emergence of a new oligarchic elite. Indeed, the next paragraphs empirically demonstrate that political upward mobility for a given family, as defined by the number of consular appointments, was coupled with trade participation.

*Lineage Dynamics and Politics.* We can infer from the payment of the *dime*, the Church's levy on agricultural revenues, that urban aristocratic families derived income from land ownership to add to their various feudal dues. In addition to these regular revenues, the product of plunder

---

[70] A blip in "new" families' trade volume toward the last quarter results from the Zaccaria clan's large trading activity.

from all across the Mediterranean has been recognized by Lopez (1937) as seed money for many commercial ventures, investment in which would dwarf those of the traditional feudal economy. For example, Zaccaria de Castello's investments of 1205 and 1206 seem suspiciously linked to his pillage of the city of Syracuse in 1205.[71] It remains that the urban aristocracy never abandoned their agricultural activity, which provided not only income but also feudal legitimacy, as lords could draw military enrollments from their estate. In fact, the notarial record shows many real estate purchases by members of the nobility active in commerce. In a sample of 475 transactions between 1154 and 1225, the urban nobility were net buyers of real estate (buyers totaled £3,128, sellers £2,308). Conversely, I have found no evidence of an asset allocation shift from land to commerce. Indeed, in the same sample there is almost no sale that can be directly connected to long-distance investment.[72]

Real estate was for the urban nobility a crucial political and economic asset, and the historical theory that pits real estate owners against the expansionists does not seems plausible. However, traditional income did not suffice to maintain one's political position. Indeed, an analysis of Table 3.1, which reports the change in political importance (as measured by number of consular appointments) for two successive periods by family trade volume, confirms the relation between success in trade and political relevance. To compute the figures contained in Table 3.1, I started by counting the number of consular appointments for every aristocratic family in the data set. Next, I ranked the families by number of appointments[73] for two periods, the first before 1191 and the second from 1191 to 1270.[74] Then, for both periods, I divided families into five quintiles. After that, I assigned for each family two numbers ("the rank pair") that identify the rank for both periods. The numbers here take values from 1 to 5, with 1 assigned to families whose number of consular appointments places them in the first quintile and 5 to families whose number of appointments places them in the bottom quintile (using a

---

[71] GI#1327, #1328, #1329, #1812.

[72] This is actually true across social groups. Many smaller sales of land seem to follow the death of the owner. Indeed, often the seller is still identified as a deceased person (*del fu*).

[73] For details about consular appointment procedures, see pp. 34–38, this volume.

[74] The year 1191 was chosen as the cutoff date because it divided the period of consular appointment records almost evenly, and corresponds to the emergence of the *podesta* regime. Checking the political dynamic using more cutoff dates would have dramatically increased the number of families with no observations and would have made the result of the analysis conditioned on sequence picking, as opposed to upon the historical dynamics.

TABLE 3.1. *Average commenda trade volume per family according to change in consular appointments (measured by "rank pairs")*

| Rank prior to 1191 | Rank from 1191 to 1270 | | | |
|---|---|---|---|---|
| | 1st | 2nd | 3rd | 4th & 5th[a] |
| 1st | £11,413 | £1,204 | £920 | £1,313 |
| 2nd | £8,872 | £4,670 | £1,982 | £2,015 |
| 3rd | £3,396 | £480 | £3,345 | £702 |
| 4th & 5th | £8,400 | £3,631 | £2,578 | £0 |

[a] Rank 4 and rank 5 could not be differentiated because for each period between 30 and 40% of the families did not have any appointments.

comparison of the actual number of appointments instead of rank was impossible because the yearly number was not constant throughout the period under study). Finally, I computed the average value of all commenda contracts per family per pair of quintile ranks. Thus, for example, the average commendae amount engaged over the whole period per family whose number of consular appointments ranked them in the second quintile prior to 1191 and in the third quintile from 1191 to 1270 (cell (2, 3)), stood at £1,982.

A first remarkable finding is that 104 out of the 110 consular families participated in long-distance trade. Conversely, every large aristocratic commercial operator before 1270 is represented in the political data set. But as the results reported in Table 3.1 indicate, the amounts invested were wide-ranging. The ancestral feudal nobility, such as the della Volta, Spinola, and Doria families, who maintained their political power – that is, who ranked first for both periods (thus cell (1,1)) – were large commercial operators (average trade volume = £11,413). At the same time, on average, the newcomers (those who ranked low in number of consular appointments prior to 1191, but high later – for example, cells (2,1) and (4,1)) who were active in the long-distance trade replaced those families whose declining political standing (cells (1,2), (1,3), and (1,4)) was associated with their relative lack of participation in trade. Establishing a positive relation between political appointments among the aristocratic groups and their commercial investments might not be a very surprising finding; however, for such a remote period of history, this empirical evidence is a rare confirmation of the analysis of scattered biographies that have, up to now, served as evidence of the increasing relation between political power and commerce in medieval Italy. Even more to the

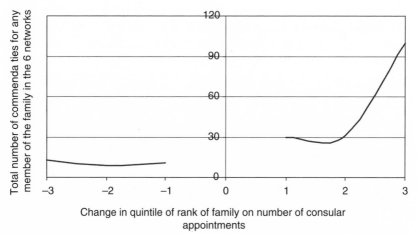

FIGURE 3.5. Families' political appointments and commenda ties, 1154–1295.

point of this research in demonstrating the tight relation between commerce and politics is Figure 3.5, which plots the relationship between change in political importance and the average number of commenda ties per family in the six networks from 1154 to 1295.[75] Thus, unlike in Table 3.1, here it is the number of relationships, and not trade volume, that serves to measure the relationship between commerce and politics.

As Figure 3.5 confirms, those families who exhibited the most political upward mobility (+3) were also those most central to the Mediterranean network.[76] It is good to remember that during the first half of the thirteenth century, the change in the composition of the ruling elites happened inside the aristocratic group, where fighting skills and lordship were prerequisites. However, the positive relationship between number of trading ties and political ascendancy indicates not only that monetary wealth was taking its place along with traditional "honor" as the main value of the aristocratic corporatism (H. C. White 2008), but also that actual commercial ties could provide the raw material for the weaving of a new elite social organization, which is formally described in the next section.

---

[75] 1154–64, 1182–97, 1198–1215, 1216–39, 1245–68, 1269–95.

[76] I did not include those families who did not move ranks (cell x,x). Indeed, the leading families who maintain their position (cell (1,1)) have on average a very high number of commenda ties and dominate the cells (x,x) group. As such, the average degree centrality for the cells (x,x) is the confirmation that the leading families who maintained their rank in political appointment were central commercial operators, but is not an indication that all "static in rank" families were active trade participants.

## 3.3. NETWORK DYNAMICS: FROM CLIENTELISM
## TO CORPORATISM

The previous pages have illustrated that, while Genoese from all segments of the community participated in the Mediterranean trade throughout the thirteenth century, for the overwhelming majority of them long-distance trade was a rare event and certainly not their main occupation. However, despite the fact that most operators lacked specialization, commerce was making an increasingly important contribution to the organization of social structure, foreshadowing the central role that trade was to play in defining social relationships during the Renaissance. An investigation of this transformation requires one to analyze not only the behavior of persons, but also the way in which the structure of the Mediterranean trade network changed between the end of the First Crusade and the beginning of the fourteenth century, when commendae lost their preeminence as the main partnership framework.

In this section, I begin by reviewing two basic network measurements in order to explore the morphological changes that the Mediterranean's commenda network was undergoing, changes that reflected the rise of a commercial elite as well as a shift in Genoa's social organization. Then, in the second part of the section, I connect the network's macrostructural dynamics with the microsocial interaction of partner selection patterns to demonstrate how overseas commerce became salient in the definition of relational ties among the nobility and, to some extent, among occupational groups.

The analytical strength of network analysis resides in the fact that it can be used systematically to examine relational data. My objective, therefore, is to compare standard parameters across time in order to follow the commenda network dynamic. It should therefore be remembered that, although the previous section dealt with groups of persons and their occupations, status, and gender, here the unit of analysis is the networks of relationships that linked the thousands of men and women who invested in trade in the medieval Mediterranean, and those who traveled all around it by sea.

As Mark Bloch (1953) observed, it is as comparative tools that analytical concepts should be deployed when referring to medieval history. Formal network analysis did not exist when Bloch made his recommendations, but following his methodological suggestions remains relevant. Bearing this in mind, my objective is to unearth empirical regularities of graph features that are scalable and transposable in time, rather than precise indicators of the stand-alone social structure for individual periods. As with any other theory, the idea is that the hypothesis behind the parameters' signification will allow us to understand the concatenation and sequence of social dynamics in a way that would otherwise be hidden. As a result, in an effort to simplify my analysis, I elected to use basic measures because I realized that a marginal gain in indices' precision might be mistaken for an increase in veracity, and that such a gain would not yield much when considering the length of the time series, the size of the data set, the low density of the networks, and the remoteness of the period under study.

I have displayed in Figure 3.6 a graph that represents the commenda network from 1198 to 1215. The reader can also refer to Appendix C to view a representation of six other networks from 1154 to 1315[77] that serve as the basis for this chapter's analysis. Each dot (node) in Figure 3.6 represents a participant in the commenda network, and each line represents a relationship between a traveler and an investor (86% of all ties), a relationship between two coinvestors in a venture (10% of all ties), or, more rarely, the agency relationships that linked one or more investors to agents investing on their behalf in a commenda (4% of all ties).[78] Little can be determined just by looking at the graphs, other than the fact that, despite being only a sample of the total network, the number of nodes in each figure confirms a large involvement on the part of the Genoese community. Note, however, that the number of records available to me for coding varies, and thus the variation in the sample size over time is not representative of the social dynamic. This said, the disparity in the size of the seven networks actually offers an unexpected methodological benefit, in that the number of records coded for each period is not a function of time. Thus, empirical regularities in the change in the network measurements cannot be attributed to the network's size.

## Occasional Partnerships and Sampling

In network language, the number of ties that are incident to a given actor is termed the "nodal degree." A quick examination of the nodal degree

---

[77] I chose the number and the periodicity of the networks to maximize the period covered while maintaining enough data density for each network. Unless otherwise indicated, every commenda network analysis in this book is based on the parameters of those seven networks.

[78] Direct co-traveling relationships are very rare. Out of almost 7,000 commendae in the database, only 34 involve more than one traveler.

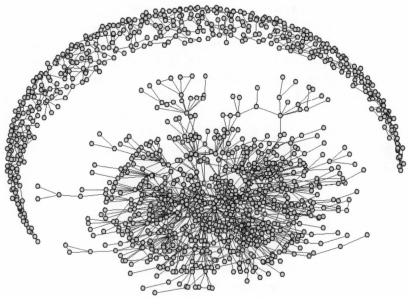

FIGURE 3.6. Commenda network, 1198–1215 (n = 1112, mean nodal degree = 2.45, average transaction per tie = 1.09).

frequency distribution (see Appendix D) and of its average in each network from 1154 to 1315 confirms that the overwhelming majority of Genoese traders were occasional participants in long-distance trade. More informative network measures indicate that, even among those who were party to multiple contracts, very few selected the same partner twice. Obviously, this lack of a "repeat" in the data set could be the result of two possible sampling biases, both of which I will consider now.

The first possible sampling bias stems from the fact that the distribution of the notarial records I coded for each network is not uniform with respect to time, as the data entries are more abundant in certain years. Therefore, the data set might provide an adequate picture of the trade network as a whole, but not of each individual pattern of action, because few consecutive years in the time series have sufficient data points. However, I tested those years in which the data was dense for more than two out of five consecutive years, and I found that the average "repeat" was not statistically different from that of the period as a whole. Additionally, the difference between the much higher proportion of "repeats" among the investor/investor ties, on one hand, as compared to the traveler/investor ties, on the other, demonstrates that the data set indeed picks up repeated relationships when they happened.

The second possible sampling bias that could explain the lack of "repeats" in partner selection might be a result of a change in the population sampled. Indeed, a dynamic analysis of the notarial records could underestimate the "repeats," simply because once the partners had had one successful venture, a rise in trust could have decreased the need for a written notarial agreement, which would mean that "repeat" partners would be underrepresented in the cartularies. However, though this is possible, it is unlikely because the records are full of contracts between members of the same nuclear family who have, as a group, relationships that are founded on the strongest degree of trust. In fact, because in some cases overseas ventures might, whether they were expected to or not, last several years, written documents were necessary to supplement faltering memories and to serve as evidence in case of the death of one of the partners. The careful maintenance of written records was also essential not only because litigious issues could arise between partners, but also because an adequate inventory had to be kept of the shares of several investors recorded in separate contracts into one traveler venture. Indeed, it was not uncommon for a traveler to collect funds on different days of the venture from different people, people who might otherwise have been unrelated.[79]

Thus, the low number of "repeats" in investor/traveler ties in our data base represent the commercial reality of the time: With little control over the length of each venture, and thus over the cash flow and its timing, participants in the commenda network were able to plan their investment decisions to only a limited extent. This meant that opportunistic behavior was the norm. Investors selected travelers who were about ready to leave, as opposed to waiting for their previous partners, as the timing of their departures would be unpredictable (if they were to leave again at all). Similarly, and especially in the early phase of the commercial revolution,

---

[79] This said, the "change in population" argument used to explain the lack of repeat partnership should not be completely ignored; the change in population may be due to the rise of agreements other than commenda during the period of my equity data set. Mentions of *compania,* or of overseas venture partnerships that were delimited in time, which I at first found to be rare, become a little more common toward the beginning of the fourteenth century. It is likely that most of these agreements, as well as those related to the employment of overseas agents, were not recorded by notaries but as private documents. However, it remains that, at the very least, the timing of appearance of such agreements in the notarial records is strong evidence that the institutional change in question did not take place before the end of the thirteenth century.

those travelers who decided to take to the sea again could not necessarily take it for granted that their previous investors would provide them with access to cash or goods. This is especially true in the case of Mediterranean trade, where credit instruments did not yet leverage existing equity investment. The best evidence that investors did not have much cash sitting around and did not wait to invest their cash – a factor that severely limited the number of "repeat" partnerships – is the very small ratio of cash to commenda contracts apparent in the thirteenth-century wills that have been studied by S. A. Epstein (1984).

### Hierarchy

In network analysis, an actor's "centrality," a measure of his or her activity level and/or "distance" from others,[80] is arguably the most common parameter corresponding to the "importance" a given node has to a network's overall architecture. This is especially true in symmetric relations, where the direction of the ties is not relevant. As such, systematic measures of network centrality variation provide indications of inequalities between actors, and thus of the hierarchal nature of social organization. An example is the intrinsically hierarchical nature of the feudal system, the historical starting point of our inquiry. Thus Figure 3.7, a graph representing an "ideal type" feudal organization, is composed of a series of star-shaped clusters in which everyone is indirectly connected through mutual ties to the local lord.

As an illustration of an ideal type of exchange, Figure 3.7 contrasts with other ideal types of economic relationships such as markets – which vary from the hyper-classic economic models of disconnected dyads that are randomly linked together, to more connected networks that take into account the interactional regularities that produce the social construction of markets (H. C. White 2002, p. 318). It also contrasts with more collaborative schemes characterized by dense and robust ties and reciprocal cliques[81] (Windolf and Beyer 1996; Stark 2001).

There is an abundant amount of literature that considers individual and group centralization, and the properties of several operational parameters have been well analyzed (Freeman 1979; Marsden 1981;

---

[80] Those "others" have different degrees of prominence, and the "importance" of a given node is a function of the "importance" of the actors to whom he or she is linked.

[81] "Cliques" refer to subgraphs where every node is symmetrically related to every other one.

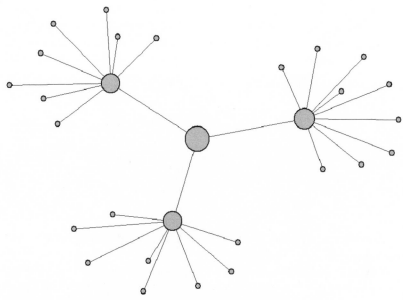

FIGURE 3.7. An ideal type of feudal social organization.

Bonacich 1987). For our purposes, those parameters that take into account how "close"[82] actors are to each other (such as "betweeness" and "closeness" centrality) can be deployed only when considering a subgraph of the entire network. Indeed, the very large number of components – subgraphs of nodes that are directly or indirectly linked to each other – in each network is a graphic representation of the apparent lack of commercial connection between many operators in our sample. Thus the distance between them cannot be computed.

As a result, I have relied on network degree centralization – an index that measures the dispersion of a person's activity as represented by the number of his or her ties – when assessing the hierarchical dynamic of the Mediterranean trade network. In other words, since this centralization's index is the variation in the number of ties of each operator divided by the maximum degree variation for a network of this size, the change in the index value from 1154 to 1315 reported in Figure 3.8 is an indication of

---

[82] Most distance-related parameters are based on the shortest path between two nodes, also called "geodesic distance."

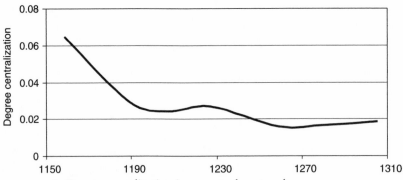

FIGURE 3.8. Degree centralization in commenda networks, 1154–1315.

how isomorphic each trade network is to a star[83] and thus to an ideal-type feudal clientelist configuration.

Evidently, the trade network's centralization decreased during the early phase of the Genoese commercial revolution, as trade opportunities opened up to all, and remained low during the thirteenth century. A closer look at the network for the period 1154 to 1164 in Figure 3.9 in which the size of plotted nodes is proportional to each individual amount of ties shows that during that period, aside from isolated and smaller operators, the Mediterranean trade was controlled by a few large operators, each surrounded by clients who were only indirectly connected to each other by their exclusive client tie to a central node. As such, network analysis confirms earlier findings – based on the surviving records of that time – which show that a group of larger-scale operators dominated the long-distance trade around the mid twelfth century (Byrne 1920; Day 1988).

One interesting point, however, is how tenuous the indirect commercial relationships among these operators were during that time. Indeed, while we have evidence to show that the large operators interacted socially and forged temporary political alliances with each other, the network indicates that they did not necessarily deal directly with each other commercially. There is also little evidence for indirect paths of commercial interaction. This is another indication that the exclusive

[83] In a star network of x nodes, the index (variation of degree) is maximal since the central node's degree equals x−1, while all others equal 1. Conversely, in a network where all nodes have equal degree (for example, if each node belongs to a clique of a similar size), the index is equal to zero.

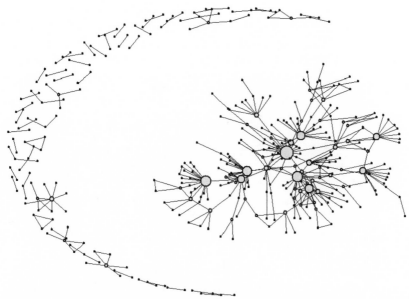

FIGURE 3.9. Commenda network, 1154–64 (node sizes are proportional to nodal degree).

character of feudal clientelism permeated not only the social organization as a whole but also the commercial network. While the measurements graphed in Figure 3.9 demonstrate the change in the hierarchical nature of the network and the lack of connection between larger traders, Figure 3.10 (which represents the commenda network for the period 1296–1315) offers visual confirmation that by the end of the thirteenth century, this had changed: Here the largest operators were directly connected to each other, and their ties were spread all around the network. By then the elite were collaborating more, not only with regard to the political and military organization of the city, but also with regard to matters of long-distance trade.

Traces in the earlier network of the transition to come are hard to find. However, while it may not be remarkable that, during the earlier period, none of the four clans – Spinola, Doria, Grimaldi, and Fieschi – who came to dominate later medieval and Renaissance Genoa were among the largest operators, it is noteworthy that the two that were already firmly involved in long–distance trade established key positions in the network by providing connections between important traders. Indeed, the Spinola and the Doria rank much higher with regard to betweeness centrality – a measure usually associated with the idea of power – than they do with

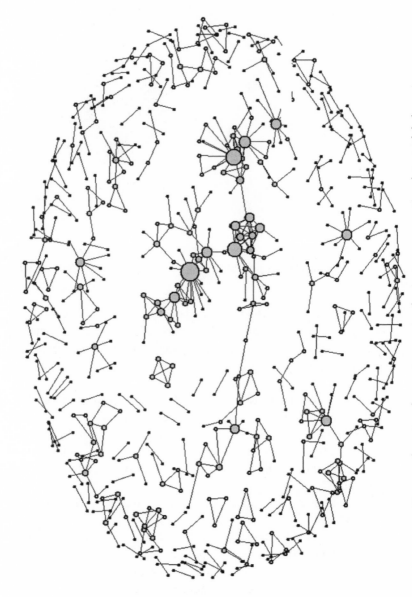

FIGURE 3.10. Commenda network, 1296–1315 (node sizes are proportional to nodal degree).

regard to the volume of their trade. During the 1154–64 period, Doria ranked seventeenth in trade volume but fourth in betweeness centrality, and Spinola ranked twenty-fifth in trade volume and eighth in betweeness centrality. These network measures are significant because – as Freeman notes – everything being equal, an actor who is between other individuals has more "control" over the flow between them. This is especially true because the betweeness centrality index takes into account the proprietary position of the in-between actor and the nonredundancy of his network position (1979). This means, therefore, that in comparison with other clans, the position of these two preeminent families in the trade network was, on average, more on the path that indirectly linked large operators. As the network measurements show, what mattered in determining the influence wielded by one's clan was not only the clan's commercial volume, but also the position it held in the network.

### Integration

The centralization index makes clear the changing hierarchical nature of the networks. However, the measures provide no information either about the integration of the network or, in general, about the social cohesion of trade. Indeed, centralized networks always exhibit some degree of connection, but the reverse is not true. For example, our centralization parameters will be equally low for networks in which integration varies from none (if they consist of dyadic relationships only) to maximal (if all the nodes are tied to each other).

Integration is naturally related both to the idea that the actors are connected and to the social concepts of cohesion (a more robust version of connection that involves more intensively organized mutual relationships) and adhesion (which refers to the idea of social partition) (D. White and Harary, 2001, pp. 308–12). While density of relationships springs directly to mind when examining social connection, this criterion is not very helpful when comparing a large network of tangible social ties such as that considered here, because of the inherent maximum number of social relationships that any given person can have.[84] Thus, density indices are a function of a network's dimension, and the difference in sample size for each period of this research makes this measure

---

[84] Obviously, that statement varies depending on what kinds of ties are analyzed. For example, density might be a meaningful parameter to assess the integration of an internet network based on hits on common web sites.

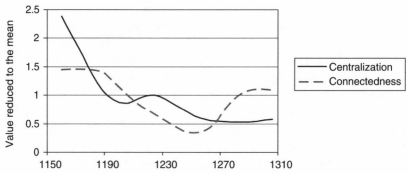

FIGURE 3.11. Centralization and connectedness indices, commenda network, 1154–1315.

nonoperational. Similarly, parameters that include graph measures of distance between operators in a network are also naturally deployed to assess a social organization's integration. However, as noted earlier, the commenda networks consisted of many disconnected clusters of ties, and, therefore, the distance between all operators simply cannot be computed. As a result, as in other studies on large networks, I relied on the parameter *connectedness* – an index that is based on the number and variability of the size of a given network's components (i.e., connected subgraphs of the network) – to assess the integration dynamic of the commenda networks.

Figure 3.11 presents *centralization* as well as *connectedness* indices from 1154 to 1315. As already noted, the integration of the earlier networks was based on their centralized architecture, as most trade connections passed through a central operator. However, as feudal-like control over the network declines, the trade network's integration decreases sharply, before commercial ties knit the whole back together to form a more integrated – yet more decentralized – trade architecture. Unsurprisingly, however, the historical increase in the interactions occurring between operators, as well as the slow build-up in specialization, followed the more dyadic construction of the early thirteenth century, which involved many smaller components. In many ways this developmental model (moving from an isolated cluster of operators to a more integrated network) intuitively fits both with the historiography (which recognizes that an increase in trade opportunities for the population as a whole followed the more restricted access to long-distance trade that was associated with the earlier period) and with theoretical market models that recognize that a market's integration correlates with its maturity.

***Economic Growth.*** It is especially noteworthy that the period of mini-mum centralization and connectedness corresponds to the highest level of growth in Genoese long-distance trade. Indeed, although there is insuf-ficient consistent data to plot annual trade growth rates in Figure 3.11, historians specializing in medieval Genoa have still been able to piece together enough about the period to recognize that it was during the thirteenth century that the city experienced its most rapid growth before long-distance trade slowed in the early part of the fourteenth century, even before the demographic impact of the Black Death.[85] Thus inte-gration was not synonymous with economic growth, but rather with economic consolidation.

## Partner Selection[86]

Earlier in the book, I outlined some of the evidence that illustrates that long-distance trade in the early Middle Ages was connected to specific ethnic groups, members of which were often considered strangers in the communities they supplied. Next, in Genoa's case, I showed that, when trade first grew following the success of the Crusades, the conquering aristocracy, in association with a handful of merchants of foreign origin (Byrne 1918), built up its commercial control through a familiar pattern of exclusive patron–client relationships that mirrored the city's feudal organization. While Figure 3.11 leaves little doubt about the change and the timing of the social "rewiring" that occurred in the trade network after the mid thirteenth century, its partner selection processes need to be investigated if we are better to understand how the early medieval long-distance commercial organization was being replaced by the involvement of the community as a whole.

Partner selection analyses of contemporary social organizations often rely on a sample or census that explicitly ascribes several pieces of sociometric data to each person in order to produce multivariate

---

[85] See Heers (1961); Day (1963); Kedar (1976); Balletto (1983); Jehel (1993); and Greif (2006, p. 243).

[86] The term "partner selection" seems to imply decision by the actors. However, this is not the case here. Commercial operators certainly used some initiative in a restricted menu of social choices, but on average, structural regularities operated in partner selections.

equations that define the likelihood of social pairing. My medieval
Genoese data set does not pretend to such systematic sampling, and
several promising hypotheses cannot be tested. For example, spatial
proximity certainly played a crucial role in partner selection, especially
in a city divided into eight distinct political entities, each with its own
client–patron relationships. However, twelfth- and thirteenth-century
records are just too scant to establish the long-distance trade operators'
domiciles.

In light of this, my objective here is to assess the incidence of the
status and of the occupation-related homophilic propensities in
the "rewiring" of the trade network that occurred toward the middle of
the thirteenth century. Note that the incidence of kinship ties in trade-
partner selection is not eluded; however, although family ties are often
cited as the backbone of the medieval trade network, this assertion is
not confirmed by our commenda data set. As a result, I have decided to
analyze the role of kinship in the trade network as part of the fifth
chapter's focus on the rise of clan relationships in the social organization of the city.

I operationalized homophily – "the tendency for individuals with
similar attributes, characteristics, or practices to form partnerships"
(Bearman et al. 2004) – by coding each commercial tie with a pair of
binary attributes corresponding to the connected nodes, in order to
generate a set of 2 by 2 tables for each of the networks from 1154 to
1315.[87] In each of the four cells of the tables, I recorded the total amount
of one of the four possible combinations of attributes for each period.
From these 2 by 2 tables, the simplest way to assess the propensity of
commercial operators to form homogeneous partnerships with respect to
the attributes coded would be to use percentages. However, this metric
does not take into account the availability of "alike partners." As a
hypothetical example, consider a case in which 30% of artisans form
partnerships with other artisans, and 70% select nonartisans as their
commenda partners. If only a few artisans took part in the commercial
network, this could indicate a very high propensity for homophilious
selection with respect to occupation. However, if artisans were to represent the majority of the commercial operators, it might actually
represent the opposite. Indeed, everything being equal, artisans in this

[87] The occupational data is sparser than the status data. As a result, I decided to use a longer
period to group information.

TABLE 3.2. *Value of S14 for status homophily, 1154–1315*

| 1154–64 | 1182–97 | 1198–1215 | 1216–39 | 1245–68 | 1269–96 | 1297–1315 |
|---|---|---|---|---|---|---|
| 0.191 | 0.117 | 0.223 | 0.348 | 0.451 | 0.499 | 0.604 |

second hypothetical case would be more likely to select a nonartisan as a partner.

As a result, I selected a measure that takes into account the availability of "alike partners." From among the measures suggested by Gower and Legendre (1986), which were suitable for use with a 2 by 2 table, I elected to use the point-correlation statistic, which those authors label S14[88] in their article. Following Krackhardt's suggestion (1990, p. 350), I also deemed S14 appropriate because it exhibited sensitivity to large variations in cell sizes and a low distortion at the extreme values that could result from such variation.

The calculation of S14 generates values that range from $-1$ to $1$, with a positive value indicating that there exists a propensity to form homogenous partnerships given appropriate availability. Measures close to zero indicate that, on average, the attribute is not salient in the partner selection process.[89]

*Status as a "Rewiring" Attribute.* Table 3.2 reports S14 values for a status-homophilic propensity for the seven periods that correspond to the

---

[88] For a given 2 by 2 table with four cells denoted x11, x12, x21, x22, S14 is defined as follows: $S14 = \sqrt{[(x11/x11+x21 - x12/x12+x22)(x11/x11+x12 - x21/x21+x22)]}$.

[89] I noted earlier that I will trace the role that kinship played in the rise of the commerce in Chapter 5. In this context, though – and solely for the purposes of furthering our understanding of the trade network rewiring that took place toward the end of the thirteenth century – we have to be satisfied with following the pattern of the proportion of intrafamily trade in the whole trade network. Indeed, it would be impossible to take into account the availability of "alike partners" in the way that parameter S14 did for occupational and status attributes, as it would require a separate index for each family. Moreover, considering the total number of selection alternatives, the random selection of kin would, even in large families, be a rare event, and this would force us to accept that all kinship selection is an indication of high levels of intrafamily partnerships. As I show in Chapter 5, the proportion of intrafamily partnerships increases only slightly during the thirteenth century, and when considering that most intrafamily trade occurred among the nobility, it is perhaps more useful to note that, among intra-status partnerships, the selection of kin as commendae partners did not increase until the end of the thirteenth century, which is consistent with the notion of a more highly integrated network.

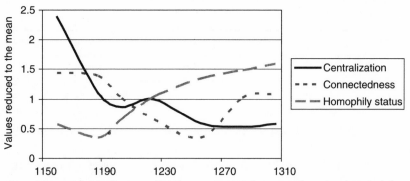

FIGURE 3.12. Network centralization, connectedness, and status homophily, 1154–1315.

seven commenda networks that serve as the basis for the network analysis. The index shows that, following an earlier period of heterogeneous partner selection, from the end of the twelfth century onward formal status became increasingly salient in commercial partnerships. This is not to say that cross-status commendae disappeared; however, it does indicate that, given availability, an aristocrat was increasingly likely to form a partnership with a fellow aristocrat.

In Figure 3.12, for the sake of comparability, I have reduced the seven homophilic S14 indices to their means. I have then supplemented these values to the hierarchy and integration parameters reported earlier in Figure 3.11.

In light of the changes in both network measures, the rise of homophilic selection among the aristocracy takes on greater meaning. From the middle of the twelfth century onward, the decrease that occurred in centralization expresses the loss of the preeminent position previously enjoyed by those of the ruling aristocracy who benefited from long-distance trade. In addition, the feudal nobility's monopoly of financial surplus was eroding, as the marginal saving rate of non-noble participants in long-distance trade increased. While the loss of this economic monopoly did not translate into significant loss of political power until the middle of the thirteenth century, it remains obvious that the nobility as a group increasingly had to compete for resources with the rest of the population. For the nobility, one logical outcome of this situation was an increase in intra-status ties. As a result, over time, status-based selection became salient, giving rise to a social mechanism that contributed to the formation of a commercial network that was, as a whole, more integrated but less hierarchical. There is no evidence to indicate, however, that the desire for intra-status partnerships was the result of a deliberate control strategy. But, this said, the data certainly does show that, as aristocrats lost some of their feudal prerogatives, commerce became an increasingly significant factor in the definition of their social ties.

*Occupation as Network "Rewiring".* Next, using a methodology similar to that applied to status attributes, I measured the homophilic tendencies of three occupational categories – artisans, professionals, and merchants. Because notaries wrote down some operators' occupations, establishing a sample of artisans (including drapers, whose occupation constitutes a hybrid) or professionals in the commenda network is a fairly straight-forward matter. However, the lack of the term *mercator* in any contract before the mid thirteenth century poses coding problems. While I used my analysis of credit instruments to refine the notion of "merchant" (see the next chapter), for the purposes of the commenda network I aggregated bankers, *mercator* (when the term appears around 1250), foreign traders, and some local commercial operators (the criteria for coding were length of career, use of multiple financial instruments, and high centrality) in order to create a regular, if not specialized, merchant category. In Figure 3.13, I report the homophilic tendency for the three occupational groups for the period 1186–1315. As the long-run trend indicates, as the commenda network became more integrated in the second part of the thirteenth century, intra-occupational partnerships among artisans, as well as merchants, increased. Professionals, however, were no more likely to associate themselves with other professionals than with the population as a whole.

The increasing use of occupational categories as a salient characteristic for partner selection by artisans can be considered to be constitutive, as well as a result of economic factors; however, it was also a reflection of the increase in political and social stratification seen in medieval Genoa. Economically, the records show a disintermediation in the trade network. This was expressed by the increase that occurred in the export of small manufactured goods, either directly by the artisans who made them or by travelers practicing the same craft. However, political history also provides clues concerning the rise of broad occupational categories: We see from the mid thirteenth century onward, a system of representation that relegated the artisans to a separate category, as contrasted with the traditional feudal system, which had been organized around patron–client relationships in well-defined spatial units.

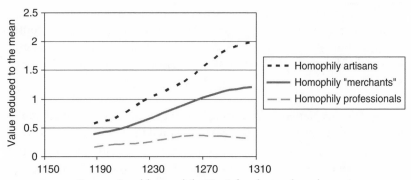

FIGURE 3.13. Occupational homophily (S14) for three selected groups.

The lack of partnerships between professionals is, in that context, less surprising. Unlike craftsmen, who sometimes worked together or supplied each other, and who exhibited a higher level of solidarity than other groupings (Hughes 1975), professionals had no goods to export and had no particular occasion to interact with each other. In fact, their primary professional and social ties were often with the aristocratic clan they served. Indeed, it is apparent that even some notaries, the largest professional subgroup recorded in the commenda data set, displayed an increasing tendency to work exclusively for a single clan. As a result, it is unsurprising that, as a group, professionals were, during this period, increasingly likely to enter into partnership with the nobility rather than with the common population.

The dynamics of merchant group formation will be developed in the next chapter, where I will show that one of the differences between these men and the population as a whole was their use of credit instruments as an aspect of their intra-occupational ties. It is thus logical that, for the most part, merchants used commendae when entering into commercial relations with unspecialized operators.[90] And, although the end of the thirteenth century shows a slight increase in homophilic propensity, this might have been the result of the growing rate of adhesion to this group by people who carried on, for a while, the practices of the more occasional operator.

---

[90] Remember that Figure 3.13 reports the value of parameters reduced to the mean to represent an historical trend. In fact, the merchant S14 parameter is much lower than that of the artisans.

In this light, it is relevant to note that the homophilic selection pattern displayed by drapers (who are sometimes seen as merchants and not craftsmen) did not conform to that displayed by other merchants. Indeed, the data indicates that partner selection on the part of drapers was, on average, similar to that displayed by artisans as a broad category. This reinforces the claim that, in twelfth- and thirteenth-century Genoa, even among those who were most involved in unprecedented growth in the commerce, few could really have been called merchants.

In the medieval East, the commenda had been a standard contract that covered a variety of economic relationships. In picking up the same framework to organize long-distance trade partnerships, Italians found a stable institution that accommodated the participation of all segments of the population. In this chapter, I have shown how the lack of repetition of most names, and the presence of a wide variety of participants in the record, points to the occasional nature of commercial activities for many Genoese and indicates that, before the middle of the thirteenth century, it is difficult to define a social structure with respect to trading activity. During that period of strong growth, the commercial expansion was characterized by a growing number of transactions. Oddly, though, the average size of those transactions remained relatively constant, or even decreased, which provides further evidence of the participation of some of the less well-off in the long-distance trade. However, the range of transaction sizes was expanding, and the corresponding heterogeneity of social pairing increased the capital formation of the largest families. As trade became more routinized and more polarized with respect to size, occupational categories became salient in partner selection. Conversely, as the rise of commerce provided a new social currency, nobles responded to the threat to the status-based political organization by increasingly selecting their own as long-distance trade partners.

# 4

# Credit Network for Routinized Merchants

The previous chapter showed that, before the end of the thirteenth century, the Genoese who participated in the long-distance trade were, for the most part, multivalent actors. In that context, commenda contracts were an efficient norm-based framework that fostered heterogeneity of ties. However, the mercantile routinization and specialization that had already developed in a few other European regions was emerging in Genoa, and credit was increasingly defining the relationships between local specialized operators. So, whereas we have been so far concerned primarily with those Genoese whose occasional participation created the conditions for the commercial revolution, this fourth chapter focuses on those for whom, in increasing numbers, long-distance trade became a main occupation and career.

It is the emergence of these merchants' networks that Braudel singles out to explain the rise of capitalism in late medieval Italian city-states. Brushing aside alternative explanations, such as the rise of agricultural productivity, the demographic impulse of the late Middle Ages, and the rise of protoindustrialization, he notes that long-distance trade was "the only area which favored the reproduction of capital" (1992, p. 239). Accordingly, he firmly assigns the origin of the sustained accumulation of financial resources to those who were increasingly able to dominate long-distance trade through their deployment of specialized networks – around the Mediterranean first and across the rest of the world next – in order to take advantage of the differences of price in space and time.

Braudel describes the merchants' predatory endurance, which made them unlike any other network before them, but he does not focus on the social origins of his leading economic class. In writing that the merchants were foreign to their surrounding social context (1979, p. 239), he even implies that their emergence was exogenous to the preexisting social system. In this chapter, I analyze 250 years of credit ties in order to show the role of credit in the formation of the merchant network, and to show that this was not the case. Indeed, my description of the network's participants illustrates the social endogeneity of the rise of capitalists. In analyzing the social origins of the network's members and the partner selection patterns, I also analytically confirm the continued blending of military repertoire and commercial success. The men who waged wars and controlled trading routes were, thus, able to build enormous wealth because financial opportunities arose not so much from fair market competition but instead, as Braudel points out, from gaining control over resources.

I begin the analysis of this chapter with a brief history showing how wealth-building among the commoners induced political change in Genoa. Then, in section 4.1, I review the formal functioning of the four most important types of medieval credit instruments, concentrating on those characteristics that were most relevant to the change in social relationships. For example, I indicate how the emergence of an international payment system necessitated network connections that had not been a prerequisite of the commenda relationships.

Next, in section 4.2, I provide an analysis of the credit network participants, empirically confirming that, for the most part, credit was an instrument that, unlike the commenda, did not involve the Genoese community as a whole, but instead involved experienced traders with different career paths.

Finally, in section 4.3, I analyze credit-tie dynamics over almost three centuries in order to trace the changes in the social makeup of merchants active in Genoa. Reviewing, successively, the place of origin, occupational distribution, and status distribution of the credit network, I begin by explaining the role of foreigners, who at first constituted the majority of routinized long-distance traders. Next, I round out the occupational description started in Chapter 3 by pointing to two occupations that originated in a craft but became central in the credit network architecture. I then conclude with an analysis of the status distribution of the emerging mercantile community. I point to the increasing role of the aristocracy in the credit network toward the end of the thirteenth century, when, along with a few commoner clans, the nobility replaced the itinerant foreign merchants. As a result of the rise of specialization, commendae, which had provided occupational mobility opportunities and introductory selection into the long-distance trade network, declined sharply. By contrast, credit instruments thrived as a robust framework for social exchange among the mercantile class and solidified the social categories apart from the dichotomic status-based division that had organized feudal relationships up until then.

## The Rise of Commoners

The object of the following paragraphs, which will precede the formal analysis, is to explain how – while credit increasingly defined relational ties among the routinized long-distance operators – the rising wealth of the commoners gave them an independent strength, and how political dynamics became an integral part of the rise of commerce as a social exchange currency.

Historians of medieval Genoa often point to internal strife among the elite to explain its medieval political history (Tabacco 1989). In particular, the beginning of the *podesta* regime in 1190, which provided for delegating the administration of the city to an outsider in order to overcome factionalism, is often cited as clear evidence of continual discord among the urban elites.

Evidently, internal rivalries were intense, but, as S. A. Epstein noted, those were not always motivated by "high minded differences" (1996, p. 109) and do not always explain much about economic relationships.[1] In addition, small random personal altercations[2] that could start a cycle of violence among armed clans also occurred in most other Italian

---

[1] Aside from the more cultural explanation for the Guelf/Ghibelline antagonism, historians often point to the divergent interests between, on the one hand, the landed aristocracy and, on the other, the mercantile urban elite in order to make sense of factions. Although this might hold true in explaining the antagonism between the Genoese urban center and the *contado*'s aristocracy, it does little to help us understand the city's contentious internal history. From the mid thirteenth century onward, almost all the protagonists, including the powerful Guelf "land-based" clans of Fieschi and Grimaldi, were heavily involved in the long-distance trade (for example, LO#63g/March 1253; DO#1481/June 1290; BA#3571/August 1349). This common commercial interest does not mean that infighting was necessarily caused by cultural antagonism or by the perpetuation of personal vendettas. Indeed, in medieval Italy, holding political office provided material benefits. As S. R. Epstein remarks, "Political authority was a source of economic rent just as much as the market was"(2000).

[2] The Genoese official Chronicle reports many such small personal altercations. Most often, those small events were not, by themselves, enough to start major strife. They were, instead, a manifestation of the antagonism between individual clans, each of which had to protect its members from encroaching clans.

towns, even those under the *podesta* regime.[3] Such violence was a legacy
of the feudal social organization, whose survival depended in part on the
eruption of violent episodes to justify its response function (Bloch 1961),
which had become less significant since the receding of outside threats. As
S. R. Epstein noted, those who "claimed seigniorial rights over trade and
people" had "a comparative advantage in warfare," and "political fragmentation was both the prerequisite and effect of their independence"
(2000a, p. 289).

In Genoa, the *podesta* certainly acted as the head of the formal executive, but his role should not be exaggerated. Greif (2006) relies heavily
on the *podesta* to explain how the Genoese resolved their factionalism,
which, in turn, according to him, explains their economic prosperity. But
this view overstates the *podesta*'s influence on communal peace. For
example, in an effort to establish a causal relationship and to demonstrate
empirically the efficiency of the *podesta* (2006, p. 246), Greif uses S. A.
Epstein's data (1996, pp. 325–6) to show that, after the *podesteria* regime
stopped being "self-enforcing" in 1339, the next 200 years witnessed 39
revolts. A large number, indeed, but, according to the same data source,
Greif does not note that the rate of revolt per year was almost identical
*when the podesteria was self-enforcing* (sixteen revolts from 1257 to
1339).

In fact, the Genoese did not lose their grip on the city administration.
Indeed, a town council elected by a group of members of the nobility was
still in control of finance and monitored the *podesta*'s decisions. For
example, a group of eight "*nobile*" administered the city's public finances
(Sieveking 1898, p. 48), and, according to Vitale, the *podesta* needed the
approval of the parliament when he decided to fight the dissidents and
those who disturbed the peace (*dissidenti e i perturbatori*) (1951, p. 51).
This permanence of the town council underscores the fact that, despite the
emergence of trade in the definition of relational ties to supplement the
preceding political organization around centralized and topodemographic affiliation, access to the political process on the part of the
commoners was still very limited until the 1257 revolution (Vitale 1956;
Pavoni 1992).

That year, members of the lower class, assisted by the trade-oriented
aristocratic clans of Doria and Spinola, brought to power Guglielmo

---

[3] As Hyde notes, the *podesta* became a permanent institution throughout communal Italy
(1973, p. 101).

Boccanegra, who took the title of "captain of the people"[4] and ran the city along with a council of thirty-two commoners (Petti Balbi 1997). The historians Sieveking (1906, pp. 61–3) and Lopez (1975, p. 27) noted that the 1257 revolution had been preceded by a banking crisis that had threatened the interests of those commoners who had managed to accumulate some capital through long-distance trade. This wealth building among commoners had actually been facilitated by a decade of economic prosperity and relative stability, as Genoa was able to fully assert its control over the whole of Liguria by the mid thirteenth century.

Hence, it appears that the revolution was the sudden expression of slow-building social changes, which, during a period of relative peace, led to the replacement of the previous political system, which had relied on its response to constant military engagements to maintain its authority. As part of the same process, peace also facilitated cross-status alliances because the nobility, which had, up until then, always managed to reunite itself when the city was in danger, was deprived by the lack of military emergencies of its own periodic integration mechanism.

Boccanegra, the new city leader who was born into a rich family closely linked to the mercantile elite,[5] led a regime that provided increased political access to citizens of all conditions. However, his lasting accomplishments served primarily the mercantile group, as he is mainly remembered not only for disentangling Genoa's poor geopolitical situation in order to bolster its commerce, but also for restoring the public finances. Although his stewardship lasted only five years and was followed by seven decades of aristocratic leadership, his tenure constituted an historical break. From then on, appointments to public office were divided equally between aristocrats and commoners (Vitale 1956, p. 86).

The grip of the most powerful feudal clans over the city's formal administration definitively ran its course in 1339, when a coalition of merchants – aristocrats and commoners alike – under growing pressure from the lower caste to see one of their own as the ruler, anointed Simone

---

[4] The similar title had been used in Florence in 1250. The regime there was supported mainly by the *popolo grasso*, the emerging middle class, which comprised professionals, the wealthiest craftsmen, and the merchants.

[5] The Boccanegra family was involved in trade at least from the early thirteenth century onward (LA#157/March 1203, #394/July 1203; LA#1704/December 1225) and – according to the database – became increasingly active in the year preceding the 1259 revolution (DO#780/December 1252; JE#10/March 1253, #744/July 1253, #749/July 1253, #910/May 1252; DO#953/May 1254). See Sayous (1937) and Petti Balbi (1991) for more on the Boccanegra clan.

Boccanegra – the grand nephew of that Guglielmo Boccanegra who had run the first revolutionary regime – as Genoese doge (Agosto 1981, p. 97; Pistarino 1993, p. 173).[6] The popular elements of the city had hoped to nominate the *abate* – an official who since the 1257 revolution had directly assisted the "captain(s) of the people" on behalf of the commoners – to the highest office. However, the new doge, Simone Boccanegra, successfully undercut the popular surge demanding additional self-representation by immediately taking the title of "defender of the people" and by excluding the aristocrats from the government (Petti Balbi 1991; Airaldi 2004).

Over time, the increasing social division between the mercantile commoners and the lower economic classes became formalized in the political organization of the city, which provided separate representation according to occupational criteria. Henceforth, the formal division, which divided the commoners into two distinct groups of merchants (*mercatores*) and craftsmen (*artifices*), was added to the original communal separation between status groups.[7]

In the rest of the chapter, I analyze the credit network to track the change in the social makeup of this mercantile class. I show how credit consolidated the elite commercial network and how the nobility increasingly relied on credit in the definition of relational ties to catch up with those commoners who had taken advantage of the upward mobility of the twelfth and thirteenth centuries. Before getting to that, in the next section I set up the analysis by describing the standard agreements that organized credit ties. Using the example of tangible credit relationships, I especially point to those characteristics that facilitated the rise of medieval merchants.

## 4.1 MEDIEVAL CREDIT INSTRUMENTS

There is a persistent perception that medieval credit – other than that extended to feudal and public authority[8] – was mainly usurious and

---

[6] As such, Genoese history differs from that of the other two great Italian Renaissance republics. In Venice, the nobility never shared power with the *populares*, whereas in Florence the fight between *magnati* and *popolani* (1290–95) ended in the complete triumph of the rich bourgeoisie.

[7] For details, see Forcheri (1974, pp. 50–3).

[8] Those loans often escaped the mechanism of credit markets as they were often a disguised form of either forward sale of taxes (Kaeuper 1973) or tribute extorted in exchange for political and military protection.

confined to consumption loans.[9] In this understanding, the lending role is often confined to non-Christian minorities – Jews in particular – who were not subject to the Church's interdiction against receiving interest (Dubois 1990, p. 756; Favrier 1998, p. 206). Against this view, well-documented quantitative studies have demonstrated that medieval credit transactions were widespread, that not all were usurious in the sense of abusive or secret, and that medieval lenders came from a variety of geographical origins, ethnicities, and religions.[10] My analysis of the Genoese record certainly complements the work of these authors, as the countless consumption loans extended by local citizens attest to a wide participation in credit markets.[11] Among those, many contracts involved ecclesiastics charging interest for collateralized loans,[12] which certainly puts the Church's activities in perspective.

An analysis of the notarial record, which I start next with a description of the sample that will provide the empirical evidence for my formal analysis, also confirms, on a large scale, previous studies (Usher 1943; Dubois 1990) showing that, while personal loans and real estate mortgages were indeed plentiful, medieval credit transactions were not restricted to consumption, but were an integral part of trade and production.

## Sample

As was the case in my analysis of the commenda network, for the credit data set I consider all the instances of commercial credit from 1154 to the end of the fourteenth century that I found among the more than 20,000

[9] See Heers (1974) or Udovitch (1979) for a summary of the various studies of this issue.

[10] See Postan (1927); Reynolds (1930); de Roover (1952); Poliakov (1965); Pugh (1968); and Murray (2005). For example, Poliakov documents the medieval Jews' wide variety of occupations. He also demonstrates that when Jews were indeed lenders, they were often acting as intermediaries by loaning to Christians money that belonged to other Christians (1965), and Murray lists a variety of lenders in the Bruges market (2005, pp. 19–48).

[11] It remains true that in many parts of medieval Europe, where financial markets were undeveloped, foreigners (not necessarily only Jews, but also Lombards and Cahorsins, for example) played a large role in local credit markets. The explanation, though, is not related to the Church position on usury (for exhaustive comments on usury in the Middle Ages, see LeGoff (1999, pp. 1265–1305), but rather to the social proscription against extending loans to friends and acquaintances, as well as the contempt and anger toward those who profited from the precarious circumstances of members of the same community.

[12] For example, S#358/March 1158; CA#77/January 1191; CA#351/March 1191; LA#665/August 1210; LA#1189/ September 1216.

TABLE 4.1. *Credit data set, 1154–1406*

|  | 1154–99 | 1200–49 | 1250–99 | 1300–49 | 1350–1406 |
|---|---|---|---|---|---|
| Number of contracts | 970 | 1,315 | 909 | 380 | 242 |
| Total amount (£) | 51,151 | 57,461 | 229,325 | 210,903 | 83,568 |
| Mean amount (£) | 53 | 44 | 252 | 555 | 345 |
| Std amount (£) | 67 | 65 | 416 | 940 | 401 |
| Number of ties | 2,206 | 2,191 | 1,744 | 795 | 301 |
| Number of individuals | 1,164 | 1,584 | 1,161 | 717 | 373 |
| Number of ties per individual | 3.79 | 2.77 | 3.00 | 2.22 | 1.61 |

notarial minutes I reviewed. Altogether, I selected more than 3,800 contracts organizing a total of 7,238 credit relationships among 4,687 persons. In Table 4.1, I break down some of the credit sample statistics by periods. It is well to remember when referring to empirical patterns over time – perhaps even more than with the commenda sample analyzed in Chapter 3 – that, because the number of records available for coding varied through time, the size of the credit data set is neither an indication of the trade volume dynamics nor a way of determining the commercial loan's relative importance in medieval long-distance commerce. For example, one should be careful not to interpret the low mean number of ties per person in the fourteenth-century data set as exemplifying an historical trend. The data points per year for that period are much sparser and come from smaller and more disparate portions of notarial records than those for the earlier period, which explains why individual careers are underrepresented. When considering the denser period of data entries, those of 1300–15 and 1340–55, the average number of ties stands at 2.78, and is in line with the average over the whole period.

What the sample does provide, though, is empirical evidence that can be used to compare changes both in the architecture of the commercial network and in the social makeup of the participants. In addition, and keeping in mind my introductory precautionary comments about comparing monetary values over time, the data set confirms the mid thirteenth century's large upsurge in mean transaction size observed in Chapter 3.

*Sample selection criteria.* For the most part, when analyzing the record, the differentiation between international credit and smaller consumption loans or local commercial borrowing, such as that of a shoemaker to buy nails, is fairly straightforward.[13] Indeed, both the exchange contracts, which included either the repayment of principal in a foreign currency and/or the borrower's travel plans, and the short-term promissory notes, which backed large trade credit, can be safely categorized as directly or indirectly funding long-distance commerce. More difficult to sort out are those far less common loans that are not identified by a specific purpose and that do not stipulate international payment instructions, but whose terms resemble those of long-distance trade credit. In some cases, the identity of the borrower provides a clue for differentiating between personal and commercial loans. This is, for example, the case with the brothers Simone and Nicolaio Grillo, who, in 1253, lent more than £1,000 to an Arabian prince who pledged "precious stones and silk fabrics enriched by golden thread" as collateral (Belgrano 1866, pp. 119–20). Another example is Bishop Ralph of Liege who, in 1191, upon returning from Syria with a suite made up of his nephew, archdeacons, chaplains, seneschals, butlers, and a secretary, borrowed 200 marks of fine silver (Byrne 1920, p. 216).

In other cases, straight debt notes are more difficult to classify. When in doubt, I have usually aggregated these few credit transactions to the clearly commercial contracts that pertained directly to the international trade. However, those represent a very small number. If I overestimated the size of the long-distance credit network sample, the quantity of these contracts certainly does not constitute a meaningful portion of the credit data statistics reported in Table 4.1.

In addition to the direct credit relationships, I have complemented the data set with two types of ties that have proven important in the organization of Genoese medieval credit. First, I coded the guarantor/borrower and guarantor/lender ties for those loans that include a personal guarantor. This was especially common before the first decades of the thirteenth century because many lenders required the guaranty of a third party. Second, I also coded those proxy/principal relationships that linked a lender to a traveling merchant because, for cases in which the principal of a loan was payable abroad, lenders increasingly empowered fellow merchants to recuperate the funds on their behalf. The proxy/principal ties should not be confused with those of an employee, or even of an exclusive agent, which were more common in the organization of European trade beginning in the late fourteenth century. Had the lenders been

---

[13] GI#531/1210; GI#1996/1211.

employers, it is doubtful that each delegation of authority would have necessitated a separate notarial record. In addition, the notarial records show that those recuperating funds might do so simultaneously for several different merchants and were often themselves active traders.[14] For example, during his career Bonifacio de Tiba,[15] a nobleman whose family had recently emigrated to Genoa and who had been asked by Luchetto Grimaldi to recuperate a debt at the Champagne fairs (April 1263), also entered into a £400 commenda partnership to Constantinople with Simona Fieschi and received 200 Provinese pounds in an exchange contract with Dagano Spinola. As an aside, what is remarkable – although it was not unusual at the time, which confirms that when it came to long-distance trade, boundaries between factions were a lot less sharp than what the historiography portrays – is that Bonifacio de Tiba entered into transactions with families who, as the historiography goes, were arch-enemies throughout the medieval period, and during the second part of the thirteenth century in particular. The Grimaldi and Fieschi were the leading Guelf clans, while the Spinola, along with the Doria, led the Genoese Ghibelline party, which was then controlling the state.

*Periodicity.* Before getting on with the analysis, it will be helpful to say a word about the periodicity of the credit network data set in order to clarify the scope of the analysis. Unlike temporary equities, which declined sharply toward the beginning of the fourteenth century, credit-based relationships span the whole period covered in this book. As such, a preliminary contrast, which will be further elaborated later in the analysis, can be drawn between commenda and credit-based instruments. While the commenda induced social changes, which in turn precipitated its own demise, credit-based institutions provided a framework for consolidating the social architecture and, therefore, lasted longer.

As Table 4.1 indicates, the concentration of entries in the data set declines with time – not because the amount of credit drops, but because the data available to me did – so that the methodology, which relies on a

---

[14] The data set shows that agents (n = 328) also entered into, on average, 4.94 transactions as principals [(mean general population = 3.06 (n = 9,958)].

[15] See, for other examples, Ambrosio Ferrabo (CA#173/February 1191; CA#491/April 1191; CA#527/April 1191; CA#572/May 1191; CA#603/May 1191; CA#746/June 1191; CA#787/June 1191; CA#870/August 1191); Guglielmo Lercario (JE#746/April 1254; JE#766/June 1259; DO#1196/December 1262; JE#800/June 1267; BA#636/August 1282; STU#513/February 1388) and Leonardo Gentilis (BA#4040/March 1388; BA#4228/August 1395; BA#4327/June 1401).

very large sample, cannot be applied evenly for the almost 300 years that pertain to credit-based instruments in this book. It remains true, however, that for the period coinciding with the commenda's golden age (1154–1300), the credit sample is large enough to establish a comparison between, on the one hand, the temporary equity network and, on the other, the credit networks. In addition, I was able to gather a large sample of credit relationships from 1340 to 1355 (n = 682).[16] The analysis of that network provides measurements that will help extend the trend analysis of the earlier centuries.

In the next pages, I describe the functioning of three varieties of standard medieval credit agreements that together constitute almost all debt instruments related to long-distance trading in the notarial cartularies. In decreasing order of risk to the lenders, I will start with a description of the *foenus nauticum*, a sea loan that transferred all traveling risks to the lender. I then explain the mechanism of terrestrial and overseas exchange agreements (*cambium*). I show the similarity between these two types of contracts, including the clause providing for repayment of the principal in a foreign location, a circumstance that necessitated an increasingly sophisticated organization of trade. Finally, the last categories of credit agreements described are the short-term promissory notes that financed many long-distance transactions.

Although these three categories of credit proceeded from distinct legal clauses pertaining to obligations that organized different commercial purposes, they shared a common base that differed fundamentally from the temporary capital ventures analyzed in the previous chapter. Indeed, the terms of the credit contracts are not concerned with the outcome of a business venture,[17] but rather with the conditions under which the debtor had to repay the principal and interest.[18] As for all credit transactions, the question for the creditor was not so much – as was the case in a temporary equity venture – how the borrower invested the funds; the creditor was more concerned with how to structure deals that compelled the debtor to reimburse in time. Obviously, good trading practices could only help the

---

[16] Unless indicated, the credit network analysis is based on the parameters of eight networks whose periodicity matches the commenda networks used in Chapter 3, except for the last one (1340–55). Here also I chose the number and the periodicity of the networks to maximize the period covered while maintaining enough data density for each network.

[17] Maritime loans might sometimes stipulate the commercial value of goods, but this refers to the collateral and not to the obligation of the borrower. In addition, in a handful of contracts the lender had a direct interest in the return of the venture.

[18] Notwithstanding special provisions for transport risks.

debtor's access to credit, but, for a creditor, it was the ability of a borrower to come up with the money at the due date that was key, not the profitability of his transactions per se. As a result, as in any debt transactions, and notwithstanding the pledges and formal personal guaranties provided in many loans, the odds of paying back were also associated with the debtor's capacity to borrow from someone else[19] at the settlement date. By contrast, a failed commenda venture did not require the traveler to pay anything back to the debtor and, therefore, did not involve his social connections to the same degree.[20] An unprofitable commenda was a legal, albeit not desirable, business outcome leaving little recourse for the investor. That this was a possibility is made clear in the will of Pietro della Croce in January 1192. He warns his heirs that his wealth might be less than expected because he invested in commendae.[21] However, failure to pay back a loan was wrongdoing, and the borrower could be forced to pay or go to jail.

## Sea Loans

The sea loan, called *foenus nauticum,* was an agreement stipulating that the repayment of the principal upon returning to Genoa was contingent upon the safe arrival of the cargo or the ship carrying the borrowed money or goods to a specific destination. This type of loan was not much different from the antique bottomry loans whose essential elements are already described in the Hammurabi code issued around 2250 B.C., with the exception that, in most cases, the antique lender was also the original owner of the goods transported and was thus, unlike the situation during the medieval period, also an equity participant (Millett 1983, p. 37).

Most scholars agree that the sea loan continued, uninterrupted, from the time of antique trading (Hoover 1926; Lopez et al. 2001). However, during the early Middle Ages, it had disappeared from the western Mediterranean when commerce considerably slowed down. When, toward the end of the millennium, Italians again regularly took to the sea for voyages to the Levant, they probably revived this sea lending practice. The customary contingency clauses confirming that the lender assumed

---

[19] Most large and successful modern commercial enterprises would be insolvent if it were not for the ability to borrow when a debt is due.

[20] Because many commenda operators were occasional participants, a failed venture did not necessarily carry subsequent business consequences vis-à-vis the ability of the traveler to find new investors.

[21] *"de predictes rebus maior pars est super mare"* (CA#1546/January 1192).

the sea risk, such as *sana eute nave* or *risicum et fortunam dei maris et gentium*,[22] can be found with precisely the same wording in the commercial records of many Mediterranean[23] cities with a variety of legal foundations. Thus, as was the case for the commenda, the sea loan was in use all around the Mediterranean under a uniform framework derived from customary commercial practices.

The records show sea loan agreements involving almost all common Mediterranean destinations, such as Alexandria, Tripoli, Maiorca, and Montpellier, and the interest rates recorded in our data set for the twelfth and early thirteenth centuries did not vary much for a given destination.[24] Depending of the distance, the rates varied from 25% to 33% for a trip to the western Mediterranean basin, and from 40% to 100% for a voyage to the Levant. Historians are quick to point out that this difference in rates for a given destination is an indication that the Levant was more profitable. That is not at all evident, however, because the capital would be repaid much faster when invested in the western Mediterranean trade.

Sea loan interest rates might seem prohibitive to the modern reader, but the borrower must have been confident that the ventures would yield even higher returns, leaving a profit after deduction of interest expenses. This appears to have been a reasonable assumption considering that the scant record of profit from twelfth-century commendae shows that temporary equity ventures could certainly return more than the sea loan's interest rate. The extremely high interest rate is yet another evidence of the relatively small role at the time of business acumen, as understood in the modern sense. The management of the strictly commercial risk (that is, the risk of selling the goods at a price that would not cover expenses) was not the key to a venture's success. The real trading exposure was the traveling risk, as is evident from the enormous premium paid to the sea loan lender. With a totally inelastic continental demand, the emphasis was not so much on which, or how, goods were traded but on securing supply and transporting them safely.

---

[22] "Only if ship is returned safe and sound" or "At the risk of the god of the sea and the people (on sea)."

[23] See, for example, Venice (Lopez 2001), Marseilles (Pryor 1977), and Barcelona (Sayous 1936).

[24] S#231/August 1157; S#1238/July 1164; OB#478/May 1184 and GI#920/October 1203. The notary would mark the interest rate as *quatuor quinque* (25%) or *tribus quatuor* (33%) or as a certain amount of *denarii per libram*.

Sea loans did not constitute a large portion of the credit market,[25] most likely because the terms were not flexible enough (remember that round-trip specific destinations were the norm for sea loans) for the opportunistic nature of medieval trading. In that regard, it is thus unsurprising that an analysis of the sea loan network shows the providers of funds to have been the most frequent long-distance operators. Indeed, the routine nature of the operations of people such as Bongiovanni Malusfiliaster, Idone Mallone, and Giacomo de Bombel[26] benefited more from their predictable outcome than those of commendae. This is confirmed by a systematic analysis of the data set: When pooling the eight credit networks from 1154 to 1355, I found that on average the number of ties of those extending sea loans was twice that of the whole population of creditors. The mean standardized nodal degree of those extending sea loans was 0.7708 (n = 84) versus 0.3232 (n = 2272) for the whole population of creditors. The standardized nodal degree parameter is not as easy to interpret as the nodal degree or number of transactions. However, it is an appropriate measure when comparing the activities of operators in networks of different sizes. A simple interpretation of the difference between the two mean standardized nodal degrees is that the mean share of the credit network's total degree for those who extended sea loans was more than twice that of those who did not.

## Exchange Contracts[27]

Toward the end of the twelfth century, sea loans declined and were increasingly replaced by the maritime exchange *cambium maritimum* or *cambium nauticum,* which combined some of the elements of the secular

---

[25] Before the fourteenth century, out of more than 6,000 credit ties I recorded only 275 sea loan ties.

[26] For Malusfiliaster: S#106/June 1156, #180/May 1156, #224/July 1157, and #665/August 1160. For Mallone: OB1#405/April 1184. For Bombel: GI#228/June 1201.

[27] The letter of exchange in many ways replaced the medieval *cambium* from the late fourteenth century onward (de Roover 1952). It would have been valuable to code letters of exchange in the context of this research, but those credit agreements were private documents. As a result, there is no exhaustive record dating from the fourteenth and fifteenth centuries other than those of a few merchants whose sampling is neither large enough nor random enough to give us a picture of the letter of exchange network. However, what can be safely advanced is that any switch from the *cambium* to the letter of exchange implied merchant routinization. Indeed, one of the biggest advances of the letter over the *cambium* was its liquidity, which was directly associated with the size of the web of relations of both a given debtor and his creditors. This was especially true in the beginning as the parties still needed to recognize the borrower's handwriting.

Mediterranean sea loan reviewed earlier with some of the clauses of the terrestrial exchange – usually referred simply as *cambium* – which had been used by foreign merchants who visited Genoa beginning in the eleventh century.

**Overland Cambium.** On September 19, 1191, Rolando de Soler, a merchant from Asti, 120 kilometers north of Genoa, received a sum from three Genoese. Further, Rolando promised to repay the principal and interest, not in Genoese pounds, but in Provinois deniers (the money of Champagne) at the fair in Lagny, Champagne. In addition, Rolando pledged some (unidentified) goods (*pignori*) and strengthened the loan by receiving personal surety from two fellow merchants from his hometown, one of whom was a close kin.[28]

The contract between Rolando de Soler and the three Genoese partners can be regarded as a typical exchange, or *cambium*, contract. It is best described as a credit agreement between two or more persons providing for the repayment of principal in a different place, at a later date, in a foreign currency, to the lender or his proxy (*missus*). Thus, the supplier of local currency was the lender, and the supplier of the foreign coins was the borrower. In almost all cases, the contract does not include the payment of interest, as the lender's return on investment consisted of the difference in the currency exchange rate. Scholars insist on using the word "undervaluation" to qualify this difference (de Roover 1953). This implies a strategic pricing mechanism. However, the reality was probably much simpler. Medieval currency quotes exhibited very large bid-offer spreads, and the conversion operations might very well have been the largest part of the lender's profit. In fact, in the exchange agreement, the loan and exchange operations were inseparable, and, aside from a classic lending and currency exchange operation, the agreement provided the lender with an ability to transport funds to faraway markets without any risk and while being paid.[29]

In the case of Rolando de Soler, it is likely that he used the Genoese pounds to buy merchandise that had been imported to Genoa from the

---

[28] CA# 1044/1191. The Soler family was one of the most active in late twelfth-century Genoa. The mean nodal degree of the six most active family members is 14, more than four times the long-distance trade network average.

[29] The contention that the *cambium* was primarily a transfer-of-funds operation can easily be dismissed because the provider of local currency was not paying any kind of compensation to the taker. Instead, the difference in currency rates clearly indicates that the transport of funds was not as valuable as its availability.

East. He then was to carry it to northern France with the intention of reimbursing the *cambium* with the proceeds of the sale. For one or all of the three Genoese partners, the money received in Champagne would probably have been used to purchase northern merchandise to carry back to Genoa. Over time, the creditors would not need to travel to recuperate the funds, as almost every *cambium* contract was to include arrangement for payment to a proxy, which, in turn, enlarged the pool of potential lenders.

Exchange contracts were particularly suitable for trading in Champagne; because of the high level of participation at the fairs, the gatherings functioned as a large clearinghouse. However, while Champagne is by far the most common destination of exchange contracts in the data set, *cambium* contracts can also be found in trading to a variety of cities such as Rome, Verona, Milan, and Paris.[30]

*Maritime Exchange.* The share of all exchange transcations in the credit network grew in the course of the thirteenth century from 12% for the period of 1150–1200 to eventually reaching almost 65% of all long-distance credit ties recorded by notaries in the fourteenth century. The bulk of the terrestrial exchange in the data set is dated before the end of the thirteenth century, before the proportion of overland *cambium* to maritime exchange declined. This reflects the fact that transportation by way of land to northern Europe began to be replaced by maritime shipping after the first Genoese galleys turned to the Atlantic around 1280.[31] As such, the inverse proportion of exchange contract types in the total debt recorded for the periods 1250–1300 and 1300–1400 confirms the tight connection in usage between the terrestrial and maritime exchange contracts. Indeed, the maritime exchange, *cambium nauticum* or *cambium maritimum*, which replaced the straight sea loan toward the end of the twelfth century, was very similar to the overland exchange in stipulating the repayment of the principal in a foreign currency in a foreign city[32] to the lender or, more

---

[30] CA#338/1191; OB#3/1190; GI#454/1201; and LA#181/1203.

[31] See de Roover for crisp analysis of the decline of the Champagne fairs (1969, pp. 24–5).

[32] Raymond de Roover, the most widely cited authority in texts related to medieval exchange contracts, notes, "As a matter of fact, a *cambium* maritimum differed little from an ordinary *cambium*" (1952, p. 23). When referring to a maritime exchange to southern Italy, the principal was usually due in ounces of *tarreni*; when to Provence, in *regalium coronatorum*; when to the Magrhebian cities, in bezant *masumotinus* or *miliarensis*; when to Syria, in Saracen bezants; and when to the Byzantine Empire, in *perperrus* or *yperperus*.

often, to his proxy (*missus*). The only real difference was that, while the maritime exchange almost always borrowed from the sea loan the conditional nature of the repayment, which "depended upon the fortunate outcome of a voyage" (de Roover 1969, p. 17), an equivalent clause for overland exchange (*salvum terra*) was extremely rare. This absence of the clause *salvum terra* in overland exchange contracts provides strong counterevidence to the still-dominant cultural explanation of the "life cycle" of maritime loans advanced by de Roover (1952), Hyde (1973, p. 162), and Lopez (2001). According to that explanation, the maritime exchange maintained the sea loan's conditional payment upon the goods' safe arrival because of a need to evade the Church edict against usurious loans. Lopez even goes so far as to say that "the popularity of the contract of exchange as an instrument of credit seems to have been connected primarily, if not exclusively, with the fact that it could be used instead of loan contracts, which, by law of the Church, must be made without interest" (Lopez et al. 2001, p. 163). Genoese indeed did not use such terms as *mutuum* (loan) and *proficuum* (profit) when drafting exchange contracts. Likewise, because the profit of the lender was the differential in currency rates, it was difficult for the Church to figure out how much the investor was getting for lending the funds. Nevertheless, because overland exchange did not include a conditional payment of the principal, the most plausible explanation for the maritime exchange having kept its conditional clause is the fact that overseas transport was more dangerous, rather than that it was in response to the Church edict. To back their theory, the economic literature also accepts the same authors' assertion that, when the contract included a provision that allowed the borrower to repay the loan in Genoa if he had been unable to pay abroad, it was usually a fictive exchange (de Roover 1954, p. 202), also called a "dry exchange," which concealed a regular commercial loan. However, they cannot provide evidence that this was the case. To the contrary, two pieces of evidence point to the local reimbursement provision as an extra flexible clause for the borrower. First, the very high exchange rate that these provisions quoted demonstrates that paying back in Genoa was at a high premium. Second, the data set involved many mandates from lenders who instructed their proxies to recoup in foreign cities the proceeds of loans that, nevertheless, also included the option of local repayment. I am not suggesting that "dry exchange" transactions never took place. However, if "dry exchange" transactions were the rule, why would the creditors bother with the proxy instructions, and why do we have records of payment to foreign agents?

Instead of seeking a cultural explanation for the emergence of sea loans, we find that their use responded to an increased routinization of commercial practices. First, instead of being tied to a predetermined return trip to Genoa to pay back the principal and interest when they contracted a sea loan, the borrowers in exchange contracts were free after they met their obligation at destination. Depending on the contract, the travelers were allowed between eight and sixty days after arrival to repay the principal, enough time for them to sell the goods they carried before reinvesting the profit in whatever business they deemed appropriate. Incidentally, the payment at destination also meant that the risk premium was reduced, because the lender did not have to bear the traveling risk on the return voyage. Second, both the increased variability and the difficulty of assessing borrowing costs conferred to the more knowledgeable trader an advantage in the bargaining about currency rates for the repayment of the loan. Thus, unlike the case of commendae, and, to some extent, the more stable sea loan's interest rates, the regular traders were at an advantage because they could count on information networks built from repeated commercial encounters. As Gobel has demonstrated, this is especially important when markets are illiquid and fragmented (1998, p. 168). Third, and of special interest to this research, possibly the most significant change from previous arrangements was the role of the lender's proxy (*missus*), a role that limited network entry to only those investors who maintained ties within a network of international commercial operators.[33] It comes, thus, as no surprise that exchange contracts became an agreement for regular and increasingly specialized commercial operators. As with other forms of long-distance credit (as was the case for the sea loan lenders, but here for lenders and borrowers both), from the mid thirteenth century onward, the mean share in the total degree count in the long-distance trade of those engaging in exchange contracts was almost twice that of those who engaged in commenda contracts only.[34]

## Promissory Notes

The third broad category of credit instruments reviewed in this section is short-term promissory notes, which formalized sales credit–deferred

---

[33] Unfortunately for the modern researcher, in many cases the documents do not mention the name of the proxy.

[34] For exchange contracts, the standardized mean degree was 0.52 (n = 1,275), while for the commenda-only operators it stood at 0.27 (n = 2,738).

payment for goods sold. Without much information about cash transactions, it is difficult to estimate the proportion of trade credit in the
overall movement of goods. However, the very large number of those
agreements in the notarial records indicates that the practice was probably widespread. For example, in my sample of promissory notes for the
year 1210, the draper *Enricus draperius* was a principal in twenty-seven
different sales credit transactions ranging from just £3 to £240, for a total
of over £2,300.[35]

The promissory notes Enricus signed were standard for the time. The
contract began with the recognizance by the buyer of having received a
specific amount of goods for which he promised to pay at a future date,[36]
which was usually no more than three or four months from the date of the
notarial agreement. The interest portion of the proceeds payment is difficult to assess because the records provide neither a way to compare cash
prices with delay payments nor a data series on prices paid for merchandise at different times. But with medieval interest on commercial
loans running sometimes as high as 4% per month, any credit extensions
must have been very valuable for the buyer. In that light, it is noteworthy
that, despite the high cost of borrowing, the promissory bills were often
not paid on time. Even in the middle of the fourteenth century, when
business was becoming more routinized and, supposedly, more sophisticated, a small sample of thirty-one promissory notes, for which we have
receipts of the repayment of principal, shows that four-month notes were,
on average, reimbursed only after more than nine months.[37] This suggests
that business practices and enforcement of contracts were dictated neither
by market pricing nor by systematic application of rules. It is, however,
unlikely that the operative enforcement mechanism was akin to that
described by Greif with regard to eleventh-century Maghribi traders, that
is, that a creditor "acted honorably solely to maintain his reputation"
(2006, p.69). Indeed, the Genoese market was much more socially heterogeneous than Greif's traders' community. Thus, his theory is much less
applicable because size of network is associated with the efficiency of his
enforcement mechanism theory.

Certainly, some promissory notes probably went unpaid. But, for the
most part, it seems that late payment was simply part of usual business

---

[35] See LA#501, #504, #510, #536, #580, #585, #608, #687, #693, #696, #787,
#828, #881, #887, #888, #894, DO#236, #241, #244, #248, #249, #256, #268,
#269.

[36] At the time, this was not a numeric date, but at a holiday (Carnival, Easter, Christmas).

[37] n = 31; mean maturity of notes = 4.035 months; mean repayment = 9.45 months.

practices and, despite the high cost of borrowing, no late-payment penalty was stipulated in contracts. By the same token, medieval trade credit may have included a way to differentiate among buyers by offering preferential rates and conditions, as is often the case today (McMillan and Woodruff 1999, p. 1286). However, I could not detect any pattern of pricing difference. The differentiation among buyers thus expressed itself not on the basis of price difference but in the binary decision to extend credit or not.

The data set shows that trade credit was extended for the purchase of a wide range of merchandise, such as lead, skins, grain, pepper, and, above all, products related to the textile industry.

The high proportion of items such as cloth, cotton, and alum in the sales credit notes data set indicates that promissory notes also served as working capital for artisans, such as the drapers and dyers. The notes financed the stock of cloth, which the artisans cut and dyed in their workshop, before selling the finished goods for cash to commendae operators, who would then carry them overseas.[38]

As in the case of exchange contracts, promissory notes also often involved proxies who could settle the transaction on behalf of either party if the party were absent, which confirms the international nature of the participants' activities and their need to have access to a network of colleagues to represent them when away.

## Personal Surety

In any credit transaction, a key issue for the lender is to make sure the borrower will repay in time (Guseva and Akos Rona 2001). In medieval Genoa, the notarial records show that the protections from insolvent debtors can be divided into two main categories. The first has to do with the creditor selection process and the second with adding material or personal surety in case of default, as well as stiff penalties. For the most part, my records do not show that a third classic protection, that of raising interest rates – which poses the problem of adverse selection and reduces the market size (Steglitz 2000) – was common for commercial loans related to the long-distance trade. I do not mean to say that interest rates did not vary, just that they do not seem to be associated with the identity of the debtor.

---

[38] Further evidence that promissory notes served as working capital was the near absence of sales credit in regard to manufactured goods.

No doubt, the selection method was the primary protection for the lender, and credit-worthiness was certainly assessed according to wealth and reputation in the professional network of traders (Tilly 2005, pp. 14–15). However, as shown in the second chapter, the Genoese traders did not, during the early phase of the commercial revolution, enjoy the tight connection of their eastern counterparts, or that of the ethnic group that had dominated the early medieval trade, nor did they necessarily experience at first the regularity and repetition of transactions that foster high credit. This is why the notarial records indicate that creditors often relied on material and personal surety. First, almost all loans provided a penalty of double the principal in case of default.[39] Second, and probably of a more efficient nature, the majority of loans were collateralized by the debtor's entire asset base and often, more specifically, by the goods that he eventually bought with the loans (*pignus*).[40] Finally, and especially before the mid thirteenth century, that is, before the emergence of a commercial network of specialized Genoese merchants, creditors often required the personal surety of a third party in case of the primary debtor's default. This does not mean that the credit network, as a whole, was strongly embedded in a "trust" or "reputation" network. In fact, the need for a guarantor indicated just the opposite. However, belonging to a tight cluster of fellow merchants would ease access to credit from a different cluster.

An analysis of the data set shows that the incidence of personal surety was associated with the size of the loan, but the difference in both the sample average and the standard deviation is not very significant. However, an examination of the guarantor/creditor and guarantor/debtor ties shows that the loans included in the countersigning of a personal surety usually involved transactions between foreign merchants and Genoese. In most cases, the guarantor shared his or her place of origin with the borrowers.

---

[39] It is difficult to assess whether this clause is more a matter of rhetoric than an actual threat to the debtor.

[40] Borrowers routinely engaged their entire belongings (*obligatione bonarum meorum*) and those of the family and successors (*successors et habentes causam a me*). For other collateralized loans, the records usually don't provide a way to calculate the "loan-to-value," and it was most likely often close to 100%. In some cases, part of the purchase was in cash, and the creditor's protection was therefore better. For example, Soler and Belardungo borrowed £305 and gave £400 worth of merchandise as collateral (CA#566/May 1191).

As expected, the guarantors were more central than the average credit operators. Indeed, using the densest portion of the data set that refers to guarantors (1184 to 1225), I calculated that the mean share total degree of all credit network participants stood at 0.54 (n = 2268), whereas the guarantors' stood at 0.82 (n = 219). However, neither the borrowers – who received – nor the creditors, who requested personal surety, turned out to have an average degree centrality different from that of the general population of credit participants (the lenders' stood at 0.55 and the borrowers' at 0.53.). Thus, at a time when the Genoese involved in the long-distance trade were still mostly multivalent actors, the request by a creditor to a potential debtor was not motivated by market exposure or any other strictly economic parameter,[41] but simply by the place of origin of the borrower. Over time, the use of personal surety declined, and by the mid thirteenth century it was rare. This dynamic is consistent with the emergence of a Genoese mercantile class who induced credit practices superseding the social division according to place of origin.

## 4.2 CREDIT NETWORK FOR REGULAR TRADERS

In Chapter 3, I described how commenda agreements formed the primary institutional framework that organized the financial participation of Genoese of all social origins. I also pointed to the occasional nature of their activities to make sense of the meaning of the Genoese saying *Ego mercator sum*: A great many were involved, but few were regular traders, especially before the mid thirteenth century. The Genoese who are part of the long-distance credit data set of almost 7,300 ties, dating from 1154 to 1404, also exhibit a large degree of heterogeneity in social characteristics. However, they do not all exhibit it to the same extent. In fact, the purpose of this section is to demonstrate that credit-based instruments associated with long-distance trade formed an institutional framework for routinized traders.[42] Thus, unlike commendae, credit-based agreements did not derive their historical importance as revolutionary social institutions, but

---

[41] Merchants mutually guarantying each other's loans. The "round robin" certainly solidified credit relationships, but of course diminished the credit solidity of the system as a whole.

[42] One must be careful not to mistake occupational routinization and specialization for professionalization. As H. C. White notes, professionalism should be set off against corporatism and clientelism (2008, p. 196). Specialization, in our context, is set off against the occasional participation of the Genoese population at large. The style of merchant organization does not concern us here yet. Nevertheless, while clientelism pervaded the feudal economic system, and corporatism organized the artisans' ties within

rather as consolidators of commercial identities that induced occupational categories. Consequently, an analysis of the change in the social
composition of the credit network over the course of the twelfth and
thirteenth centuries provides clues as to where the mercantile elite who
dominated the Renaissance came from.

   Before getting to that analysis in the last section of this chapter, I will
first, in this section, justify my choice of the credit network as the more
suitable empirical site of analysis for illuminating that process. In order to
do so, I review three characteristics of the credit operators – occupation,
gender, and career – and demonstrate that, unlike the commenda, the
credit network referred to a more specialized commercial network.[43] I
found that, in the medieval world of wide and heterogeneous participation in long-distance trade, an analysis of the credit data set indicates that
those receiving and extending credit had longer trading careers, and were
less likely to have another principal occupation outside commerce. In
addition, while women's participation in commendae was clear evidence
of the social heterogeneity of the Genoese long-distance participation,
their near absence from the credit network constitutes a further indication
of the more specialized profile of those using credit in their participation
in long-distance trade. Finally, I bring in one more piece of related evidence when I conclude this section by briefly comparing the commenda
and credit network parameters over 175 years. Indeed, I show that the
credit network architecture is both denser and more structurally stable
than that of temporary equities and, thus, refers to a more specialized and
more routinized set of participants.

## Occupation

As mentioned earlier, the wide distribution of occupations was one of the
characteristics of the commenda network heterogeneity. The credit network was different. Figure 4.1 reports the artisans' and professionals'
combined share of the long-distance trade network population, not only
for networks credit but also for commenda agreements. As the figure
indicates, when excluding clearly commercial occupations directly related
to long-distance trade, the proportion of Genoese identified by the

---

and without their communities, merchants' interactions were also corporatist. However,
the difficulties in marking boundaries sapped the system and made control difficult.
[43] This is true only because most credit transactions did not involve intermediaries. Lending
organizations, such as banks, occupied only a very small portion of the overall network.

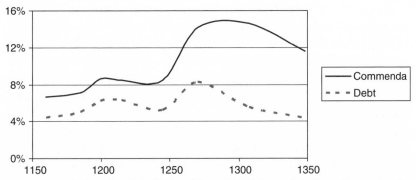

FIGURE 4.1. Artisans' and professionals' combined share of the long-distance trade network population, 1154–1355.

notaries according to their craft or profession is much lower.[44] As such, the lower heterogeneity with respect to occupation is the first evidence that credit was an institution more often linking specialized long-distance operators when compared to the commenda.

I have found that the pattern of lower participation in the credit networks vis-à-vis the commenda networks holds for both craftsmen and professionals. While artisans' share of the commenda networks rose throughout the thirteenth century to more than 10% of operators, their level of participation in the credit market was much lower. In fact, and leaving aside the 1350–1400 period, for which the sample is too small, this proportion is almost constant for any given fifty-year period and never exceeds 3.5%. In addition, artisans' credit ties often took the form of promissory note agreements extended by suppliers for the raw material they needed in their shops. This was, for example, the case when, in March 1253, Pietro Doria, on five occasions, sold alum to dyers who each received trade credit facilities.[45]

This does not mean that all alum transactions involved dyers, or that all animal-skin buyers were shoemakers or furriers. However, artisans' involvement in the credit market was often more industrial than commercial in nature, and, as a result, I probably overestimated the proportion of commercial debt contracted by that occupational group.

---

[44] I excluded from the calculation drapers, bankers and – obviously – *mercatores* when they started to be referred to as such in the fourteenth-century notarial cartularies. Also, I aggregated to the clearly professional occupations, such as teachers *(magister)* and doctors *(medicus),* the members of the clergy involved in the long-distance trade.

[45] LO#97f, 98f, 99f, 100f, 101f/March 1253.

Grocers[46] constituted the only craft where the proportion of debt in the total network was higher than that in the commenda network. In itself, this exception confirms the more routinized characteristics of those who participated in credit networks. In the course of the medieval period, the grocers' occupation shifted; the art of knowing and handling spices became less important than the ability to trade. From the fourteenth century onward, some grocers became large international merchants. Indeed, the mean size of the transactions involving at least one grocer jumps from an average of £38 in the twelfth and thirteenth centuries to more than £300 in the fourteenth. Although our sample of grocers is small, and inference should be interpreted cautiously, the jump in average volume is a strong indication of some grocers' change of business activity. Their business has little relationship to that of shopkeepers or artisans, and their transactions cover a variety of products and a variety of markets.[47]

The data also shows that professionals, while increasingly well represented in the commenda network as the commercial revolution unfolded, constituted only a very small portion of the credit ties. This is especially true when excluding both land and maritime exchanges, where the sole profession of notaries artificially boosted the average participation of professionals in the credit market. But notaries seem to have been mainly trading either as principals, when they traveled to their postings in Genoese enclaves around the Mediterranean and leveraged their international professional network, or, toward the end of the fourteenth century, when acting as agents of merchants.

## Gender

Many entries in the notarial records regard women borrowing small amounts of money, most likely for personal needs, as, for example, when on July 24, 1203, Soleste de Pilosis and her sister-in-law, Anna Nalsca, borrowed 20 sols from Oberto de Costa.[48] Similarly, women also lent equally small amounts – this almost always on their own, whereas

---

[46] Grocers constituted only 1.1% of the total debt network sample and only 0.68% for the commenda network. My hesitation to code grocers as long-distance merchants stems from the difficulty in differentiating the numerous grocers who held retail shops and who did not fully participate in the long-distance trade from the few who did.

[47] Despite the change in the nature of their business, Genoese grocers never occupied the same type of central position in the trading network as their counterparts in other European cities such as Venice (Lane 1973, p. 314) and London (Thrupp 1948, p. 2).

[48] See GI#431/August 1210.

borrowing was frequently done together with their husbands[49] – but as far as the record tells us, these were one-off agreements for both creditors and debtors. In many cases, the agreements involved mortgaging real estate properties, presumably because the borrower did not possess any other assets to put up as collateral.

Thus, women were not strangers to the idea of credit, and there seems to have been no specific cultural prohibition against them extending or receiving loans. Indeed, the long-distance credit–related data set also includes some women, who were as often debtor as creditor.[50] However, unlike commenda agreements, in which women constituted a significant part of the commenda network, they very seldom extended or received commercial loans.

Indeed, only 151 ties, out of almost 7,300 commercial credit relationships in the data set, involve one or more women. In fact, it is likely that I overestimated women's participation because I probably coded some personal loans – where the proportion of women's participation is around 25% – as commercial. As a result, the tiny proportion of the total financial volume of commercial credit involving at least one woman (less than 0.3%), as opposed to the proportion of the number of transactions (2.05%), might, in this case, be more representative of the near absence of women from the long-distance credit market. Moreover, and also indicative of the restricted nature of women's involvement, when a woman borrowed in the commercial credit market, she often did so jointly with her husband,[51] who added his wife's assets to his own in order to bolster the value of the collateral. For example, on the 27th of March 1313, Iohanna, the wife of an innkeeper (*tabernarius*), Alegio of Bonifacio, along with her husband, received a trade credit of £20 for groceries (*tantan speciaria*).[52] The plan called for Alegio to travel to Flanders to sell the goods and then repay the principal and interest upon his return.

---

[49] I did not systematically record personal loans, but a sample of eighty-two personal loans recorded between 1154 and 1225, which involved at least one woman, shows that in more than 34% of the cases women borrowed together with their husbands.

[50] Out of 151 ties coded, women borrowed 79 times while extending loans 84 times (79 + 84 >151 because some were intra-women loans).

[51] While there was no specific prohibition against women extending loans, in the majority of cases the women acted on the advice *(consiliatores)* of one, or possibly two, male acquaintances, usually outside the nuclear family. For example, Iohanna's advisers were Pietro de Clavica, *qui facio vestites* (who makes clothing), and Iacio de Carpono, *accimator* (shearer). It may be that these advisers could diminish the ability of husbands to coerce their wives to invest their own funds against their will.

[52] DO#1776.

During the husband's absence, Iohanna probably ran the tavern by herself.

Next, I continue my study of credit network participants by analyzing the distribution of career length.

## Career

In January 1191, Martino de Albaro borrowed £12 from Giovanni de Canneto – a draper – that he promised to pay back within one year. From that date onward, until September 1213, when he entered into an exchange contract payable in Syria, I found no fewer than forty-nine credit agreements tying him to forty-four different people. Martino de Albaro can certainly be classified as one of the early Genoese merchants. He borrowed both from grocers and drapers in order to trade a variety of goods, traveled around the Mediterranean, and used an array of commercial instruments to finance his operations. Many of his counterparts were foreign merchants – from Flanders and closer Italian cities. His commercial world was that of the routinized merchants. As far as the record shows, he never entered into transactions with women, aristocrats, or artisans – unless it was to deal in goods related to their craft.

Martino de Albaro's egonet is one of the densest I have recorded, but the length of his career was not unusual among the most active long-distance operators. A study of individual career dynamics is relevant because a trader's career unfolds through time, and the meaning of the social network that knits the long-distance trade together is associated with the duration of individual trajectories (H. C. White 2008, pp. 185–97).

Figure 4.2 reports the comparison of the mean career lengths of credit users and the rest of the long-distance trade operators. Although during the earlier period of the commercial revolution the career-length variation was not large, the difference became increasingly wide after the mid thirteenth century. In the portion of the database which refers to the fourteenth century, the career of a given long-distance trade participant who was using credit instruments was on average almost three times longer than that of one who wasn't.

This dynamic certainly confirms the increasing routinization of the trading networks and further validates the theory that credit best identifies the emerging mercantile group.[53] This pattern also holds true when

---

[53] It might be that credit ties in turn make careers longer, too.

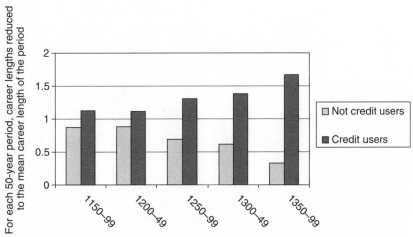

FIGURE 4.2. Comparison of career lengths of credit and noncredit users among all long-distance operators, 1154–1399.

controlling for the discrepancy in the average number of ties per trader observed in each group. Indeed, next, in Figure 4.3, I report the same ratios as in Figure 4.2, but this time only for those who were the most active participants.[54]

The pattern revealed in Figure 4.3 is slightly different from that reported in Figure 4.2. In the earlier period, the career of those not using credit was actually a little longer than that of those who did borrow or lend funds. A logical explanation for this lies in the fact that, at that time, foreign merchants were not yet as active as they would become toward the turn of the thirteenth century. In the first part of the twelfth century, commerce was mostly in the hands of multivalent persons, many of whom were men-of-arms. The subsequent period witnessed an increasing difference in career length between credit users and the others. This difference is in line with the temporality of the rise of specialization and the emergence of Genoese everyday merchants. This explains why commenda ties, which had provided strong threads in the fabric of the trade network, almost disappeared as temporary, and often changing, medieval

---

[54] I defined the most active as all of those for whom I was able to record at least ten trading interactions. For the less dense 1350–99 sample, I chose a cut-off of six interactions, which was the closest integer matching the average percentile cut-off for the rest of the period.

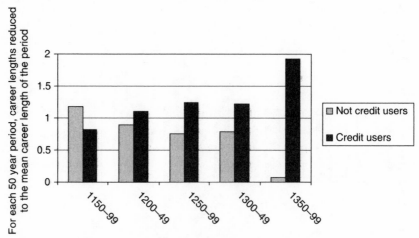

FIGURE 4.3. Comparison of career lengths of credit and noncredit users among routinized long-distance traders, 1154–1399.

partnerships were replaced by more static long-term ties that served to congeal trade relationships, a process that is consistent with the slow-down in upward mobility that historians[55] have noted. This, in turn, further provided fertile social ground for the growth of credit – a type of agreement that is more dependent on preexisting ties and wealth.

Next, I wind up section 4.2 by comparing the density of the commenda network and that of the credit network and bring forth another piece of evidence demonstrating that unlike the commenda, long-distance trade–related credit was a framework for routinized traders.

### Density of Credit Network

Against the widely held neoclassical view that markets are animated by individual utility functions, economic sociologists are focusing on the shared social practices that organized economic exchanges and in the absence of which markets would break down.[56] Indeed, the "stable

---

[55] For example, see Kedar (1973, pp. 43–57) and Balard (1978, pp. 697–700).
[56] See, for more on this approach, Granovetter (1985); Powell (1990); Thomson (2003); and White (2002).

TABLE 4.2. *Density ratio between credit and commenda networks,*
*1154–1315*

|  | 1154–1164 | 1182–1197 | 1198–1215 | 1216–1239 | 1245–1268 | 1269–1295 | 1296–1315 |
|---|---|---|---|---|---|---|---|
| Ratio of density | 1.93 | 1.72 | 1.43 | 1.43 | 2.81 | 3.35 | 2.96 |

memberships and structures" of markets (Leifer 1985, p. 442) are fostered by repetitive and transitive interactions (H. C. White 2002, 2008) that are initiated and reinforced by social relationships occuring outside the economic exchange context (Adler 2001, p. 218; Tilly 2005, p. 39).

As such, the institutional site of encounters by regular traders should prove dense because the organization of exchange naturally gives rise to clusters of people (Burt 1992). Table 4.2 reports the density[57] ratio between credit and commenda networks throughout seven consecutive periods. Because, in the case of the routinized exchange system, clustering is underpinning density, we should expect a higher density in the credit networks regardless of the size of the network. This difference is clearly reflected in Table 4.2.

Next, in Figure 4.4, I report the evolution of the credit network density up to 1355. Notice how, despite the large variation in network size, the density remains stable across the time period, thereby indicating equilibrium in the proportional size of the cluster's distribution (density would otherwise be inversely proportional to the size).

As I mentioned in Chapter 3, one of the reasons why the commenda network developed its particular architecture was the irregular availability of a given partner, both because of uncertainty as to each venture's duration and because of an irregular cash flow for both travelers and investors. As a contrast, credit contracts fostered more regular transactions and concerned more experienced traders. The movement of people and funds follows a pattern allowing for embryonic strategic planning and the formation of clusters of regular associates. Except during the earlier period, when merchants from northern Europe and from other Italian towns had not yet formed the basis of the first routinized mercantile network in Genoa, the credit network architecture was relatively

---

[57] Comments about the caution needed in interpreting density measures as a measure of cohesion (see p. 109) are relevant as well. Interpretation here is not about cohesion but about conformity to the ideal network structure.

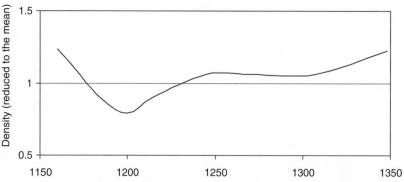

FIGURE 4.4.  Credit network density, 1154–1355 (values are reduced to the mean).

stable.[58] Thus, it is not by the pattern of change in the network's construction that the emergence of the Genoese mercantile group can be explained. Rather, the study of the social makeup dynamic of the credit participants reveals the mechanism that gave rise to the Renaissance mercantile oligarchy. It is to that analysis that I now turn in section 4.3.

## 4.3  MERCHANTS

The first two sections of this chapter examined medieval debt instruments and showed why the credit network was a site of exchange among the more routinized long-distance traders active in Genoa. Building on this analysis, I now turn to a study of the medieval men who shaped and enacted the credit exchange system. The objective is to provide the reader with a sense of the historical dynamics shaping the composition of the mercantile group that gave rise to the fifteenth-century Renaissance oligarchy.

As with any classification process, stratification studies require the identification of salient social characteristics.[59] For the purpose of this research, and considering the limited information available for such a

[58] Keeping in mind that the sample I used to build the 1154–64 network is smaller than the later one and concerned only with the records of a single notary, note that the earlier-period credit network is more centralized and corresponds to a more hierarchical architecture, which, in turn, corresponds to the command/authority mode of coordination of the town as a whole.

[59] It would have been methodologically more satisfying to use block-model testing to single out ex-post-salient stratification characteristics as opposed to determining, a priori, which ones are most suitable. However, the low density of network makes the block clustering statistically insignificant, so the result does not provide any meaningful conclusion.

remote period of history, I have picked three: place of origin, occupation, and status.

I begin with the distribution of the places of origin of credit operators in order to show that, initially, foreigners constituted the first dense clusters of merchants active in Genoa. Then, I complete the occupational review started in Chapter 3 by describing the roles of drapers and bankers, two lines of work that naturally became central in the emergence of the Genoese long-distance credit network. Finally, I consider the status distribution of the mercantile elite in order to illuminate the economic and social mechanisms underpinning the fourteenth century's upward mobility. Each of these three parts corresponds to three occupational recruitment processes into the long-distance trade.

First, foreigners who visited Genoa as itinerant merchants organized themselves on the model of those early Middle Ages commercial networks of specific ethnic groups described in Chapter 2. Although we do not always know the precise kinship relationships of many credit partici-pants, localism bound various network clusters according to distinct geographic places of origin (Bearman 1991). For those, the likely recruitment process was the spatial bases relationship, which welcomed new cohorts of itinerant merchants who could be trusted and integrated as part of a broader social organization (Greif 1989).

Second, I consider the consistent proportion of debt operators, whose occupation originated in craft but who naturally shifted into mercantile activities as long-distance commerce grew in the twelfth and thirteenth centuries. Silvia Thrupp indicated that the difference between some craftsmen and merchants was not always very large (1948, pp. 3–6). The database confirms that the occupations of drapers and bankers, in par-ticular – yes, bankers did not occupy in tenth-, eleventh-, or even twelfth-century Europe the same lofty status they have today, and their occupa-tion originated in the manual handling of coins – provided logical recruiting grounds for the long-distance credit network. For those two occupations, credit relationships escaped the tighter clustering of foreign merchants and, for the most part, corresponded to a more modern con-ception of an economic network as defined by a group of agents who, while pursuing repeated and enduring exchanges with each other, restricted their relationships to their occupational activities more than the previous commercial network did. Thus, for those two mixed occupa-tions in particular, while recruitment into long-distance trade was surely also based on kinship and social opportunities, craft skills acquired by following a long apprenticeship period could matter as well.

Third, in considering the status distribution dynamic of the elite mercantile group, I first demonstrate that, for the most part, commoners struggled to access elite status unless they could leverage their wealth build-up either into participation in ventures that sought the monopoly control of colonies, or into political appointment to high office. Then, turning to the nobility, I show that as a corollary to the equity partners' selection dynamics described in Chapter 3, from the late thirteenth century onward, aristocrats increasingly used credit in the definition of their relational ties and provided the bulk of the replacements of the foreign itinerant traders of the earlier periods. For aristocrats who had, from the years that followed the early twelfth century, participated in the commercial expansion in the form of commenda partnerships with fellow Genoese of all social backgrounds, the increased intra-status ties observed in Chapter 3 induced specialization and routinization, and new generations of the feudal aristocracy increasingly shifted part of their control repertoire from that of men-of-arms to that of long-distance traders.

### Places of Origin

Genoa was, from the early days of the commune, always willing to accept "outsiders." This is made evident by the city's granting, as early as the beginning of the twelfth century, a special status of participation in the Commune to anyone swearing they would abide by the rules and residing in town at least three months per year. This status of *habitatores* did not provide full citizenship and carried various fiscal obligations, but conferred certain rights, such as real estate possession and permission to participate in overseas ventures, to the regular visitors.

Those whose names in the commercial records show an origin outside Genoa can be divided in two groups. The Ligurians – habitants from nearby communities under Genoese control – formed the first. The other is composed of traders from more distant communities. These could be either from other parts of Italy or from political entities outside the peninsula.

An analysis of the data set indicates that the proportion of outsiders – across place of origin – in the credit network rose toward the end of the twelfth century and remained major throughout most of the thirteenth century before declining in the fourteenth century.[60] The bounding of the

---

[60] The percentage of outsiders in the total sum of degrees of credit networks stands at 16% for the period 1154–64; 54% for 1182–97; 52% for 1198–1215; 48% for 1216–39; 45% for 1245–68; 38% for 1269–95; 19% for 1296–1315; 15% for 1340–55.

TABLE 4.3. *Percentage of long-distance trade volume involving one or more Ligurians, 1154–1355*

|  | 1154–1164 | 1182–1197 | 1198–1215 | 1216–1239 | 1245–1268 | 1269–1295 | 1296–1315 | 1340–1355 |
|---|---|---|---|---|---|---|---|---|
| Percentage | 1.2 | 8.6 | 11.3 | 8.7 | 4.0 | 4.5 | 5.5 | 6.5 |

period of a large presence of outsiders in the credit network conforms to an earlier finding in this book: on one end, the rise of the presence of foreigners in the twelfth century corresponded to changing commercial opportunities and, on the other end, the decline corresponded to the increased active participation of the Genoese nobility in the long-distance trade.

Although for a long time outsiders constituted an important part of the credit network, the distribution of places of origin inside that group changed over time. Starting with Ligurians, I continue my analysis in the next paragraphs by breaking down the places of origin to explain the specific participation dynamics of different groups.

*Ligurians.* Studies have insisted on, but not quantified, the important role of the members of the nearby countryside, often of modest condition, in the rise of Italian medieval commerce.[61] Table 4.3 reports the share of immigrants from Liguria – as the Genoese region is called – in the long-distance trade. While the participation of this group in the trade expansion is clear, at the same time, the impact is not large.[62]

In addition, the members of nearby communities were not, in the strict legal and political sense, "aliens." In this light, it is well to remember that the definition of Genoese was not at all simple in the twelfth and thirteenth centuries. Some Genoese were originally residents of communities under the legal jurisdiction and protection of those Genoese feudal lords who combined their urban power with feudal possession. Others lived in towns that were gradually falling under the city's control as Genoa extended its power over the whole of Liguria throughout the twelfth century.

---

[61] See Plessner (1934); Padovan (1941); and Luzzatto (1961).
[62] Caution is necessary in interpreting the numbers in Table 4.3 because the onomastic identification of a place of origin can be prone to confusion. A family might have been living in Genoa for generations and still be referred to as "from a nearby town."

No doubt, before the twelfth century, some of these people visited Genoa for commercial reasons, but their proportion of the population was comparatively smaller than in later periods. Indeed, my analysis of the first surviving notarial commercial agreements from 1154 to 1164 shows that, unlike in later records, the proportion of surnames indicating origin in a nearby town is very small. This is probably not the result of a bias in the sample because the same surviving registers contain numerous real estate transactions for which the proportion of agreements between members of nearby communities is the largest (70%). Further evidence that Ligurians did not participate much in the long-distance trade before the end of the twelfth century is the lack of names from outside Genoa in the list presented to the Byzantine emperor in 1174 to recover Genoese losses from the attack on their colony in 1162 (see also Balard 1978, p. 506, for similar comments). This lack of Ligurians is yet another reminder that, before Genoa's expansion in the late twelfth and the thirteenth centuries, the local economy and the long-distance trading opportunities did not yet warrant the migration that occurred subsequently. For the men of places such as Nervi and Langasco, the economic incentives were not clear enough to cause them to leave for the larger urban centers. Unlike those foreigners who repeatedly came to Genoa to trade goods, when Ligurians immigrated it was not as specialized merchants. As a result, it is logical that the Ligurians used commenda contracts to organize their commercial interactions in a proportion equivalent to that of the native Genoese. Like other Genoese, a few of them became everyday merchants, but most remained occasional participants in the long-distance trade.

*Foreigners.*[63] Foreign merchants did not regularly visit Genoa as early as they did some of the other Italian cities. The lack of local consumption explains the relatively low level of commercial activity in Genoa before the commercial expansion that followed the first Crusades. As Spufford (2002), and MacCormick (2001) have noted, the early medieval European trade was essentially driven by the demand of local courts. In Milan, for example, the abbey of Saint Ambrose created the kind of demand that justified the presence of foreign traders – and the emergence of local

---

[63] Note that in medieval Europe, the word "foreign" related not to a geographical but to a status criterion, and referred to the disenfranchised segment of the population. Those born overseas were described as aliens. For the purpose of this discussion, "foreign" will have a modern signification, i.e., "subject of another political unit."

*negociantes* (buyers) (Lestoquoy 1947, p. 15). Similarly, Pavia, the capital in succession of the Lombard, Frankish, and Italian kingdoms, enjoyed a privileged position as the seat of administration of the courts and was, de facto, the only outlet for silk. As a result, traders from beyond the Alps, and, above all, from England and Saxony (*gens Anglicorum et Saxorum*), who brought horses, slaves, woolens, and linen goods, regularly visited Pavia (Lestocquoy 1947).

By contrast, the Genoese feudal overlords – the *Marchese* – never really held court in the city, and the bishop of Genoa was, until the middle of the twelfth century, under the control of Milan. Thus, Genoa had no such concentrated economic and administrative center to attract early medie-val long-distance traders, nor did it have a large enough sedentary wealthy population to make up a consumer base for luxury goods. This situation started to change around the time of the first Crusades. The Genoese purchasing power increased as military expeditions brought wealth to the victors, which directly fed the emerging international commerce and established the city as a hub of long-distance trade. We know of the presence, among the first itinerant merchants in Genoa, of northern merchants around 1125, as attested by a surviving document recording the Commune's decision to impose a tariff upon "*Hominess de Ultramontanibus partibus*" (men who came from beyond the mountains). This document confirms other research showing that some Flemish merchants traveled to Genoa to sell woolen fabrics in the early part of the twelfth century.[64] The operations of those northerners have been the object of the classic Genoese commercial historiography.[65] However, whereas the northerners' transactions are part of almost all the post-1190 cartularies that I have analyzed, there is little trace of them in surviving records prior to that date. Even taking into account the evident selectivity bias inherent in any notary client base, this evidence indicates that it is only toward the end of the century that the northerners expanded their activities.

These men who came from faraway Flanders were not the only Frankish visitors. Commercial treaties, often as part of broader military and political agreements, with cities such as Narborne in 1141 and Montpellier in 1143 confirm the emergence of a commercial flow between Provence and Genoa that was carried on by the merchants of these towns. This is confirmed by our database, which contains thirty-four persons

[64] See Reynolds (1930, pp. 496–7) and Laurent (1935, p. 146).
[65] See, in particular, Reynolds (1929, 1930, and 1931).

who can safely be traced to Provence. Among them, for example, were *Belengerius de Nerbona* (Berenger from Narbonne, CA#1368/1191), *Faber Martellus de Montepesulano* (Martellus, the blacksmith of Montpellier, DO#268/1210) and *Wilielmus de Provincia* (William from Provence, LA#844/1210).

Merchants from those Italian towns that had developed routinized commerce practices earlier also started to visit Genoa. In the twelfth century, we know of the presence of traders from Asti – a town located on the main road to the northern fairs through the alpine Mt. Cenis pass – as well as of cloth merchants from Lucca and of a group of men from Piacenza, some seventy miles east of Genoa, who lent funds to the city in 1149.

The first visitors from these inland towns considered Genoa not only a growing consumption center, but also a convenient maritime hub for their overseas commerce (Racine 1979), and as trade grew in the twelfth century, so did their share of the long-distance market. Unsurprisingly, it is in the debt network that the concentration of foreigners was largest. The foreign merchants consisted of tight clusters of people who sometimes reinforced their geographical links with kinships ties. I have already mentioned the de Soler family from Asti. Another example, out of many, is that of the Artesian (from Arras) kinsmen Simone, Nicolaio, and Giliotto de Iser. Localism (Bearman 1993) was key in the partner selection process. Merchants traveled together from their home regions and helped each other when in Genoa.

When the foreigners maintained credit relationships with the Genoese, their counterparts were more active and more experienced than the network average. Indeed, before 1250, the mean career length and mean nodal degree of Genoese interacting with foreigners stood respectively at 18.6 years and 4.95 (n = 515) versus 7.2 years and 3.32 for the whole sample of credit users (n = 1,350). While I will come back later in this section to the status stratification of the long-distance trade, a look at the names of those active with foreigners shows that many of the most commercially active aristocratic families are also among those who most frequently transacted with the foreign merchants, often even hosting them in warehouses (*statio*) that had been outfitted with living quarters. The Mallocello and Spinola were known to host the men of Lucca and Piacenza, the Stancone Romans and the della Volta, Pisans.[66] In fact, twenty-seven out of the thirty-three aristocratic clans who we can safely say

---

[66] See Grossi Bianchi and Poleggi (1979, p. 100).

entered into commercial ties with foreign merchants are found among those long-distance clans who would become the most active[67] in later centuries. By contrast, and notwithstanding a few families such as de Fornario and de Goano, the list of those nonaristocratic operators who maintained credit ties with foreigners is full of names that do not show up among those in the most active Renaissance mercantile families. For those clans, being involved early did not necessarily translate into lasting upward mobility. Genoese society was still experiencing ups and downs that limited the stability of wealth and occupation.

Before the mid thirteenth century, foreign merchants – as a group – were net creditors in the debt system[68] and were thus a crucial igniting force in the emergence of routinized mercantile activities. Over time, the men of Arras, and of the northern Italian towns of Asti and Alexandria, who undertook the long journey to Genoa to sell Flemish cloth, and who had constituted an important cluster of merchants in the late twelfth century, lost part of their business when the Genoese first accompanied and then replaced them at the Champagne fairs (Vitale 1949, p. 36). Around the mid thirteenth century, other foreigners – Piacentine and Tuscans, in particular – remained very active in the Genoese markets (Bautier 1987). However, by that time the Genoese did not need their credit as much, nor did they need to copy commercial practices that the foreign merchants had brought to them 100 years earlier. Their own class of routinized traders was emerging.

Although the foreigners clearly constituted the bulk of the credit market in the first part of the thirteenth century, in the next few paragraphs I continue my description of the social makeup of the merchant network by showing how two early medieval crafts,[69] those of drapers and bankers, naturally evolved into commercial occupations and constituted a second broad category of recruitment into the mercantile class. In doing so, I also complete the description of the occupational distribution of the long-distance trade begun in Chapter 3.

## Mercantile Craft

*Drapers.* As Ph. Wolff (1986, pp. 256–7) notes, the status of drapers, known as *draperii*, was often referred to, toward the end of the medieval

[67] See footnote 54 (p. 145) for the definition of "most active."
[68] The data set empirically confirms the comments of Reynolds (1930, p. 504).
[69] I have already covered grocers in section 4.2.

period, as "*mercatores sive draperies pannorum lanne*," which indicates that the *draperii* were also merchants. Although, in the Genoese notarial records, the word "draper" is never followed by a supplemental word indicating a more strictly commercial activity, the volume of long-distance trade–related transactions shows that drapers were as much wholesale clothiers as they were artisans, working and dealing not only with wool – *drapi* was the trans-Alpine term for woolens – but also with linens, Lombard's fustians, and textiles in general. For example, in the year 1210, *Enricus draperius*, the most active draper of that period in the data set, sold and bought at least £3,003 worth of textiles of all kinds.

It remains that drapers were artisans. Their apprenticeship into their manual occupation was long (four to five years), and their guild was organized as a craft like any other. In addition, in all fiscal and electoral lists, drapers are always classified among the *artifices*. Nevertheless, it is clear from a fiscal list of 1404, calling for drapers to pay from two and a half to five times as much in taxes as other crafts, that the profession was lucrative and probably enjoying higher status than other textile crafts.[70] This is also because drapers stood at the end of the manufacturing chain and often benefited from asymmetric work relationships. Indeed, in many parts of Europe, drapers controlled other artisans, such as master shearers and dyers.[71] There is no evidence that such formal control existed in Genoa. However, the notarial records show many employment agreements offered by drapers to other textile trades. For example, on January 10, 1192, two dyers, Widotus and Pinellus, agreed to color precious fabrics that Rufino del Canneto, a very active *draperius* as per our data set, had bought from two northern merchants, Belardo Belardungo and Guala de Rugiasco.

Higher earnings provided the drapers with disposable income with which to build up financial capital. How the increasing wealth translated into upward mobility is difficult to assess empirically, mainly because of the lack of stable surnames, especially prior to 1250. Indeed, many drapers are referred to in notarial contracts by their first names followed by the word *draperius* or, more seldom, by the district where we know many drapers occupied their shops.[72] Despite this onomastic difficulty, I

---

[70] This 1404 list was transcribed by Sieveking (1909, pp. 76–8). With the exception of grocers, drapers paid the largest amount. The large tax imposed on foreign *draperii* also indicates that the guild was powerful.

[71] See Pirenne and Espinas (1909, pp. 219–23).

[72] Of the 115 Genoese families that I identify as drapers who were active in the long-distance trade before 1250, more than 60% include at least one member referred to as

established a sample of more than fifty families who counted at least five long-distance transactions by a *draperius* in the data set. From those 50, 10 ended up among the top 140 commoner mercantile Renaissance families (see Appendix E). Obviously, not knowing what happened to the other forty families – and surely some family names became extinct – we have to conclude that the 20% upward mobility is underestimating the social reality of the time. However, if at first this number seems high, I have found only a couple of drapers' families whose descendants later assimilated into one of the wealthiest mercantile *populares* oligarchic clans, such as those of Giustiniani, Sauli, Promontorio, Adorno, and Campofregoso.[73] Thus, being a draper conferred a certain amount of wealth, but social upward mobility ended up being limited. Part of the reason can be traced to the drapers' early specialization, which, while providing superior income, at the same time limited their wealth-building capacity for two reasons. First, while technical skills and the network embededness of routinized business operators provided opportunities for them to lower their costs, and thus to gain a competitive advantage in mature markets, the drapers' focus on textiles did not fit the opportunistic nature of medieval commerce. Certainly, the records show some *draperii* dabbled in nontextile goods (for example, the *draperius* Iohannes Bavosus bought a large quantity of pepper in November 1259),[74] but this was a rare event. Second, the record shows that most drapers were net debtors in the Genoese financial markets, and the high proportion of promissory notes indicates that they used the international credit market mainly to buy whole cloth that they enhanced in their shops before selling it for cash to exporters. As a result, drapers focused on using their international financial relations to build up inventories – thus using debt as rolling capital – and not on financing their own distribution in partnership with traveling operators. Their commercial relations with the

---

*draperius* or are from the "Canneto," a district where many of their places of business stood.

[73] The Longo and de Corso families integrated into the Giustiniani clan, and the Barbavaria family became part of the Centurioni clan in 1395. In addition, a Fornario declared himself a draper, but that lineage is difficult to follow. One could argue that the most prominent families did not have to be referred to by their occupations in order to be identified, and that – as a result – the count of drapers among them is underestimated. However, this argument does not hold for two reasons. First, the computation referred to a period prior to the given family's prominence. Second, for the occupation "banker," even persons from the most prominent clans are occasionally referred to by their occupation.

[74] JE#943.

wealthier Genoese elite were often cash transactions, and did not develop into the more long-lasting relationships that could be solidified by repeated financial agreements with longer duration. As we have seen in Chapter 3, in the case of professionals, commercial ties to the Genoese elite, especially to the aristocracy,[75] were a salient factor in an occupation's commercial growth potential. As a result, and unlike the situation among bankers (who will be the subject of the next paragraphs), the specialization of drapers to some degree prevented them from having that opportunity. In fact, from 1154 to 1400, fewer than 10% of the *draperius* ties in the long-distance network were with aristocrats, and, among those who transacted with the nobility, upward mobility to the status of merchant was much more likely: Of the 10 *draperius* families who made the list of the top 140 Renaissance commoner families, at least 8[76] had regular transactions with the nobility, thus more than 8 times the *draperius* population average.

**Bankers.** Along with drapers, bankers constituted the second occupational group that originated in a craft that was intrinsically connected to long-distance trade expansion. The revival of European banking has been the object of a controversy as to what technical service, credit, deposit, or money-changing activity gave rise to the profession,[77] and the early Renaissance bankers are often portrayed as sedentary businessmen providing an increasingly sophisticated array of financial services throughout Europe (Usher 1943). However, up to the time in the early twelfth century, when the present research picks up with the Genoese long-distance activity in the notarial records, bankers had been – as Manucci (1910, p. 275) and Lopez (1979) both note – more akin to craftsmen working with precious metals than to emerging commercial

---

[75] Of all noble clans, only the Barbavaria family – who probably emigrated from Milan – has any member specifically referred to as a *draperius*. However, the aristocratic status of the Barbavaria was not among those who won in military service. Nicolas Barbavaria bought feudal rights in the early thirteenth century from the Marquese di Ponzone (Vitale 1951, p. 44). Unsurprisingly, though, the Barbavaria family was atypical among *draperii* in its equal involvement in equity and debt markets and in its transacting business with the prominent aristocratic families of the time, such as, for example, Nepitella in 1295 (GI#1216), della Volta in 1213 (DO#309), and Streiaporco in 1225 (LA#1372). As a result, the Barbavaria family had the highest average transaction volume in the long-distance trade network of any *draperius* family of the time.

[76] Corso, Campanario, Monleone, Longo, Formento, Costa, Pignatario, and Nantono.

[77] Banking existed in antiquity; Greek banks began to receive deposits and make loans and money transfers (Westermann 1930). For the controversy regarding occupational origin, see Hall-Cole (1938); Sayous (1936); and Reynolds (1938).

entrepreneurs. Their original name of *cambiatores* or *composores*, as well as their craftsmen origins, certainly gives credit to de Roover's idea that banking originated in the physical handling of coins (1952, pp. 24–5). In particular, the bankers' money-changing operation was necessary because of the great variety of medieval currencies in circulation as well as the unevenness of conditions. In order to determine the respective values of a wide variety of coins, a banker had to be skilled in assessing the quality of metal alloys. Naturally, it is on that basis that bankers provided the first currency-exchange services. Further supporting the idea that depositing and lending were not the banker's primary focus is the Latin origin of the word "banker" – *bancherius*, a term derived from *banca*, the bench at which money changers laid the small piles of coins of various origins and the scale they needed to conduct their business.[78] Working in the open certainly could not have been conducive to safeguarding large amounts of money.

Elements of individual biographies indicate the rise of the profession toward the second part of the thirteenth century. However, the occupation was already established around the mid twelfth century, as evidenced by the purchase of the city's banking rights by a group of investors in 1145 for £400 and by the names of eleven bankers appearing in the cartulary of Giovanni Scriba from 1154 to 1164.

It would be wrong to assume that the commercial growth of the *bancherii* arose from innovative operations that provided them with a competitive advantage in recognizing financial opportunities ahead of other operators. It is generally agreed that, given that the early bankers lacked formal training, most advances in financial technique originated with traders and not with bankers (Hall-Cole 1938; de Roover 1952). Likewise, it would be a mistake to assume that bankers' success could have resulted from their ability to deploy sums left under their care to invest in the long-distance trade, because deposits were relatively small and almost always repayable on very short notice. Indeed, with the exception of a £50 deposit by the priest Guglielmo of Langasco in the care of *Ingone bancherius* on February 17, 1158,[79] which was repayable in a

---

[78] In Genoa, "erano chiamati bancherii perche non lavoravano in uma bottega o laboratorio, come solevano fare i negozianti e gli artigiani, ma dietro un tavolo (bancum) posto nella piazza del mercato" (Manucci 1910). [In Genoa, "they were called bankers because, unlike other craftsmen and shopkeepers, they did not work in a workshop or an office, but at a bench on the market square.] Note, though, that the butchers also used an open-air stand (*bancum macillarie*) made out of stone (Di Tucci 1933, p. 82).

[79] See S#357.

year, twelfth-century banking deposit agreements I have seen regarded small amounts (£6 to £25) that were repayable on short notice (seven days) if not on sight.

In the early part of the commercial revolution, medieval banking was not yet much about lending and fiduciary services. As Cole noted, at the onset of the commercial revolution "bankers occupied no exalted place in the business world. They played only a very minor role in the financing of commerce and industry. Compared to the merchants of their day, they were small businessmen, indeed" (1932, p. 79). Lopez added, "their cash reserve was so modest that some of them took it home in a box every night" (1979, p. 11).

However, if the volume of their transactions was small in twelfth-century Genoa, the *bancherii* benefited from a central position in the trade network, since anybody involved in long-distance commerce inevitably used coin-exchanging services. Thus, it comes as no surprise that, among those whom we can clearly identify as practicing an essentially commercial occupation in the twelfth and thirteenth centuries, bankers, as a group, interacted the most with the rest of the less routinized long-distance participants, which interaction was – as we saw in Chapter 3 – a key to trading growth. Indeed, when defining such essentially commercial occupations as drapers, foreign merchants, bankers, and those who do not declare an occupation but whose network nodal degree is in the top tenth percentile, I found that – before the fourteenth century – only 32% of bankers' long-distance ties were with fellow commercial operators, whereas for that population as a whole, the proportion was almost twice that (58%).

As bankers became more and more professional, they left the open-air piazza and the manual operation of checking alloy in coins. Their business regarding long-distance trade also changed, and the database shows that, to an ever-increasing degree, bankers were involved in large transactions with the wealthiest commercial families. Here again, heterogeneity in commercial ties, a key to success during the early phase of the commercial revolution, was in time replaced by more homogeneous relationships that consolidated social boundaries.

Banking became increasingly lucrative. However, the nobility remained underrepresented, at least until the mid fifteenth century. Dealing exclusively with money and belonging to an occupation that had clear roots in craft was, most likely, unacceptable for an aristocracy that was still impregnated with feudal culture, and an examination of the data set indicates that aristocrats were ready to be called "*mercatores*" before they would be called "bancherius." Indeed, in the twelfth century none of the fifteen bankers in the data set belonged to the *nobiles gentes*, and in the thirteenth century, I counted only a couple. This gradually changed throughout the fourteenth century, but, even still, out of the thirteen bankers mentioned in a document of 1359, only two – Giovanni Lomellino and Iodisio Vivaldi – belong to the nobility.[80] By the early fifteenth century, however, the situation was different. The record shows many members of aristocratic families designated as *bancherius*.[81] In addition, while bankers' recruitment in the earlier centuries was, for the most part, from lesser families among the *populares*, the bulk of the late fourteenth and fifteenth-century banking volume in the data set is contracted by the wealthiest families, such as the de Podio, Giustiniani, Franchi, Sauli, and Adorno.

The shift of control of the banking occupation to the wealthiest, and often aristocratic, families signals a social change. Indeed, the acceptance of money as a currency of control by those clans, who, up until then, had buttressed their privileged position by right of birth, shows the increasing significance of commerce in the definition of relational ties among the elite. It is thus fitting that, in the next few paragraphs, I conclude this chapter with a short analysis of the status stratification dynamics in the formation of the mercantile elite.

### Commoner versus Aristocratic Mercantile Elite

I will begin my comments about the credit network's status distribution by first addressing the commoners. Then I will take up the dynamics of participation in the debt market by aristocrats before briefly commenting on credit partner selection among the Genoese elite as a whole.

*Commoners.* As I showed earlier in the book, the routinization of long-distance trade induced the social and political category of *populares mercatores,* a reference to those plebeian families who counted as regular and everyday long-distance traders. Continuing this chapter's study of the social makeup dynamic of the merchants, the objective of the next few pages is to provide the reader with an idea of the path to the *populares*

---

[80] Note, however, that, even if these two families categorically classify as *nobiles,* neither one seems to have much in the way of feudal antecedents.

[81] Grillo, Lomellini, Vivaldi, and Mallocello, in particular.

*mercatores* occupational status in the late fourteenth and fifteenth centuries.

Tracking commoners' lineage historical path is hard for two main reasons. First, immigration and assimilation to aristocratic families through marriage and name association make it difficult to follow the microdynamics of merchant families. Second, *populares* surnames could be unstable, which makes onomastic tracking over a long period of time fairly complex. For example, the records provide information about *Ansuixus de Sanctus Genesius*, an active long-distance trader in the late twelfth century. We know that during his career he established credit and commenda ties for sizeable ventures to a variety of Mediterranean ports.[82] During that time, Ansuixus accumulated enough capital to provide a comfortable income for future generations of his direct family. While my database shows several long-distance traders with the same surname over the next 200 years,[83] it is almost impossible to assess whether Ansuixus indeed began a commercial dynasty, or, if all these men were related only by their residence around the *Sanctus Genesius* church in central Genoa. In addition, over time, the use of surnames with toponomic origin declined, which would suggest that the incidence of name changing among those families was higher than for the others.

This said, while dynastic origins are sometimes difficult to assert, their end point is much easier to determine. Here, I refined the merchant list used for my analysis of drapers by using the 1440 tax records on assets to identify the wealthiest clans. I found that among the thirty leading *populares* mercantile families, only five (Longo, Corsio, de Campis, de Vialio, Vignoso) were among the thirty most active prior to 1250. This finding is quite robust as it stands using a ranking based on nodal degree in our data set, the custom payment for 1376–77, or the tax assessment of 1440. Thus, while nearly all the aristocratic families active in the twelfth- and thirteenth-century long-distance trade were still thriving, this was not true for the *populares*. Maybe a few changed their names or became naturally extinct, but for many others who had been very active traders

---

[82] For examples of commendae, see CA#1093/1191 and GI#1599/1206; for sea exchange, see GI#842/1203; for straight debt, see CA#1094/1191; and for promissory notes, see CA#447/1191. For a sample of destinations: to Naples, see CA#134/1191; for Sicily, see CA#359/1191; for Ceuta, see CA#425, 426/1991; for Alexandria, see GI#639/1203.

[83] *Wilielmus de Sanctus Genesius,* 1244–50; *Andriolus de Sanctus Genesius,* 1252–53; *Faciolus de Sanctus Genesius,* 1281; *Odoardus de Sanctus Genesius,* 1282; *Franceschinus de Sanctus Genesius,* 1288, *Iohanninus de Sanctus Genesius,* 1292; *Antonius de Sanctus Genesius,* 1343–49.

for multiple generations, the decline is evident from the loss of rank in commercial activity as measured either by the fourteenth-century notarial contracts I coded or by the custom records.

It is hard to pinpoint the reasons for the commercial downfall of these families over such a long period, as it would require further systematic research into each clan's microdynamics. However, it is possible to recognize why some rose in prominence. Aside from a handful of smaller elite clans (Sauli, Premontorio, and Maruffo), every single other wealthy commoner dynasty can be traced to one of two processes: either to the adhesion of a large group of merchants who set out to invade and control the trade of foreign settlements, or to the leveraging of political appointments into the extraction of wealth and formal privileges. The first process is best exemplified by the wealth-building activities among those merchants who participated in and financed the conquest of Chios and Phocea in 1347 by a fleet led by one of their own, the Admiral Simone Vignoso.[84] For the next 200 years, associating to their own name[85] the common appellation of "Giustiniani," this group of merchants privately controlled Genoese colonies, where the export of mastic and alum made them the wealthiest mercantile group in the city (Heers 1961, p. 565). Well organized, their colonies resisted until 1566 not only the fall of the Byzantine Empire in the mid fifteenth century, but also the Genoese political and institutional turmoil.

In the Giustiniani's wealth-building process, military control and monopolistic extraction were key elements. However, the coordination of commercial operations among several families was also a factor in their success.

The Franchi clan is the other wealthy group of merchants who originated in a military venture. Indeed, at the onset, as Petti Balbi (1976,

---

[84] The Vignoso had been active in long-distance commerce since at least the second quarter of the thirteenth century. The data set shows members of that family trading all over the Mediterranean (the Levant in 1227, Tunis in 1239, Romanie in 1274, Tabriz in 1307, Caffa in 1393) and in the northern country as well (Champagne in 1263, England in 1384). The historical selection sequence in our data set is indicative of the institutional dynamic that brought about the use of debt, as opposed to temporary equity, among routinized operators. From 1216 to 1250, as beginners in the long-distance trade, the data set shows members of the Vignoso family contracting thirteen commenda ties as compared to only two credit ties. Then, from 1253 to 1401, I counted twenty-four commercial ties involving the Vignoso in the sample, twenty-one of which were debt ties.

[85] In Chapter 5, I will explain the *albergho* phenomena, which regrouped families into a single clan. It is enough for now to note that the level of Giustiniani business integration was high, and that the group organized itself via formal representation.

p. 155) and Heers (1989, p. 26) note, the merchants who eventually took the common name of Franchi hoped to take commercial control of Corsica by military means.[86] While the military venture did not prove as lasting or as profitable as that of Chios, the families nevertheless stayed united in a single organization, which conferred on the clan leverage in the long-distance trade. This said, the large difference in wealth between the Giustiniani, on the one hand, and the Franchi, on the other, demonstrates that while the pooling of resources certainly provided certain commercial benefits, the key was the monopolistic control of commercial resources.

The second process of wealth building for *populares* mercantiles families was leveraging the highest public offices into various fiscal and feudal privileges. Among the wealthiest commoner families members of the Adorno, Campofregoso, and to a lesser degree Zoalio and Montaldo families, had accumulated seigniorial privileges and countless estates granted to them by the city while they served as doges. In addition, their relations with the highest local and international aristocracy provided them with enfeoffment of land and with marriage opportunities to consolidate their elite status (Heers 1961, p. 568). These families were still involved in long-distance trading, but not nearly as much as other leading *populares* clans. As Heers notes, their lifestyle was comparable to that of the most prominent European aristocratic families. They often lived outside the urban center, tending to their feudal prerogatives while maintaining political networks that ensured their reappointment to the highest offices.

Evidently, these two types of wealth-building processes,[87] political appointment and monopolistic extraction, had little to do with the type of superior strategic business acumen that is portrayed in historical economic literature. This is not to say that Genoese merchants' commercial techniques did not become increasingly sophisticated. It is only to point out that maintaining strong ties with the political elite and participating in war still constituted the paths to success in an early Renaissance world that increasingly mixed commerce and political hegemony.

In turning next to an analysis of the nobility's increased use of credit in the definition of their relational ties, I will show that the path to

---

[86] It should be noted that the operation was led by an aristocrat.

[87] As Heers (1961, p. 564) notes, aside from the Giustiniani and the Franchi, only the two smaller *populares* clans of Sauli and Premontorio count the *"grands commercants"* (large merchants) among them.

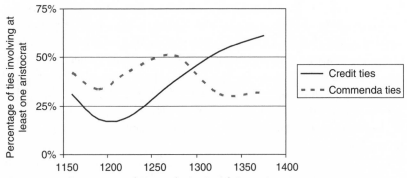

FIGURE 4.5. Percentage of network ties involving aristocrats, 1154–1400.

commercial success was a little easier for them than for *populares*, because ascribed formal status was still a salient variable in accessing the elite commercial network.

*Aristocrats.* Figure 4.5 reports the percentage of commercial ties involving aristocrats in the long-distance trade network over a period of 250 years for both commenda and credit relationships.[88] Note not only the overall increase in the nobles' participation in the long-distance trade after the mid thirteenth century, but also the shift to credit ties. This pattern is consistent with this research's earlier findings regarding the transfer of part of the aristocracy's resources into more routinized and univalent commercial practices than the earlier multivalent activities of the feudal men-of-arms. Similarly, the decrease in the number of credit ties during the very first period covered by the database is consistent with this historical shift. Indeed, as I have shown in the third and fourth chapters, at a time when Genoese trade had not yet attracted foreign traders the way it had in other Italian cities, long-distance commerce was dominated by the ruling elite, along with a very small number of specialized traders inside a hierarchical network that naturally reproduced the patronage structure of the feudal social organization. At that time, aristocrats were, for the most part, either passive investors or involved in commercial ventures as a by-product of seafaring expeditions.

---

[88] It is well to remember the likelihood that, for the most part, long-duration equity agreements took the place of commendae. Thus, outside of cash relationships, which, for obvious reasons, are not associated with the robustness of longer-duration agreements, credit ties provided the repetitive solid raw material to knit the long-distance trade together.

Long-distance trade participation was one expression of the constant commingling of family interests with the city's expansionist policy. By and large, the nobility's role was to secure trading routes while not necessarily actually dealing with the goods themselves. It is when referring to that time that the expression "prince merchant" gained currency, and aristocrats did, indeed, use credit as well as temporary equity. But neither network signaled the rise of specialization. They were both the expression of the social organization as a whole, where commerce took its place in an unsegregated sphere.[89]

Then, the emergence of univalent long-distance traders – at first mainly foreigners, but then increasingly Genoese – modified the credit networks' architecture. It became less hierarchical and included several clusters of merchants who regularly and intensively interacted with each other. As attested by the request in 1192 by Suzobono (a very active *populares* long-distance operator)[90] for a personal surety before agreeing to a small loan to Marchesio della Volta (a member of one of the leading feudal families),[91] status in this increasingly segregated sphere did not confer a privileged position in the negotiation of relational ties to the same degree that it had in other social interactions up until then. As a result, and because of the well-documented importance of reputation, trust, and repetition in the credit network, aristocrats were less likely to use credit, which emerged as the framework of choice for regular traders. When they did, it was – for the most part – as creditors pumping their capital into the long-distance trade in the segment activated by routinized operators, but not necessarily as active participants.

[89] While this book argues that the timing of aristocratic participation in the credit market signals the rise of occupational categories in the definition of their social ties, it is important to flesh out here why a counterargument about the impact of the Church's position on usury is not salient in this discussion. Much has been written about the Church's position on usury (Le Goff 1999; de Roover 1952; Lane 1969) and it would be logical to believe that the aristocrats, whose piety has been well documented in other research (Kedar 1976; S. A. Epstein 1996), did not enter into credit agreements because they simply wished to comply with the canon law. This cultural explanation might have some appeal, but historical evidence shows that Italian aristocrats knew of and used the credit market extensively before the rise of the long-distance trade. In addition, unlike the rest of the European nobility, who were probably, as a whole, net debtors, the Italians were net creditors to public authorities (see Vitale 1955, p.107). As the history of Genoese public finance indicates, the nobility were not afraid of Church interdiction when they charged very high rates of interest to the Commune. Thus, cultural norms were not an obstacle, but occupational dynamics were.

[90] Suzobono's nodal degree in the 1182–97 long-distance trade network is 20.

[91] Ingo della Volta, possibly the uncle of Marchesio della Volta, guaranteed the £10 loan (CA#1813/ February 1203).

As Figure 4.5 also reveals, by the latter part of the thirteenth century, when mercantile wealth accumulation had induced formal political and social changes, aristocratic families increasingly turned to commerce in order to participate in the new control repertoire.

Evidence of the nobility's increasing operational control over commerce can be seen in my analysis of the Genoese customs records for the years 1376 and 1377.[92] Having coded the status affiliation of each importer, I found that the proportion of nobles among the custom-duty payers represented roughly 65% of the total trade volume. Those numbers are slightly higher than the proportion of the total degree aggregation in the 1340–55 network that referred to aristocratic operators,[93] and thus confirm the steady rise of occupational category over formal status.

In addition, every one of the forty leading aristocratic families, as measured by trade volume in the customs records of 1376–77, was active in the credit network in the late thirteenth and early fourteenth centuries. For those aristocratic clans, being passive investors, as in the early days of the commercial upsurge, was no longer enough, and participating in the increasingly routinized credit-ties dynamic had become a necessary condition for their sharing in the control of the city.

As the previous paragraphs make clear, throughout the fourteenth century, ventures including aristocrats constituted an increasing portion of the trade volume. By then, a growing number of noblemen could be considered everyday merchants, not hesitating to be called *mercator* in official documents.

Next, I conclude the chapter with a short analysis of the credit partner selection process to show how it was still easier for the nobility than for commoners to access the mercantile elite. However, my analysis also indicates that social advantage was closing in on the nobility: By the fifteenth century, the occupational category "merchant" became the salient characteristic in credit partner selection among the elites, confirming thereby the consolidation of the social organization around commercial exchange.

---

[92] It is possible that, in some cases, the name on the customs records is that of an agent. Assuming that agents were less likely to be aristocrats than the actual importers, the actual share of aristocrats in the total trade volume is probably higher than that computed from the customs records. It is also well to keep in mind that privileges, exemptions, and frauds are always inherent in historical fiscal records and, consequently, that the information might not be as precise as it first appears.

[93] The total nodal degree of noblemen represents 46% of the total (1,212 out of 2,658) for almost 58% of total volume (£250,075 out of £438,898).

TABLE 4.4. *Closures index (S14) for homophilic credit partner selections,*
*1300–1400*

|  | Status | Occupational (Merchants) | Mercantile Elite + Aristocrats | Mercantile Elite + Commoners |
|---|---|---|---|---|
| Value of S14[a] | 0.25 | 0.58 | 0.36 | 0.09 |

[a] See page 113 for methodological background and definition of S14.

***Credit partner selection among the elites.*** In Chapter 3, I reported the
value of a closure index that measured the propensity for status and
occupational homophily. As the reader may remember, the index took
values from minus one to plus one, with a positive value indicating a
propensity to form homogeneous partnerships given the appropriate
availability. Measures close to zero indicated that, on average, the attribute was not salient in the partner-selection process. Table 4.4 reports the
value of the index for four different credit networks' binary partitions.

First, as expected, the closure index for formal status homophily (0.25)
indicates that status was only marginally salient in credit partner selection. This is, indeed, consistent with the increasing occupational commingling of the mercantile *populares* elite with those members of the
aristocracy who, at this point, openly adopted the title of *mercator*. It
should be noted, however, that the cross-status commingling, which
during the early period of the commercial revolution characterized all
long-distance trade partnerships, was now limited to active and more
routinized traders. Indeed, for the limited number of commenda contracts
that still took place in the fourteenth century, thus concerning a more
heterogeneous population than that of the routinized traders using credit
instruments, the closure index for status jumps to 0.63.

Conversely, the much higher intramerchant closure index (0.58) is
consistent with the rise of occupational categories. In fact, the progression
of the closure index from the period 1300–49 (0.38) to 1350–1400 (0.62)
(not reported in Table 4.4) suggests that the occupational boundaries
were getting tighter.

More surprising, perhaps, is that the network autocorrelation for
credit networks during the 1340–55 period among three trade-volume
parameters – average and total volume, as well as nodal degree – were
low, which suggests that the data does not indicate that credit partner

selection was a function of individual amounts traded or the number of commercial ties. While this is surprising, the difference in the value of the closure index reported in the last two columns of Table 4.4 provides an explanation of why strictly quantitative economic variables were not the only salient partner selection criteria. Indeed, the value reported in the third column concerns a binary partition that separated all aristocrats and the top mercantile clans – nobles and commoners included – from the rest of the population. The fourth column separates all commoners and the top mercantile elite from the rest of the population. While the closure index drops in both cases, it does so much less sharply when aristocrats are aggregated to the mercantile elite than when the commoners are (0.36 versus 0.09). Thus, while occupation was the main selection criteria for credit ties, status was a second choice. In other words, the difference between the closure indexes in columns three and four shows that in the hybrid social organization of the late fourteenth-century Genoa, where lords involved in long-distance trade at the same time continued to impose their political authority in their countryside estates or even in town, formal status still carried enough network power to provide access to the elite pool of commercial partners. However, the rise of occupational categories was threatening that privilege, and as the analysis in the next chapter reveals, status lost its saliency in fifteenth-century commercial dealings.

As I show in Chapter 3, in the early part of the commercial revolution, commendae had been a fine institutional framework that facilitated the pooling of resources from heterogeneous social origins. However, that framework declined not because of its economic obsolescence and its replacement by a more "efficient" institution, but because long-distance partnerships became more homogeneous with respect not only to status but also to occupation. By contrast, credit ties thrived in partner selection dynamics driven by membership in a small elite group. In this case, the stability of the network's social makeup, the higher threshold of wealth or status, and the frequent social interactions – not only through commercial partnerships but also through intra-status relationships – solidified the social system as a whole.

Next, in Chapter 5, I continue my analysis of the relation between the structure of Genoese social ties' temporal movement and commercial institutional dynamics by showing how maritime insurance further consolidated the mercantile oligarchy.

# 5

# Insurance Ties for Oligarchic Cohesion

In previous chapters, I have indicated that in medieval Europe, traveling risks dwarfed the strictly commercial risks of long-distance ventures. Thus, the emergence of maritime insurance contracts during the second part of the fourteenth century directly responded to an economic need, and freed investment capital. This said, in this chapter, I continue the analysis of the role of commercial institutions in the transformation of Genoa's social organization by showing that the maritime insurance market was not sustained by commercial interests alone. Indeed, although the key innovation of medieval insurance was the ability to transfer traveling risk to a third party, underwriting took place inside the mercantile community; more than the price mechanism, it was the expectation of social reciprocity that organized the insurance pairings. In fact, I demonstrate that underwriting decisions were laced with solidaristic meaning and that insurance became more than an economic tool as it cemented the robustness of the Genoese oligarchic network.

This fifth chapter differs slightly from the previous two. The first difference relates to the unit of analysis. Earlier chapters analyzed ties among individuals from which larger social aggregates were formed. This focus corresponded to the commercial reality that linked individual interests together. However, the intense social consolidation of the mercantile Genoese elite into clusters of households called *alberghi* during the fourteenth and early fifteenth centuries profoundly altered the nature of intrafamily ties and had far-reaching implications for the social organization of the city. Consequently, I have changed the focus of my analysis from individual ties to inter-*alberghi* ties to reflect the changed social and political landscape.

A second difference concerns the temporal scope. Whereas previous chapters have dealt with commercial and social dynamics over multiple centuries, the analysis of the insurance network concerns a shorter period.

The first third-party insurance contracts took place in the middle of the fourteenth century and were, thus, loosely contemporaneous with the end of the medieval period and the beginning of the Renaissance. As a result, I will focus on the significance of insurance ties in the whole medieval institutional sequence and not on comparing insurance networks over time. While boundaries between historical periods are artificial and defy both the intrinsic continuity of social life and the geographical disparity of historical dynamics, for our purposes, an analysis of third-party insurance contracts is a fitting way to conclude our examination of the rise of the mercantile social organization. Indeed, the dissociation of traveling risk from business risk introduced the potential for commercial ties that were unconnected to business at hand and signaled the objectification of economic relationships so characteristic of modernity. As will be made clear, this had not yet taken place in medieval Genoa, as insurance ties proved to be another tool that the Genoese elite could manipulate to consolidate oligarchic boundaries and, thus, to manage their control of the city. Still, insurance contained the seeds of social changes to come.

Following a brief historical introduction that places the analysis in the larger context of fourteenth- and fifteenth-century Genoese state decline, the rest of the chapter is organized as follows: In the first section, I describe the consolidation of the elite families into *alberghi* in order to provide the necessary background for the analysis that follows. In the second section, I study the insurance market and focus on those elements that were most relevant to the role of underwriting in the Genoese social dynamic. Finally, in the third and last section, I formally analyze the structure of the insurance network before applying a probability model to explain the role of insurance in consolidating social boundaries.

## State Decline

When the first maritime insurance contracts were devised in the mid fourteenth century, Italy's economy had been slowing down for several decades. However, commerce retained its vigor, and as Luzzatto noted:

Italy did not occupy the same place in the economy of Europe as in the two preceding centuries, to this extent, it is proper to speak of Italian economic decline. But to use the word "decline" in the further sense, of an absolute fall in the volume and value of production and exchange, would be wholly unjustified. (1961, p. 142)

Thus, although it is difficult to measure the historical pattern of Genoa's trade volume, it seems that the classic interpretation of Lopez and Mischkinin (1962) overstates the economic decline that preceded the great plague of 1348–51. Indeed, in aiming to establish a continuous data series for Genoese international commerce in the thirteenth century that would show a downturn in business, many scholars use a figure mentioned in 1293 by Jacopo Doria (the city annalist who, in all his chronicles, systematically exaggerated the prosperity of the city) to complement the tax records of 1214 and of 1274 and those of 1334–75. Doria's number, which is still often used as evidence by most historians, would indicate that, after rising 1.5% per year from 1214 to 1274, trade expansion jumped to an annual pace of 16% from 1274 to 1293, then contracted by an average of over 2% per year until 1340. While there is no doubt that the last quarter of the thirteenth century was a period of commercial growth, the figure given for 1293 is totally inconsistent when compared to all other, more reliable data sources. In addition, although business may well have slowed toward the end of the century, nothing in the historiography or in the number of transactions recorded by notaries that I have surveyed and coded suggests either such an astonishing increase from 1274 to 1293 or a dramatic decline thereafter.

However, other facts are not in dispute. The diminishing return on equity of overseas ventures reduced social mobility, and the increased concentration of wealth among the urban elite fostered a consolidation of social strata. Both of these historical dynamics were discussed in the previous two chapters and are supported by, among others, Benjamin Kedar (1976), the author of a study of the early Renaissance merchant mentality in Genoa and Venice, who found that a shift toward pious attitudes and a more cautious approach to business risk further amplified the stagnancy of the social structure. In another influential book, Goldthwaite (1993) argues that the Italian economy remained strong, but that the concentration of wealth within the urban elites induced a shift of financial resources from investment to consumption that further reduced upward mobility. In his account, disposable assets among the elite created the conditions for the emergence of an art market – a market in religious art, in particular, which fits Kedar's thesis – and for the rise of a consumer culture that was a precursor of modern markets.[1]

---

[1] The argument developed in this chapter – that the innovations in commercial insurance did not arise in response to market forces alone, but rather served to further consolidate the control of the oligarchy over Genoa – complements those of the latter two studies.

Nevertheless, it remains true that at the beginning of the fourteenth century, despite having equaled and probably even surpassed Venice as the most powerful Mediterranean maritime state, Genoa had seen the end of its period of rapid territorial and commercial expansion. At the same time, despite the formation of increasingly large nation states,[2] this comparatively small polity still exercised monopolistic control over distant colonies. As a result, Genoa continued to play a preeminent role in the organization of long-distance trade well into the sixteenth century, and certainly remained on a par with Venice and Florence, a fact that is downplayed in the economic historiography of the Renaissance. As S. A. Epstein asserts, the real issue is that "the hegemony Venice and Florence exercise over 15th century history, especially in America, leaves little room for other Renaissance cities and for Genoa in particular" (1996, p. 241). As such, the decline of Genoa is overemphasized in the historiography in order to reinforce the contrast between the late medieval commercial revolution and the Renaissance consolidation. In fact, even the two most significant markers of Genoa's downfall – its military defeat by Venice in Chioggia (1381) and its submission to the king of France, Charles VI, for a period of fifteen years (1396–1411) – had less significant implications for the city's economy than is suggested by their central position in the historiography.

First, the impact of the Genoese defeat in the Venetian Lagoon of Chioggia in 1381 has been overstated, probably because Genoa had been so close to invading Venice only a few weeks earlier. In reality, the toll extracted by the Venetian side was very manageable in the long run.[3] More significantly, the loss had little impact on Genoa's eastern colonies, which remained the backbone of its economy. This is further evidence that the city remained a formidable military power on the Mediterranean Sea. Indeed, although Genoa had lost its foothold in Palestine in 1291, the city had been in control of several territories around the Black Sea since 1267, particularly Pera and Caffa, and had added Chios and part of Cyprus to its dominion during the course of the fourteenth century. Years after the defeat in Chioggia, Genoese Levantine trade was still dominant. For example, of a small sample of ships that anchored in Alexandria in

---

Here, though, I interpret this commercial dynamic as an outcome of the process of social consolidation rather than as an outcome of cultural history.

[2] For a critical review of the different theoretical frameworks used to explain the historical downfall of city-states, see Tilly (1990) or Lachmann (2003, pp. 347–54).

[3] Frederic Lane even argues that Venice paid a higher fiscal cost and saw more of its trade disrupted than Genoa (1973, pp. 196–201).

1400 and 1401, more than half belonged to Genoese merchants (Ashtor 1976, pp. 533–86).

In addition, while it is true that Genoa was to lose most of its eastern settlements in the second half of the fifteenth century, the mercantile elite succeeded in reestablishing quasi-monopolistic opportunities elsewhere.[4] Furthermore, Genoa had been the first to link the eastern and northern markets by sea routes around the year 1280 (Doehaerd 1938), and any market share lost in the East was compensated for by new business opportunities in emerging markets such as Bruges and London.

The economic impact of Doge Adorno's submission to the king of France in 1396 has been similarly overstated. The submission was not welcomed by the populace (Jarry 1896), but by and large the Genoese continued to govern themselves according to their own rules and customs. In addition, little changed in the city's administration of its foreign territories because many of the colonies had been enfeoffed to various clans and thus escaped the direct control of the French. As such, the weakening of the state did not slow the emergence of the oligarchy; in some ways it even prepared the landscape for the hegemonic control of financially successful families. Some historians (Day 1958; Surdich 1970) even suggest that the submission to a foreign ruler was a strategic ploy on the part of the elite to restore order at little cost and then to regain control over the masses, who might have preferred the oligarchic rule of native lords to that of a foreign governor. However, attempts to explain historical events of this magnitude as the long-term political machinations of individuals – or even of whole factions – are at best speculative (see Bearman et al. 1999).

What is beyond doubt is that, while the Genoese population continued to strive economically, the weakening of the state's formal institutions had begun much earlier than the French occupation or the Battle of Chioggia. One likely explanation for this decline is that, beginning in 1259 and then accelerating in 1339, as the *populares* – without appropriating financial and feudal resources – forced the nobility out of many public offices, they eliminated a strong and indispensable constituency. For aristocratic families, now without direct control of the administrative offices and of the patronage opportunities that they offered, it made little

---

[4] For example: 1) the papal state's alum mines at Tolfa were rented out to a consortium of Genoese aristocrats (Grimaldi, Usodimare, Gentile, Centurione, Doria, and Cigala); 2) the Lomellini and several other aristocratic families developed sugar plantations in the Azores; and 3) Genoese bankers controlled much of the financial activities at the important Lyon fairs in the mid sixteenth century.

sense to support the state's institutions directly. In response, they invested their resources in commercial and financial institutions, away from the state organizations.

As I showed in Chapter 3, the increasing focus on commercial opportunities went along with an increase in intra-status ties. Similarly, control of the state debt by the leading urban aristocratic clans was to compensate for the loss of political representation. The Genoese historian Petti Balbi has demonstrated that the share of public debt held by the largest aristocratic clans surged after the 1339 revolution (1991, pp. 140–2). Over time, financial success, and the aristocratic elite control of the Casa di San Giorgio, a financial institution established in 1407 to manage the outstanding funded debt that the state had accumulated over the previous 150 years,[5] was to provide the nobility with the opportunity to reinfiltrate the political process informally without enduring the constant bloody feuds that characterized the jockeying between the *populares* clans[6] claiming the formal political leadership of the state.

The rise of money to replace formal political institutions as the site of hegemonic control was further solidified by an increase in the number of direct commercial relationships between leading families. It is to the examination of one of these relationships, uniting mercantile clans through maritime insurance contracts, that this chapter is devoted.

Before proceeding with the formal analysis of insurance ties, however, the next section describes the process of family aggregation that began in Genoa around the beginning of the fourteenth century and explains the significance of the rise of large clans, both to society in general and in the specific context of this book. The historical background of the emergence of these clans is necessary if the reader is to understand the analysis that follows. In placing the rise of the clans in the broader context of the role of family relations in the Genoese long-distance trade, I will also take this

[5] The Casa di San Giorgio represented the interests of those investors, and the heirs of earlier investors, who had financed the state over that period. The idea was to consolidate the debt and to pay off the creditors by directly assigning various tax collections to the Casa. As could be expected, with each financial crisis the prerogatives of the Casa's shareholders increased, because the weak and underfunded state had lost any leverage it might have had when the creditors were fragmented into smaller associations. As a result, by the late fifteenth century the Casa directly controlled most public revenues and for a while even administered several colonial territories (for example, Cyprus [conceded in 1447], the Black Sea territories, and Corsica).

[6] From 1339 onward, the Cappellazzi, a group of five or six *populares* families (Adorno, Campofregoso, Goarco, Montaldo, and Zoalio) fought constantly for control of the public offices.

opportunity to touch on the role of kinship ties over the three centuries of commercial activities covered by this book.

## 5.1. GENOESE CLANS

During the course of the fourteenth century, Genoa witnessed the aggregation of elite families into larger artificial kindreds called *alberghi*. The emergence of these large households was part of a wider Italian urban social dynamic that defied the theory of progressive nuclearization of the family. By the end of the medieval period, lineages with no common ancestors were again binding themselves into larger households in much the same manner as an earlier rural warrior stratum had in a predatory economy (Herlihy 1969, pp. 179–85). Unlike their predecessors, though, these associations – called *consorteria* – did not always combine their member's assets; rather, they formally bonded, for renewable periods, families who pledged to help and support each other. The formation of the *alberghi* followed the same aggregation pattern found in other parts of Italy but pursued this course to a much stricter level of integration. In Genoa, the formal contracts linking families were open-ended as opposed to time-bound, and members abandoned their patronymic surnames to adopt a common name that was either that of the most powerful family in the clan or entirely new.

The Genoese annalists first used the term "*albergho*" to describe the Spinola family in 1265 as a social unit that grouped members of "lineage whose identity had become fragmented" (Hughes 1977, p. 108). But it is only during the fourteenth and fifteenth centuries that the integration of families who did not claim a common ancestor became increasingly common (Heers 1977, p. 85). With a few notable exceptions, the alliance process involved aristocratic families and clients recruited and organized on the basis of territorial principles. Members of *alberghi* lived in homes that bordered common squares and streets, frequented their own churches, shared bathhouses, and regularly met in communal spaces called *loggia,* where "members met at any time of day or night for various reasons" (Grossi Bianchi and Poleggi 1979, p. 228). The neighborhood life and the daily interactions concerning financial and commercial matters, or the administration of the community, certainly sustained cohesive ties and enhanced unity.

Several theories have been proposed to explain the emergence of *alberghi*. For Hughes, the federation of families was a natural outcome of demographic as well as economic difficulties (1975, p. 28). For their part,

Agosto (1981, p. 106) and Heers (1962, p. 385)[7] posit that aggregation into *alberghi* was the nobility's response to the threat of the emerging *populares* group. By contrast, Greif (2006, p. 245) does not regard status conflict as a salient factor. Instead, he sees the rise of *alberghi* as part of the factionalist dynamic that opposed groups of similar status as a reaction to the emergence of the *podesteria*. Offering another historical outlook, Grendi notes that the city's administration had long favored alliances. He argues that artificial kindreds formally crystallized political coalitions (1987, p. 62). Raggio builds on Grendi's idea and argues that *alberghi* offered a substitute for the state's weakening authority (1990). In his case study, he finds that *alberghi* provided a stable conduit for the organization of commercial exchange, and his demonstration could be reinterpreted to highlight other facets of Genoa's social organization.

These theories offer valuable perspectives on the emergence of *alberghi*, but they do not lead to a full understanding of the family aggregation process in the context of the Italian Renaissance, nor do they hold up well when applied to a comparative analysis across time.[8] Indeed, in a town where commerce now constituted the central fabric of social interactions, it is clear – and topical to the object of this section – that the aggregation of mercantile families in Genoa was part of a trend toward large kinship-based trading houses that also affected other Italian city-states. In other words, it is the change in commercial practices combined with the social and political dynamics advanced by these historians that best explains why *alberghi* became the social building block of the elite network. The members of a house acted, as S. A. Epstein notes, "together in politics and commerce" (1996, p. 154).

Economic historians point to the importance of extended family ties in the organization of Italian Renaissance commerce.[9] For example, most studies regarding Tuscan commercial organizations note that the large merchant banking companies organized the distribution of business responsibilities among family members (blood relatives).[10] Similarly, Lane (1973, pp. 137–9) and Hocquet (1997, p. 255) both note that although the Venetian clans were smaller than those in other parts of Italy, the

---

[7] "Les groupes se forment de toutes pièces pour lutter contre les initiatives des popolari" (p. 385).

[8] Raggio's argument seems at first glance to fit a quick comparative review across the Italian social space because the strength of the family federation dynamic in a given urban center seems to have been inversely associated with the stability of that city-state.

[9] See, for example, Sapori (1952, pp. 21–30) or Heers (1961, pp. 93–6).

[10] See Kent (1977, pp. 8–11); Larner (1980, p. 62); Bloomquist (1971, pp. 173–8).

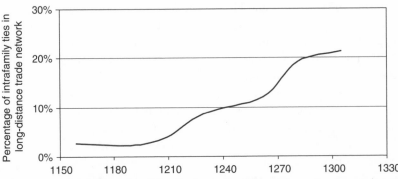

FIGURE 5.1. Percentage of intrafamily ties in the Genoese long-distance trade network, 1154–1315.


*fraterna* constituted, from the fourteenth century onward, the basic commercial unit.

After all, this must have seemed natural to the Renaissance merchants, as they did not separate business and family transactions. Even the accounting ledgers of the largest companies, such as the Florentine Peruzzi, include entries for clothing, food, medical bills, and dowries of extended family members.

In many ways, the importance of kinship in the Italian Renaissance is consistent with a variety of studies of routinized commercial networks across historical periods and geographic locations, right up to today's business organization.[11] As such, it is worthwhile to place the rise of the Genoese *alberghi* social structure in the broader context of the history of long-distance trade kinship ties in order to understand its commercial origin.

### Kinship[12] Ties in Genoa's Medieval Commerce

Figure 5.1 reports the percentage of intrafamily ties in the long-distance trade network between 1154 and 1315. For this figure, I reduce the data set population to Genoese and Ligurians (7,780 persons) and consider both debt and equity ties from 1154 to 1315 (n = 13,175). I identified all

---

[11] In international commerce requiring long-distance communication, strict kinship networks – that is, those defined by descent and marriage – are sometimes enlarged to include ethnic ties. For more, see Archer (1991).

[12] For a general discussion of kinship in medieval Europe, see Goody (1996).

ties among persons bearing the same name, but I probably under-estimated those forged by marriage alliances because notaries did not systematically supply that information, and the supplemental literature could not always help me in making my coding decisions. However, these missing relationships probably represent only a small part of the sample because – as Jehel demonstrates (1993, p. 163) – agnatic ties constituted the majority of family ties in medieval Genoese commerce.

Although the trend presented in Figure 5.1 should be interpreted with caution and may not fully represent the importance of kinship in medieval Genoese commerce, there is no doubt that, while strong family clusters contributed to the robustness of long-distance trade networks during the Renaissance, this had not always been the case in earlier times. Indeed, it is clear that extended family ties were relatively rare during the early expansion of long-distance trade, but became increasingly common during the course of the thirteenth century. This finding contradicts the accounts of those historians who, without the benefit of extensive quantitative data, have argued that kinship ties formed the basic Genoese business unit that spurred the commercial revolution. Certainly, close family relationships, such as those of the Gontardo (Hughes 1975, p. 16) and those linking the della Volta cousins (Day 1988), show the impor-tance of kinship ties in the development of commerce, but the dynamic demonstrated in Figure 5.1 illustrates how the study of individual biog-raphies can overstate their relevance when attempting to explain large social mechanisms.

The percentages reported in Figure 5.1 for the early period of trade expansion are equally low when compared to descriptions of specialized mercantile networks in the Middle Ages, such as those linking the oriental traders sending goods across the Mediterranean or the northern itinerant merchants visiting Genoa.

Although the comparatively low incidence of kinship ties in the Genoese network at the onset of the commercial revolution stands in contrast to most existing scholarship, it should come as no surprise to the reader. As Chapters 2 and 3 have demonstrated, the origin and strength of Genoese long-distance commercial growth in the twelfth and thirteenth centuries stemmed from opportunistic and heterogeneous social ties, and not from the fixed structures associated with routinized mercantile networks.

As such, the increasing proportion of family ties in commercial inter-actions during the course of the thirteenth century reported in Figure 5.1 goes hand in hand with the emergence of occupational role differentia-tion and with the emergence of a more specialized mercantile network, which led to the rise of urban kinships, and of the Genoese *alberghi* in particular.[13]

The rise of kinship during a period of commercial expansion and role differentiation might sound like a paradox for economists who believe in markets organized solely by price mechanisms, but it is consistent with other historical economic developments. As Tilly notes, "When Adam Smith argued that kinship loses it connective power in commercial countries, he got the historical facts and the causal mechanisms wrong" (2005, p. 37).

### Trade and *Alberghi*

The meticulous renderings of the fifteenth century floor plans of *alberghi* compounds by the architectural historians Grossi Bianchi and Poleggi show that clan members shared warehouses and shops (1979, pp. 225–38). While we know that for the most part individuals maintained separate assets, it is equally clear from these floor plans and from primary records that those assets often consisted of business partnerships with fellow *alberghi* affiliates. While *alberghi* affiliates account for less than 50% of the names listed on the custom records for 1376 and 1377, out of the 196 intrafamily partnerships defined by the shared custom bills, 145 (74%) consisted of intra-*alberghi* relationships.

Earlier in this section I reviewed several theories concerning the social aggregation of the *alberghi*. Next, I briefly explain why changes in the organization of long-distance trading networks – the increased differentiation of tasks and the rise of occupational categories – were directly associated with the emergence of these clans.[14]

First, as Lane observed, "the increased sophistication in business exchange and the fact that unlike in earlier times it was no longer

---

[13] Furthermore, the pattern presented in Figure 5.1 continued throughout the fourteenth century. Indeed, the custom records of 1376–77 indicate that 196 of the 749 ties (26%) defined by shared custom bills involved intrafamily relationships. In fact, 26% is a low estimate because family members were less likely to declare their joint tax liability than partners not bound by clan ties. The notarial records of the end of the fourteenth century also confirm the trend reported in Figure 5.1, but my data is less reliable than the data for the earlier period because it is less dense.

[14] Another classic economic argument concerns the switch to bulk trading and transportation on increasingly large ships, which required the pooling of capital among groups of merchants. This is not, however, very convincing because in view of the stagnant trade volume and the increased concentration of wealth, it is hard to argue that the need to pool capital was more urgent at the end of the fourteenth century than during the early phase of the commercial revolution.

necessary for traders to wander around looking for buyers and sources of supply" (1973, p. 137) created conditions for the delegation of authority to close associates, for which members of artificial kindreds were obvious candidates. In this regard, Gourdin (1995) provides strong evidence of the importance of *alberghi* in international mercantile networks. Using tax documents for the year 1445, he shows that, out of a sample of ninety-two merchants who resided in the most common stopover ports along the Genoese long-distance routes, 80% belonged to the most established *alberghi*. In addition, the clan's members were spread along the route, providing further evidence of the commercial coordination within clans.

Second, the continuing importance of maintaining monopolies and commercial privileges, as well as military relevance, in the context of the rise of occupational categories induced a division of labor among the *alberghi*. For example, while some branches of the *albergho* concentrated on providing men-of-arms and controlling feudal possessions outside the urban centers, others specialized in commerce. Such was the case with the Grimaldi clan. While part of the *albergho* worked on consolidating feudal possessions around Monaco – which they still rule today – others developed commercial interests in town. In other cases, one part of the clan might interact with the state, while others controlled the commercial traffic that often originated in faraway settlements. This was the organizational model of the Giustiniani clan. Many of the clan's affiliates lived in the colonies, where they administrated the monopolistic extractions of commodities, while others resided in Genoa, where they protected the interests of the clan and shored up the support of the public authorities. The Giustiniani provide the most famous example of this arrangement, but many other commercial privileges can be traced to the close relationships between the *alberghi* and the state. A letter sent by the Genoese doge in 1433 to the king of Aragon to confirm the trading privileges of 145 Genoese merchants illustrates the importance of the *alberghi*'s connection to the public authority. Indeed, from that list, 74% of the merchants were affiliated with nineteen of the largest *alberghi*, all of which were well represented both in the council of elders and on the board of governors of San Giorgio. In addition, the list provides strong evidence of how vital commercial and political networks were to the survival of the clan. Although from 1430 to the end of the fifteenth century the number of *alberghi* diminished by at least half,[15] sixteen of the nineteen *alberghi*

---

[15] This is a conservative estimate for aristocratic clans (Heers 1977, p. 85; Sieveking 1909, pp. 69–70). The count is a little harder to establish for *populares* clans because the

were still registered on a fiscal list of 1495,[16] and all sixteen of them took part in the grand council of 1500.[17]

Having established the importance of *alberghi* in the Genoese mercantile structure, for the remainder of the chapter I turn to an analysis of the insurance network. I start with a description of the insurance market. Thereafter, I demonstrate how insurance ties mediated the collaborating social relationships of the elite and consolidated the social boundaries around the Renaissance mercantile oligarchy.

## 5.2. THIRD-PARTY INSURANCE

The real profit uncertainty in medieval long-distance trade was rooted in traveling hazards. Price fluctuations surely affected the profitability of a venture, but by and large, if goods got to their destinations, a profit could be expected. In most cases, merchandise did indeed arrive at its destination. However, especially during the early years of the commercial revolution, if the value of an entire venture was lost, it could ruin even the most eminent families. For example, in 1162, the Mallone, one of Genoa's leading feudal clans, is said to have been financially ruined by the Pisan attack on the Genoese quarter in Constantinople, which destroyed merchandise about to be imported to Genoa (Day 1988, p. 95).

The example of the Mallone family is not an isolated one; Mediterranean long-distance trade investments did not proceed with the modern caution that comes with forecasting sequences of business ventures. As Braudel notes, the medieval Italian merchant often adopted a winner-take-all attitude and engaged his entire resources in single ventures (1967). This attitude certainly fits with the "warrior culture" of the time, which did not value mitigating risks but placed whole identities on the battlefield. This being said, medieval traders started to reduce traveling risk in a variety of ways.

First, although there was little that could be done to reduce the natural risk inherent in sailing the high seas – *riscium maris* – other than to select solid vessels and experienced crews, long-distance traders protected their

---

definition of a clan might be subject to interpretation. In any case, by 1500 no more than seven or eight *populares* clans qualified as full-fledged *alberghi*.

[16] See Sieveking (1909, pp.69–70); Squarciafico, Oliva, and Marionibo had folded into larger *alberghi*.

[17] See the list provided by Cattaneo Mallone (1987, pp. 194–8).

merchandise against pirates and privateers – the *riscium gentium*[18] – by hiring armed crews and by traveling in convoys. These precautions certainly applied to the Genoese fleet, as the administration strictly regimented and controlled the readiness of the fleet to carry out long-distance trade. The regulations included requirements detailing the ships' equipment and weaponry.[19] In addition, most transportation contracts (*nolis*) specified that seamen had to be *muniti ad ferrum* – that is, armed for combat – and the Genoese often sailed in convoys. However, whereas the public authority in Venice – and for a short while in Florence as well – organized trading convoys by allocating quotas through an auction system until the sixteenth century,[20] in Genoa the coordination remained, for the most part, a private process.

Second, as I mentioned in Chapter 4, financing a venture by contracting a sea loan or a maritime exchange could also provide protection against traveling risks. However, this option was very expensive and forced the traveler to borrow funds even if he did not need to. Furthermore, in the case of the maritime exchange, the borrower was required to reimburse the loan at the destination, which might leave him with no financial resources for reinvestment for the return trip. Finally, sea loans and exchange contracts could prove difficult to obtain for traders with no established network, as the availability of funds depended on experience and specialization (see Chapter 4).

Third, another risk-reducing alternative was indeed traveling diversification. As trade volume grew, merchants started to invest in multiple ventures. They could thus increasingly spread their parcels among different ships and different destinations. Here again the objective was often to diversify the traveling risk and not the market risk. The constitution of "galleys companies" in Venice offers a telling example of the traders' attempt to avoid the loss of a whole ship. As Frederik Lane reports, "One of these family partnerships might have born the whole cost and risk of a galley or two, but the *fraterne* divided the cost of the voyage among

---

[18] Attacks from pirates and privateers constituted the largest category of *riscium gentium*, but this category of risk also included any human intervention that caused damage while at sea or during the unloading of merchandise.

[19] For details on these regulations, see Forcheri (1974). Note that insurance underwriters almost always required that the ship be equipped as required by the law. Indeed, insurance contracts often included a provision such as "*secundum tractatus et ordinations Officci Gazariae et Officii Maris civitatis Janue.*" See, for example, KE#213/January 1416.

[20] For an exhaustive study of the Venetian convoy, see Stöckly (1995).

24 shares" (1944, p. 187). Because the family sent similar goods to a single destination on different ships, it is obvious that the pooling of resources to rent a galley was not an attempt to diversify business risk, but rather a method to avoid bearing the risk of total loss during transportation. A business diversification strategy would have been to trade different goods and/or to trade with different destinations.

Fourth, groups of traders had also, on occasion, shared traveling investments. In Genoa, this was especially true with regard to the ownership of ships, which was often divided. However, this does not mean that the capital was pooled so that, as Edler-de Roover stated, "the burden of the risk was assumed by several individuals" (1945, p. 174). More likely, pooling capital was often not a matter of choice. Ships constituted the most expensive capital investment, and isolated investors simply did not possess enough financial assets to purchase or build them.

All of the strategies just outlined mitigated traveling risk, but until the emergence of maritime insurance, none of them took this risk totally out of the hands of the long-distance traders or their creditors.

### Antecedent

The concept of insurance can be traced to antiquity. Traveling risks for overseas trading ventures had already been addressed by the Babylonians when they defined the bottomry loans in the Code of Hammurabi around 2250 B.C., and Greek and Egyptian societies created organizations that funded decent burial ceremonies for their members. Roman clubs initiated for similar purposes even seem to have developed rudimentary life insurance practices, and around 225 A.C., the jurist Ulpian seems to have relied on a crude mortality table to evaluate the value of life annuities. Closer to the epoch under study, during the Carolingian period, the formation of guilds provided a mechanism for mutual assistance to the affiliates' widows and their immediate families should the affiliates suffer certain misfortunes (Boiteux 1968, p. 38). This was true for a variety of trade brotherhoods, including those of seafaring merchants. As McLean reports, "In Denmark, we hear of 'Firth Gilds', crude forerunners of municipalities, whose memberships embraced important northern merchant families and which combined to compensate unfortunate brothers for loss from shipwreck" (1938, p. 16). Similarly, charters granted to villages by feudal overlords sometimes included formalized obligations of mutual assistance. For example, the *keuren* (charters) of Verambacht of 1240 A.D. held that the person whose house burned down was to be indemnified without delay by the whole village and was to be paid by the officers elected to serve as *keurheers*.[21]

All of these historical instances of insurance arose from an attitude of solidarity in traditional communities. The words *club, brotherhood,* and *membership* associated with these insurance practices illustrate their communal and reciprocal characteristics. Note that the word *solidarity* used in this context does not mean that mutual assistance is necessarily set in motion by selfless actors. Rather, members of the community probably helped each other out of habit or normative pressures or expectations of reciprocity.

Thus, the great innovation of medieval maritime insurance was that some uncertainties could be transferred to third parties – the underwriters – who did not otherwise need to be in any way concerned with the commercial operation at hand.

## Risk

While the first record of fire insurance dates from 1680, and other types of nonmutual personal insurance began to develop around the same time, the late medieval maritime insurance contracts constitute the first third-party insurance[22] and thus the first real possibility of transferring risk.

The idea of transferring and thus selling risk against a premium implies the ability to quantify – even if not yet to calculate – hazards and thus entails a new conception of danger, which shifted from being unavoidable to becoming the result of choice. In addition, danger could become not

---

[21] Stipulations to the same effect are also found in the charters of Berges, Furnes, and Bourbourg (Trennery 1926, pp. 247–60).

[22] My focus on maritime as opposed to overland insurance was chosen by default, as I have not found many instances of terrestrial shipment insurance during the medieval and early Renaissance periods. For example, in a sample of 165 commercial insurance contracts dating from 1345 to 1400 published by Liagre De Sturler, only 4 regarded overland shipping (1969, p. xcv). Heers, focusing on the fifteenth century, found almost no terrestrial policies among the thousands he examined in the Genoese archives (1959a, p. 9). The much higher insurance premium placed on maritime transportation than on overland transportation to similar destinations indicates that the reason for the near absence of overland insurance was that the incidence of damage was much lower on land. First, long-distance traders traveling in caravan had long paid bribes – protection money – not only to local lords but also to their suzerains, and could be protected more efficiently than when on water (Boiteux 1968, pp. 25–6; Doehaerd 1976, p. 210). Second, it is easy to imagine that natural hazards, such as a packed mule falling into a ravine or water damage by river or rain, could be more easily minimized than shipwrecks.

only a matter of the odds about actual circumstances, but also of the magnitude of aleatory outcomes.

Although merchants started to control the business environment, the rudimentary medieval methods of assessing odds could not yet bring about the modern differentiation between uncertainty and risk as defined by Knight (1921).[23] Certainly, the emergence of maritime insurance premiums contained the seeds of the modern risk/reward business decision-making process. However, while discharging risk on a third party was a key business advance that liberated disposable capital, underwriting insurance did not always make for a rational investment decision based on quantitative assessments. Nonetheless, maritime insurance was charged with enough social meaning to sustain a rapid growth. Indeed, because wealthy merchants were often underwriters themselves, maritime insurance was a device to organize the distribution of, and thus the sharing of, risk among the whole community in a way that had not previously been possible.

Before presenting evidence to explain this dynamic at the end of the chapter, I will next provide a description of the key components of maritime insurance. My purpose here is not to repeat what has been written elsewhere, but to point out those institutional elements that are most relevant to understanding the social dynamic underpinning the development of third-party insurance.

## Maritime Insurance

Scholars offer different opinions about where and when the first third-party insurance was created.[24] It is not my aim to contribute to this historical debate. It is enough for our purpose to know that between 1325 and 1375, the first third-party insurance contracts were drawn in several Mediterranean ports, and that Genoa was likely the largest center of this innovative business technique.[25] The timing of the emergence of maritime

---

[23] For Knight, *risk* refers to changes in economic context for which probabilities can be computed, whereas *uncertainty* refers to situations in which no such computation is feasible.

[24] For example, Edler-de Roover placed the first third-party insurance contract in Palermo in 1350 (1945, p. 183); for Stefani, in Venice in 1336 (1958, p. 73); for Liagre De Sturler, in 1347 (1969, p. xcv); for Daston, in Marseilles in 1328 (1988, p. 118); and for Melis, in Genoa in 1343 (1975, p. xxii).

[25] As Bensa noted, "Au moment ou le 14e siècle s'achevait et la ou commençait le siècle suivant, Gênes parait avoir été, entre toutes les villes Italiennes, le centre le plus actif du commerce des assurances" (1897, p. 48).

insurance in the mid fourteenth century was linked to an increase in individual disposable capital that could be deployed for insurance purposes, and as such, as Heers has noted,[26] is a direct consequence of the development of capitalism (1959a, p. 11). In addition, as will be apparent later in this chapter, the emergence of maritime insurance was also associated with the rise of occupational categories that increasingly linked wealthy mercantile families.

The record shows that medieval maritime contracts coexisted in two different forms. Either they followed the Genoese custom of drawing a fictive loan that was reimbursed in case of damage and that provided for separate payment of a premium, or else the contracts kept to the Florentine legal outline called *ad florentinam*.[27] This latter form already contained the basic features of the modern insurance policy, which provides for the payment of an up-front premium and which became the standard around the Mediterranean from the late fifteenth century onward. Prior to that time, the two forms coexisted and provided exporters and ship owners with similar protections against a list of traveling risks sometimes so exhaustive as to include those that "are of God, of the sea, of the men at war, of fire, of jettison, of detainment by princes, by cities, or by any person, of reprisals, of arrest, of whatever loss, peril, misfortune, impediment or sinister" (Origo 1986, p. 140). Because of the lack of systematic records, it is hard to know which of these potential hazards represented the greatest risk. However, it can be safely assumed that pirates and corsairs were high on the list. For example, of a small sample of forty insurance claims in fifteenth-century Barcelona, half resulted from the action of privateers and pirates.[28]

In the hundreds of Genoese notarial records of insurance that I have coded, the contracts almost always stipulate the name and type of the ship as well as the kinds of goods[29] that were covered as two elements that

[26] "En définitive, c'est le développement du capitalisme moderne qui a permis l'avènement de l'assurance maritime" (1959a, p. 11).

[27] Several studies provide detailed descriptions of the different legal frameworks. Bensa (1897) is still the reference. See also Liagre De Sturler (1969, pp. xc-cxxii) and Boiteux (1968, pp. 77–89).

[28] See Del Treppo (1972), pp. 341–46.

[29] Historians have used insurance contracts to provide an indication of the various types of goods in the fourteenth-century Genoese long-distance trade. Without entering into details, the data set indicates the shipment of a wide variety of merchandise such as alum (STU#261/March 1350; KE#251/October 1419), wool (KE#61/June 1410), wheat (KE#176/April 1414), cotton (KE#13/May 1405), wine (STU#223/March 1348), pepper (STU#653/May 1393), cinnamon (STU#625/October 1398), and many others.

were factored into the pricing of the premium. However, over time the descriptions became less precise and began to correspond to generic categories. For example, instead of a technical description, a contract might state only that the ship was a galley. Similarly, the descriptions of the goods insured became less detailed. Generic terms, such as "wine," replaced fuller descriptions that could have included the specific provenance of the wine and the size of the jars. The increasing use of standard norms certainly prefigured the fungibility of the modern insurance market. However, the stipulations concerning the voyage itself remained strict. The contracts invariably named the captain and stated that the ship was to follow a preestablished itinerary, leaving only limited flexibility for the captain to improvise along the way. This requirement certainly seems reasonable to the modern reader, but it is clear evidence of the routinization of shipment practices, which contrasted sharply with the earlier medieval ventures that had let the captains go "wherever seemed best" (see Chapter 3).

## Merchants as Underwriters

It is difficult to estimate the proportion of long-distance maritime trade that was insured. Historians have cited a range of 20% to 25%, and my own rough estimate, based of data compiled by Melis for the years 1427 to 1431, points to a similar proportion.[30] This number is high when it is considered that it was the merchants themselves who almost exclusively constituted the pool of underwriters. This was not only true for Genoa, but also for the insurance networks at other ports throughout the sixteenth and even the seventeenth century. The historian Tenenti, who analyzed hundreds of insurance contracts in Ragusa (today's Dubrovnik, a Croatian port on the Adriatic Sea) from 1565 to 1596, states that "when analyzing Ragusa's commercial community of the second part of the 16th century, it is difficult to distinguish between insurance underwriters and merchants because the separation between them is not clear" (1985,

---

[30] Melis, who demonstrated that his data collected from the notarial archives was exhaustive (1975), identified an average of 198,000 florins worth of maritime insurance recorded per year in the notarial records for Genoa from 1427 to 1431. At that time, the Genoese underwriters did not often write down their insurance agreements in private documents (*apodixia*) [acknowledgments]; therefore, his numbers are probably close to the actual volume. Considering that the value of total trade was probably somewhere between £1.2 and £1.6 million – that is, roughly, between 1 and 1.35 million florins (based on Heers 1961 and Day 1966) – 15 to 25% is indeed a fairly good estimate.

TABLE 5.1. *Frequency distribution of risk amount underwritten per individual per contract, 1427–31 (n = 11,209)*

| Risk amount underwritten, in £ | ≤50 | 50–99 | 100–149 | 150–199 | 200–249 | ≥250 |
|---|---|---|---|---|---|---|
| Number of underwriting commitments | 852 | 3,937 | 4,998 | 1,076 | 304 | 52 |

p. 127). He goes on to note – as I did, based upon my own Genoese data set – the low level of participation of bankers in the insurance market (1985, p. 188).[31] Another economic historian, Boiteux, reports that in Marseilles around 1635, "Almost all merchants both underwrote and received insurance coverage" (1962, p. 453).

To understand the analysis presented in this chapter, it is important to keep in mind that the Genoese merchant class represented a tight community, in which normative habits and the anticipation of reciprocity must have been important factors when making investment decisions. While third-party insurance offered the possibility of discharging the risk outside the community, the Renaissance maritime insurance network was still almost exclusively composed of ties among merchants.

*Individual Risk Covered.* Table 5.1 reports the frequency distribution of the amount underwritten per individual per voyage in a sample of 2,471 contracts forming 11,209 insurance relationships dating from the years 1427 to 1431.[32]

Clearly, the amounts of individual premiums were not large. Indeed, the distribution of individual exposures per contract is concentrated between £50 and £150, and commitments above £250 are rare (52 out of 11,209). An analysis of the same sample also shows that most policies were underwritten by syndicates of multiple insurers, as only about 1,400 out of 11,209 insurance commitments relate to contracts signed by one or two counterparties. As such, the numbers reported in Table 5.1,

---

[31] Tenenti's study is the most exhaustive study on maritime insurance. The one missing component is an analysis of the structure of the network, which would help the reader understand the social implications of investment decisions, a component that Tenenti acknowledges is key (1985, p. 371).

[32] This is Melis's sample (1975).

combined with the practice of syndication, suggest a puzzling fact: The ratio of risk exposure per contract between wealthy merchants and those much less well-off does not match their respective abilities to withstand the risks they underwrote. In other words, why did extremely wealthy men, such as Pietro Spinola, Stefano Lomellini, and Raffaele Fornario,[33] provide the same average amount of coverage per voyage as underwriters whose capital was only a fraction of theirs? I have found no trace of a regulatory limit on individual underwriting, and the existence of a few individual policies for amounts exceeding £450 indicates that it probably did not exist. Thus, any one of these three wealthy merchants could certainly have insured whole lots by themselves and still have had much less exposure than the majority of those who were underwriting £100 or even £50 at a time. Although it is very difficult to assess with precision the distribution of wealth for that period, I have, nonetheless, produced an educated guess on the basis of tax records so as to provide the reader with a sense of wealth disparity among insurance underwriters in order to further illustrate this puzzling finding. Using conservative assumptions in regard to my claim,[34] I established that the wealth of the top 22 underwriters was about 50 times that of the bottom 216, which I would put at around £2,000. I am aware that this later number is speculative. However, whatever the exact figure is, it is clear that a very large number of the underwriters possessed only a very small fraction of the capital base available to the wealthiest.

Modern economists who see in the underwriting decisions of the wealthiest the mark of virtuous operators who elected to diversify their exposure may be, to some extent, correct. However, by the same logic, the same modern observer should deem the great majority of those less well-off to be imprudent, which does not seem a very reasonable assumption because the distribution of underwriting risk with respect to wealth does

---

[33] The combined wealth of these three men, as reported by the tax assessment for the *gabella possesum* of 1440, stood at more than £300,000, and the three were among the fifty wealthiest Genoese heads of household in that year (Sieveking 1909, pp. 81–4).

[34] Using data from the tax records of 1466 *(avaria)* summarized by Grendi (1987, p. 81), I calculated that among 707 of the wealthiest taxpayers, the average asset base of the top 5% was around 50 times larger than that of the bottom 50%. (The top 35 paid an average of £96.50, while the bottom 355 paid an average of £1.98.) Then, assuming that the distribution of wealth in 1440 was similar to that in 1466, and assuming that the underwriters were indeed recruited from among the wealthiest Genoese merchants (both conservative assumptions in regard to my claim), an educated guess would put the average capital of 216 out of the 432 underwriters for the years 1427–31 at around £2,000.

not seem to have changed much over three centuries. Indeed, economic theory would have predicted that imprudence would be penalized. This would in turn lead to a change in the distribution of underwriting amounts with respect to wealth and the setting of an equilibrium price for premiums that would organize the distribution of risk volume according to available capital. However, this was not the case. Although the data series for Genoese insurance is neither long enough nor dense enough to provide conclusive support for that assertion, Melis's (1975) series on Florentine insurance from 1524 to 1526 and Tenenti's (1985) on Ragusa's from 1565 to 1591 complement the Genoese data, and provide strong evidence of the stability of the underwriting patterns with respect to wealth. It is only much later that the ratio of underwriters to policyholders slowly decreased and the average coverage per underwriter rose. For example, while in early seventeenth-century Marseilles this ratio was still almost even, as individual exposure remained small and exhibited little variation, later in the century, a newly founded insurance company reduced the number of underwriters to 78 per 474 policyholders.[35] By then, the capital was becoming strictly financial, which signals the rationalization of the insurance business. Indeed, without consideration of delivery cost, the larger the insurance capital pool, the easier it is to absorb random losses.

The next few paragraphs, and then the last section of this chapter, will demonstrate that underwriting decisions were not predicated solely on an economic rationale, but were laced with elements of a solidaristic mercantile attitude. Part of the reason wealthy underwriters did not raise their individual stakes in policies might have been a prudent diversification stance toward risk, but it also had to do with the lack of profitability of the business – which comes as no surprise, since investment decisions were a matter of social choice and not purely of economic sense.

## Premium

The Genoese records regarding insurance prior to the mid fifteenth century usually did not include details about premiums, and we do not have a large unbiased sample from which to construct an insurance price curve. However, historians have been able to piece together a few lists of premiums that provide an idea about the price of insurance for Genoa and

---

[35] For details on Marseille's insurance market, see Boiteux (1962, p. 453) and Delumeau (1985, p. 149).

several other Mediterranean ports.[36] Many of those who have analyzed these lists point to rational premium pricing with respect to distance, type of ship, and geopolitical circumstances as evidence of an accurate assessment of risk.[37] Although in some cases the premium price is irregular with respect to distance, for the most part the pricing structure was indeed coherent. Rates varied according to distance or length of contract; insuring smaller ships was – per value of goods carried – more expensive than insuring larger ones; insuring barrels of olive oil (which could float) was cheaper than insuring salt (which could dissolve in water); and the likelihood of pirate activity or maritime battles could substantially raise the premiums, which otherwise show a remarkably stable price series over long periods (Delumeau 1985, p. 148). In other words, the price distribution of premiums with respect to a series of salient variables seemed coherent to the medieval underwriter. However, while the premium price variations made sense, there is no evidence that the baseline did so or that the business as a whole was profitable. Indeed, there is no evidence that the perception of risk in itself was accurate. In fact, while our data set cannot justify definite conclusions about the profitability of the insurance industry, other studies for later periods that involve the same homogeneous social structure with respect to occupation in the maritime insurance network point to aggregate premium rates that did not leave a profit margin for the underwriters. Tenenti, in the only study of the Renaissance insurance business that relies on a large quantitative data set, notes that in Ragusa, the ratio of damage claims was around 5% of the number of ventures covered by underwriters and that the average premium was also about 5% (1985, p. 371). Similarly, in the only other comparison between premium rates and damage claims that I could uncover in the literature (Delumeau 1985, p. 147), the mean premium insurance rate for a smaller sample of voyages between Spain and America in the early seventeenth century was slightly lower than an estimate of the average loss of Spanish convoys during the same period.

Thus, considering the transactions cost of each contract, it appears that in these two circumstances the maritime insurance business as a whole was at best a break-even, and more likely a losing, enterprise. Although

---

[36] See, in particular, Edler-de Roover (1938), Heers (1959a), and Boiteux (1968).

[37] For example, this is implicit in the comments of Melis (1975, pp. 12–18), Favier (1998, p. 257), Lopez (2001, pp. 255–65), and Spufford (2002, pp. 30–2). Note that Kedar (1976) and Tenenti (1985) did not come to the same conclusion. Tenenti wrote: ". . . a field of insurance as the one in Ragusa which seemed dominated by opportunism and extemporaneity" (1985, p. 211).

we do not know for sure that this was representative of the late medieval and early Renaissance maritime insurance industry, samples of individual biographies give further credit to this theory. The great Florentine merchant Francesco di Marco Datini (1335–1410) abandoned the underwriting business for several years because after he earned "100 florins in little bits, he lost 200 in one stroke" (Edler-de Roover 1938, p. 197). Later in life he began to underwrite again, but one must wonder why such a wealthy merchant pursued this marginal business, which gave him so much worry, as evident from a letter he wrote to his wife:

I dreamed last night of a house which had fallen to pieces and all my household were therin . . . and the meaning of this dream gives me much to ponder on, for there are no tidings of a galley that left Venice more than two months ago, bound for Catalonia; and I had insured her for 300 florins, as I did the other ships for Domenico di Cambio, which perished the next day. (Origo 1986, p. 136)

Another example of how unprofitable the insurance business was is provided by an analysis of the accounting ledgers of Giovanni Piccamiglio, a Genoese merchant active in the mid fifteenth century. Piccamiglio was part of an old aristocratic lineage that can be traced to the time of the First Crusade. Like many of his ancestors, he was actively involved in long-distance trade[38] and was certainly well connected to the Genoese elite, as evidenced by his regular co-optation into the small circle of the Casa di San Giorgio board members. Like other wealthy merchants, Giovanni Piccamiglio underwrote many policies. From 1456 to 1459, his exposure totaled more than £6,600. However, his average profit per year from this business – before expenses and taxes such as the *Gabella Securitatis* (Lodolini 1967) – was a mere £14. In fact, the combined profit from three years of insurance underwriting – one of Piccamiglio's main activities as described by Heers, who wrote a meticulous study based on his accounting books (1959b) – would not even cover the bill for the food at his daughter's wedding banquet in 1459. Again, one must wonder why a man of considerable means, otherwise involved in transactions worth thousands of pounds, persisted in underwriting insurance.

---

[38] The data set contains the names of five Piccamiglio involved in twelfth century long-distance trade, thirteen involved in the thirteenth century, and eleven for the fourteenth who entered into seventy-nine different commercial relations with fellow traders. For specifics, see, for example, S#180/May 1157; OB1#436/March 1184; DO#235/January 1201; LO #92f; DO#1034/May 1259; BA#1418/March 1291; BA#3836/February 1351; STU#458/October 1384.

There are other individual accounts that confirm the unprofitable nature of insurance underwriting,[39] and I have not come across any individual biographies that suggest the opposite. Maritime insurance was nevertheless an important activity for many early Renaissance merchants. What is striking is that in almost all cases underwriters also insured their own shipments. As a result, because they continued to engage in the unprofitable underwriting of fellow merchants' ventures, they simultaneously benefited from the low premium rates. Thus, while it is relatively easy to demonstrate that the merchants could not have been motivated only by the prospective profits, insurance did play an important role in freeing individual capital, since the volatile element of business risk was now shared by all. In the next section, I will systematically analyze the Genoese insurance network in the early 1400s in order to demonstrate that the viability and growth of this key business innovation was indeed sustained not by its profitability for the underwriters, but by its social role in building ties between elite clans. In doing so, the insurance business became a locus of consolidation of social boundaries, further protecting the interests of the wealthy mercantile oligarchy.

## 5.3. OLIGARCHIC FAMILIES

Figure 5.2 represents the Genoese insurance network from 1410 to 1435.[40] Each node corresponds to a family, and the lines between the nodes represent insurance relationships. The size of the various nodes is proportional to the nodal degree of the family – that is, the number of ties that are incident to a given node. Without using algebraic methods to measure systematically and thus to reduce the complexity of this social network, it is very hard to reach any precise conclusions by looking at the graph. However, even an untrained eye could make several preliminary observations. First, most of the lines (ties) are concentrated in the middle

---

[39] For example, that of the Florentine merchant Bernardo di Cambio, who underwrote many insurance policies from the 1450s to the 1470s and who, according to his account books, "paid out more in claim than he received in premiums" (Edler-de Roover 1945, p. 194). As anecdotal evidence of how small the mercantile community was during the Renaissance, note that Bernardo was a descendant of Dominico di Cambio, a protagonist in the Datini nightmare reported above.

[40] For this section's analysis, I used a sample of 471 insurance contracts dated from 1410 to 1435. Altogether, these contracts formed 2,029 underwriting agreements among 172 families. Note that I did not consider the weaker underwriter-underwriter ties, and that the periodicity of the sample was dictated by the density of available transcribed documents.

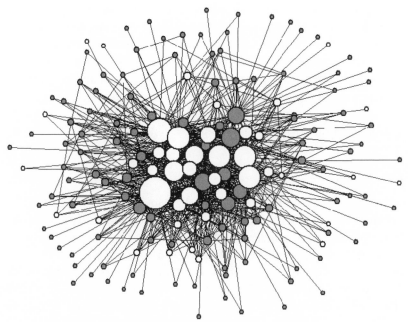

FIGURE 5.2. Insurance network, 1410–35.

of the graph. Second, the center of the graph is so crowded with lines that it is impossible to distinguish which dots are linked to each other. Third, all of the largest dots are in the middle of the graph. Fourth, the white dots (aristocrats) seem to be larger and seem to gravitate toward the center.

In network terminology, these visual observations correspond to a core/periphery structure formed by a very dense center sparsely connected to peripheral actors. These observations are consistent with an ideal type of hierarchical social organization that distinguishes between a group of cohesive preeminent mercantile families – mostly aristocrats – and others who deal with the elite center only sporadically. Indeed, it appears that the clustering takes place among the largest operators and that the hierarchical nature of the network is, as such, very different from that of the "ideal type" graph representing feudal organizations composed of a series of star-shaped clusters (Chapter 3 p. 105). It is also evident that the insurance network contrasts sharply with the centerless "spanning tree" shape of the long-distance trade network of the thirteenth century (Chapter 3, p. 108).

In the following section I will confirm some of these preliminary observations. I begin by using an algebraic algorithm to define the core/periphery structure of the network. Next, I review the composition and the cohesive structure of the core and show how it exemplifies the Genoese oligarchic organization. Then I use a probability model to explore some components of the partner-selection process, and show that insurance underwriting denoted a solidaristic attitude that eventually consolidated the social boundaries of the oligarchy.

### Core/Periphery

Oligarchy is a governance structure that, in its broadest and simplest definition, is characterized by the control of a few individuals or families over the rest of the population. As such, a focus on the core/periphery structure of the insurance relations displayed in Figure 5.2 is of particular interest to this study for three main reasons. First, formal network analysis provides computational methods to identify analytically the cluster of clans that increasingly cooperated with each other to form the ruling elite of the Genoese Renaissance. Second, a comparison between the Genoese insurance network and the ideal social organization summarized in binary matrices links the analysis to a rich social science literature. Third, common graphic measures can help to evaluate the degree of cohesiveness of the oligarchic clan and directly tie it to the concept of solidaristic behavior.

The concept of core/periphery structure is well established in the social science literature and has been applied in empirical studies to a variety of fields such as economics and organization studies as well as to studies of revolution and collective action. Closer to our substantive topic, Mintz and Schwartz (1981) refer to the concept of interlocking directorates, and Zucker and Rosenstein contrast the core dominating firms in a market with "the smaller firms constituting the periphery," which "have much less economic control" (1981, p. 870). In Zucker and Rosenstein's analysis, the core/periphery pattern is analogous to the oligopoly/competitive paradigm. Implicit here is the idea that oligopolistic organizations are not composed of independent competitors but are rich in horizontal connections. Closer yet to the historical period under study, Wallerstein's (1976) world system theory is built around a distinction between core entities, – which simultaneously control production, trade, and capital – and a periphery exploited by the center.

Intuitively, a core/periphery social structure can be represented as a bipartition of a network that separates a small cohesive cluster of actively interacting actors – in our case, Genoese clans – from the sparsely connected remaining population. Intuitively also, the reduction of a complex social network to two groups of nodes is akin to block modeling methodology. Block modeling is a theoretic reduction of a network of relationships aimed at grouping actors who are structurally equivalent, that is, actors who exhibit the same graphic pattern of ties. The objective is to summarize the network into a smaller interpretable matrix by shifting "the unit of analysis to blocks" (Bearman 1993, p. 74).[41] Thus, the bipartition of a social network into a core and a periphery of nodes proceeds with similar intentions. However, the methodology is simpler because the assignment of a given node to either the core or the periphery is dichotomic in that the reduction of a social network to a 2-by-2 matrix that represents the connection between the artificially divided subnetworks can take only two different ideal forms. Either the periphery class is connected to the core, or the core is monopolizing all ties. Empirical data, especially data regarding large networks such as the Genoese mercantile community, are unlikely to conform exactly to an ideal type. Nevertheless, the measure of density assigned to each of the four cells of the core/periphery matrix provides a sense of the degree to which a given network matches either ideal social structure.

## Leading Clans

The computational method that I use to identify the core network of the insurance organization differs in two ways from that of the more classic historiography, which readily identifies preeminent families on the basis of various criteria associated with a combination of trade volume, political position, military appointment, and/or reputation and status.[42] First, the results provided by an algorithm that assigns a family either to the core or to the periphery are not based on individual attributes or reputation, but on the objective metric associated with each family's position in the web of mercantile connections – a measure that thus emphasizes social capital as crucial to elite membership. Second,

[41] Peter Bearman's study of the structure of kinship in sixteenth- and seventeenth-century England is a standard in the empirical application of block modeling to historical social sociology (1993).

[42] See, for example, Balard (1978); Grendi (1987); and Jehel (1993).

TABLE 5.2. *Density matrix for insurance network's core/periphery bipartition (1410–35)*

|  | Core (26 clans) | Periphery (146 clans) |
|---|---|---|
| Core (26 clans) | 0.529 | 0.085 |
| Periphery (146 clans) | 0.065 | 0.005 |

algebraic methods not only analytically establish, but also measure the magnitude of the oligarchic nature of the Genoese social structure by identifying the core/periphery bipartition and by providing density parameters of ties among the elite.

Borgatti and Everett have developed an algorithm designed to generate such a network bipartition. The routine in their network analysis software package UCINET consists of permutations of the row and column of a sociomatrix so as to maximize the correlation between the data input and an ideal core/periphery pattern matrix.[43] The assumption is that the actors with the most intense ties form the core of the network. The software output 1) provides for the assignment of every node (family) either to the core or to the periphery, 2) indicates the density of network ties in each of the four cells of the reduced matrix, and 3) offers a fitness index that allows for comparisons between networks and provides for a measure of reliability.

I applied the UCINET procedure to the Genoese insurance relations among the 172 clans that form the insurance data set. Table 5.2 reports the density parameters computed by the permutation algorithm.

The program identifies 26 families[44] as the core cluster and relegates 146 families to the periphery. Clearly, the density of the core/core cell (0.529) is much higher than that of the other three. In addition, when taking into account availability, peripheral families were thirty times more likely to enter into relationships with core clans (0.065 and 0.085) than with fellow peripheral families (0.005).[45] It is also important to note

[43] See the explanation in Borgatti and Everett (1999), p. 381.
[44] Calvo, Cattaneo, Centurioni, Cigala, Doria, Fieschi, Fornario, Franchi, Gentilis, Grillo, Giustiniani, Grimaldi, Imperiale, Italiano, Lomellini, Mari, Marini, Maruffo, Negrono, Oliva, Pinello, Salvago, Spinola, Squarciafico, and Usodimare.
[45] Frequency cell (0–1) + frequency cell (1–0) compared to frequency cell (0–0). Note, though, that this does not mean that the ratio of core/periphery ties to periphery/

that the propensity to deal with members of the elite had little to do with the greater capacity of the core clans to provide insurance as a result of their greater wealth. In fact, the data suggests that the peripheral families were more likely to insure the core clans than the reverse (0.085 versus 0.065), another finding that leads us to set aside the economic argument as a reliable framework with which to make sense of the insurance selection pattern.

The composition of the core elite subnetwork identified by the UCINET routine is particularly remarkable. Indeed, whereas the twelfth- and thirteenth-century equity partnership data might have underestimated the importance of certain feudal Genoese families in the organization of the city because they were not much involved in long-distance trade, only preeminent Genoese clans, as measured by a variety of variables, are part of the insurance network core. Consider that, while it is likely that a couple of elite families are missing from the core subgroup,[46] the partition contains eighteen of the top twenty clans as measured by tax records for 1440 and 1466, and twenty of the top twenty-five as measured by political appointments and by the number of San Giorgio board seats.[47] The clustering is also a good predictor of clan survival. Twenty-three of the twenty-six core insurance clans survived the reform of 1528 that designated twenty-eight elite *alberghi*.

Note also that identifying the top twenty-six clans in the network according to volume of transaction, instead of the block model, did not yield the same partition. Indeed, the volume criterium eliminates a few preeminent families from the core (among others, Fieschi and Marrini) and add others who clearly never reached oligarchic status (for example, de Felisano and Santo Blasio). Thus, the analytical network partition can certainly be understood not only as representative of tangible commercial relationships at the time, but also as a proxy for the dense connections among almost all the oligarchic clans.

periphery ties is 30. It means that a given "member of the core" was on average thirty times more likely to have a tie with a "peripheral" family than a "peripheral" family was.

[46] This is either because of "type two" error (a family should have been identified as a core member in the insurance network but the routine did not identify it) or simply because a mercantile elite family did not participate actively in the insurance market. The Sauli family is one of the few obvious candidates for the latter case.

[47] See Grendi (1987, pp. 73–81) for the data source.

## Cohesion

Many sociological studies have centered on the concepts of group cohesion and social solidarity. These two concepts are just as central to Durkheim's works on the division of labor (1964) and on suicide (1979) as they are to Marx's theory of class consciousness (1963). Simmel's studies of the relation between social ties and network size, and his related critique of modernity, also directly tackle the issue of cohesion (1971).

However, even in these monumental works, the concept of cohesion has no clear operational definition because it often has a variety of meanings.[48] One way to develop a clearer definition would be to focus on the network structural properties of cohesion and to deduce a theory of cohesion from empirical measures. In the field of historical sociology, Gould deployed this strategy in his study of the mobilization process in the Paris commune (1991), as did Bearman in his analysis of desertion patterns during the American Civil War (1991).

Density is a key property of network structural cohesion because the more closely individuals are tied to each other, the more likely they are to behave according to homogeneous norms and interests (Coleman 1988). Because the UCINET algorithm separates the core of the network by separating the nodes according to their connectivity, to observe the cohesiveness of the elite twenty-six clan clusters on that basis alone would be trivial. It is more significant to note the large difference in density between the core and the periphery, as this demonstrates the increased monopolization of mercantile activity by a small number of clans.[49]

Leaving aside density measures, which are certainly valid in measuring group cohesion, but which in this case present obvious "circularity issues," other network parameters – in particular, the frequency of ties among members and the reachability of group members – are also associated with cohesion (Wasserman and Faust 1994, p. 250).

It is not possible to determine the frequency of insurance coverages among the core network members with precision because, without knowing the total volume of insurance underwritten during the twenty-five-year period covered by the sample, I could not calculate the proportion

---

[48] See, for further comments, Mizruhi (1990), pp. 16–18) and Moody and D. White (2003, p. 104).

[49] It should be kept in mind that if insurance were treated as consisting of symmetrical relationships, then the observed density of the core network would have been even higher (68.9% versus 52.9%). Thus, when randomly picking two out of the twenty-six families, there is more than a 68% probability that the sample contains an insurance connection between them.

of the whole population of contracts represented in the data set. However, using Melis's data (1975) for the years 1427 to 1431, I came up with a rough conservative estimate of an average per family of about 100 intra-core insurance agreements per year.[50] Knowing that insurance coverage lasted several weeks, this estimate should provide the reader with a sense of the frequency of the intra-core family insurance ties.

Proximity and reachability among the subgroup members are other widely used network properties associated with social cohesion.[51] Network parameters are most helpful here in confirming the close mercantile interactions among all of the elite families during the Genoese Renaissance. Indeed, the sample shows that the twenty-six clans formed a 2-clique,[52] which means that the longest geodesic distance between two nodes is equal to 2 (geodesic distance is defined as the length of the shortest path between a pair of nodes). Thus, in a 2-clique all members need not be adjacent, but all members are reachable through at most one intermediary. In early fifteenth-century Genoa, if a core clan was not directly connected to another core clan, then it had at most "two degrees of separation."

While reachability is a key parameter in measuring cohesion, Moody and D. White also note the importance of "multiple independent paths linking actors together" in assessing cohesion strength (2003, p. 104). This idea can be easily understood by considering the following case: Compare the cohesion of a network in which every path between two given nodes passes through a centralized actor with that of a network of maximal density minus one tie (that is to say that, with the exception of two nodes, all the other nodes are linked to one other). Both networks are 2-cliques, but the star network will have only a single path between any two nodes, whereas the other network will have [(n-2)!] independent paths. On the basis of this measure, the Genoese elite network also proves to be robust. Indeed, at least four independent paths link every member to each other without raising the minimum distance between any two given nodes. In other words, the graph of network ties for the twenty-six core families

---

[50] Melis reported an average number of underwriting ties (2,242) per year that is probably close to, but short of, the actual total. Knowing that intra-core member insurance coverage represented 60% of all insurance coverage in my sample, and assuming that the concentration of ties was constant from 1410 to 1435 (a conservative assumption for the purposes of my argument), I estimate that each core family entered into an average of about 100 to 110 intra-core agreements each year $\{[(2242*0.60)*2]/25 = 108.75\}$.

[51] For more on proximity, reachability, and cohesion, see Markovsky and Lawler (1994).

[52] The software routine for the detection of cliques assumes a symmetrical sociomatrix.

shows that each clan in the network was either directly connected or indirectly connected through at least four independent paths of a geodesic distance of two (a single intermediary separation). In addition, when relaxing the maximum-distance criteria, the elite network also shows good resilience and remains connected even when several clans are removed.

### Insurance Pairings

The reader will remember that, in the second section of this chapter, the evidence indicated that although insurance underwriting was important to Genoese mercantile community growth, it wasn't generating much profit. Consequently, and without disregarding all economic concerns – such as cash flow availability and price – in the partner selection process, it is unlikely that the classic rhetoric of market development as an allocation mechanism will be of much help in understanding the structure of the insurance network that united the Genoese mercantile elite.

In Chapter 3, and to some extent in Chapter 4, I resorted to aggregate long-distance participation on the basis of a priori attributes such as status and occupation to explain the partner selection dynamic. This methodology makes little sense when analyzing the insurance network because neither occupation nor status provides relevant characteristics to partition the network. For the most part, the underwriting business was concentrated in the hands of mercantile families, and as I demonstrated at the end of Chapter 4, status was decreasingly salient in partner selection, a trend confirmed by the insurance data. Indeed, using the methodology employed in Chapters 3 and 4, the value of a closure index $S_{14}$[53] that measures the propensity for status homophily in insurance relationships for the period 1410–35 was close to zero. By the end of the early fifteenth century, status was no longer salient in commercial partner selection, and the data indicates that, given availability, aristocrats were almost as likely to enter into maritime insurance contracts with fellow aristocrats as with anybody else.

Without a significant aggregation methodology, it is hard to make sense of the partner selection process for the whole network because I

---

[53] See page 113 for the definition of $S_{14}$. As the reader might recall, the value of the index ranges from −1 to +1, with a positive value indicating a propensity to form homogenous partnerships given availability. Measures close to zero indicate that, on average, the attribute is not salient in the partner selection process. In this case, out of a total of 2,029 ties, I counted 1,031 aristocrat-aristocrat ties, 161 commoner-commoner ties, and 837 aristocrat-commoner ties.

have records of only a few transactions for most of the 172 families coded in the data set. As I showed earlier in this chapter, the high density and the composition of the insurance network's core cluster indicate that, first and foremost, actions took place among the ruling mercantile class. This is why I focus on the core clans in my effort to bring to light the role of insurance underwriting in the consolidation of the Genoese oligarchy.

Network analysis tools are often designed to uncover patterns of social interaction by partitioning networks and then assessing the connections between clusters of actors. It is by studying not only the relations among clusters (or lack thereof) but also the common attributes shared by members of the same cluster that the analyst can come to understand the social pairing processes.[54] Even the inventive advance of block-modeling methodology did not change this principle. Indeed, while H. C. White, Boorman, and Breiger's insight that individuals did not need to be connected to each other to be part of a common structural subgroup (1976, p. 736) opened the way to engage in "positional" rather than "connectivity" analysis and relaxed the clustering constraint, it did not change the central methodological importance of network partitions.

In the case of a very dense component, such as the core Genoese oligarchy, in which every family was connected or in close proximity to every other, partitioning a network will not uncover partner-pairing patterns. However, if clustering proves to be insignificant in this case, this does not necessarily imply a random selection process, as is sometimes assumed. Think about certain social settings in which actors may control the frequency or intensity of their interactions per counterpart in order to allocate their limited resources to multiple partners, much in the way skillful cocktail partygoers ration their casual conversations in order to be able to meet as many people as possible. (Obviously, for the host, this maneuver is especially crucial and actually well accepted.) Other resources that can be socially optimized by spreading them around include, for instance, money (as in political donations to multiple parties) and eligible children (as in arranging marriages to fortify alliances).

It is with this in mind, but without presuming a purposive theory of action, that I set out to determine whether the insurance-tie pairings served as a means to consolidate the oligarchic network. The objective of the test was simple: to determine whether the mercantile elite clans entered into more insurance relationships than would be expected by

---

[54] It is this method that I used earlier in the chapter to define the core Genoese mercantile oligarchy.

random processes, in the same manner that a political candidate tries to shake as many hands as possible rather than focusing on a few electors. In other words, is twenty-two, the number of core clans recorded in the data set as having at least once insured a Vivaldi merchant, a low or a high number? And, having the answer to this question for all twenty-six core clans, what could be inferred and then tested about the insurance-pairing process of the whole core network?

*Test.* While the concept of the test is straightforward, its application is complicated and requires multiple steps. First, a baseline function is needed to quantify whether the observed number of different underwriting families in the data set was indeed "unusual." For that first step, for each of the twenty-six core elite families I established twenty-six empirical probability distributions $P_i(x_j)$, where $x_j$ denotes the number of insurance ties. Thus, the higher $x_j$, the more the policy coverage of the $i$ family was spread around fellow core clans.

Second, I compared the empirical data with the baseline for each of the twenty-six families. From that, I created a sample of twenty-six observations $y_i$ that measure the "odds" of a given family having as many or more underwriting families than the number observed in the sample.[55]

Third, I tested to determine whether the sample of "odds" $y_i$ for the twenty-six core families was different from the odds of randomly picking a number from a uniform distribution of numbers from o to 1.[56] For that, I applied the Kolmogorov-Smirnov test, and I found that I could reject the hypothesis that the sample of odds $y_i$ belong to a uniform distribution. Thus, I concluded that the odds of observing the high diversity of underwriting families coded in the sample was statistically significantly different from the diversity if randomly allocated. In addition, I found that, as a whole, the odds $y_i$ were smaller than if randomly allocated,[57] and thus that the variety of underwriting families observed was a "rare event." From that, I inferred that the Genoese insurance underwriting process created more intra-elite family ties than a random allocation

---

[55] See Appendix F for an explanation and definition of $y_i$.

[56] Note that $o \leq y_i \leq 1$; thus, in other words, I wished to test the hypothesis that the twenty-six numbers $y_i$ were chosen at random from numbers uniformly distributed between zero and one.

[57] $\int s(y)dy < \int f(y)dy$, where $S(y)$ denotes the cumulative function that specifies for each value of y the proportion of sample values less than or equal to y, and $F(y)$ the cumulative probability function of a random selection of numbers between o and 1.

pairing process – and, a fortiori, more than a market allocation where repeated interactions usually create clusters – would suggest.

Even for readers familiar with probability and statistics, the procedure just described might sound complicated because it includes multiple steps and focuses on creating and testing a sample of probabilities. For those interested in understanding the testing procedures more fully, I detail in Appendix F each of the three steps just summarized.

### Elite Cohesion

While the data certainly suggests that insurance ties provided a mechanism for social cohesion among the elite *alberghi* in fifteenth-century Genoa, there is no reason to believe that this mechanism was deliberate in the sense that everybody "pitched in" according to a well-organized partner-allocation process. Rather, the record shows that it could take weeks and sometimes even months for a merchant to assemble a syndicate willing to insure his goods.[58] This, however, was to be expected. In an unprofitable business, in which premiums did not fluctuate according to supply and demand but rather seemed to be set according to a series of fixed characteristics (destination, type of boat, etc.), merchants were often reluctant to provide coverage. No doubt some merchants received the premiums because they thought they could make a profit, but the pool of insurance capital they represented was not large enough to insure the whole community. It is thus among the pairing patterns of the more reluctant underwriters that we can learn why the insurance ties created a "denser than expected" core network of elite *alberghi*.[59] It is beyond doubt that the mercantile elite recognized the importance of maritime insurance as an institution that liberated risk capital. As such, in the ongoing process of negotiating relational ties, providing coverage to a

---

[58] See Doehaerd and Kerremans (1952) or Liagre De Sturler (1969).

[59] Before explaining why the insurance ties did not cumulate in a cluster of *families* instead of the cohesive elite network that the data analysis revealed, I will consider why the competing economic argument that explains the density of the core network by the strategically prudent diversification of insurance risk among multiple families is not valid. First, traveling risks were not associated with the identity of the policyholder but with the technical characteristics of the voyage. Spreading underwriting among many boats might make sense, but, knowing that each boat carried goods from various clans, spreading the risk among families did not reduce that risk. Second, each insurance commitment was for a period of several weeks, whereas the data covers a period of twenty-five years. Each commitment was thus an independent trial, and spreading risk around did not amount to financial diversification.

member of a fellow elite family would be viewed more as a duty or a favor than as a financial decision based on fiscal criteria.

It is difficult to evaluate the normative pressure that must have existed among the Genoese elite, as it does among all cohesive groups (Coleman 1988). It is possible that, as an underwriting syndicate was being formed, the participation of a clan member would liberate his fellow *alberghi* members from their responsibility while putting more pressure on members of other clans to participate.[60] Although norms and duties certainly played a role, I believe that another social process was also at work. Favors often lose their marginal reciprocal value when cumulated on a single alter. Indeed, although the size of a reciprocal favor is dependent on the size of the original favor, this is only one of the parameters.[61] Favors do, to some extent, escape quantification and have to be returned even when there is a discrepancy in the magnitude of the service; therefore, spreading underwriting business among many clans increased the size and the liquidity of a merchant's favor-bank. This could prove to be important if the underwriter needed coverage in the future, but the reciprocal favors probably extended beyond the insurance network. Looking back on the large insurance underwriting business of Giovanni Piccamiglio, the merchant discussed earlier in the chapter who was co-opted onto the board of San Giorgio and who obtained a preeminent political position, it is easy to believe that insurance favors could be deployed as political chips.

Underwriting decisions were not solely motivated by the immediate potential financial reward of the contract at hand. Even without speculating as to why merchants had a tendency to spread their business around, it remains that the interchanging role of the insured and the insurer in the context of the syndication of insurance policies explains how maritime insurance contracts bolstered the cohesion of the elite group. Even some historians who are attached to the rhetoric of market development based on price adjustment to relative supply and demand note that the insurance pairing process was laced with solidaristic meaning. For example, Tenenti (1985, p. 371) writes, "The occurrence of

---

[60] In addition, the reputation of a participant in the community is associated with the rate of diffusion of his actions, and, as a result, it is likely that those merchants who wanted to be perceived as "good citizens" might have had a tendency to spread their coverage.

[61] For example, imagine a colleague and a friend help you move. A year later, the colleague calls you because he is himself moving and needs help. Even if his house is twice as big as yours and you are the only one he asks for assistance, it would be most inappropriate to refuse to lend him a hand on that basis.

insurance practices was not, nor could it have been, reduced to a pure quantitative calculation, or a mechanism of contractual relationships." Likewise, Boiteux (1962, p. 453) notes that insurance consisted "in an act of solidarity that bounded the insurer and the underwriter into a real partnership." There is nothing to suggest that the Genoese insurance ties were the source of oligarchic control. They were simply one among the tools used to manage its operations.[62]

In this chapter, I have established that insurance ties were very dense among a set of core *alberghi*, who are better identified by network analysis than by the volume of their business. While insurance was a valuable innovation that freed up capital, the formal analysis of the underwriting pairing reveals that it also served to bind together core clans far more tightly than equity partnerships or credit networks did.

During the fifteenth century, the military might of the Genoese fleet, which had provided the city with a competitive advantage in long-distance trading for more than 300 years, was being supplanted by the rise of large nation-states' navies. With the loss of control of trading routes, commerce suffered.However, the now tighter core of elite families was well positioned for the sixteenth century's first wave of financial capitalism because raising funds and accessing liquidity were dependent on dense banking connections. It is, thus, no surprise that the Genoese enjoyed a revival in what Braudel (1996, pp. 433–46) called "le siècle des Génois," the period from 1560 to 1620 during which they dominated the European flow of financial resources. After that period, those who had previously replaced them in the control of long-distance routes – the Dutch and the English, in particular – caught on to the control of financial flow as well, and the Genoese were overmatched because, as is true in every capitalistic process, size became decisive.

---

[62] Mintz and Schwartz in their study of interlocking directorates (1985) assign a similar role to commercial ties in contemporary America.

# 6

# Conclusion

This study begins with an analysis of a charter from 958 – which leaves no doubt about the feudal character of Genoese social organization – and concludes with a graph theoretic bipartition of the fifteenth-century insurance network, one that identifies an oligarchic mercantile core of closely related mercantile families who may be considered to be in some way separate from the rest of the population. During the long period covered by the study (roughly the same amount of time as that which separates Christopher Columbus's discovery of America from the moon landing), western Europe underwent profound changes in its social organization and in the structure of economic exchange. These changes included the rise of the money economy and the use of nonland assets to generate capital in order to further extend business activities, both of which are now emblematic of the modern world.

This transformation is the central topic of the texts upon which the social sciences are founded. For Marx, it marks the rise of the objectification of social relationships; for Durkheim, the emergence of the division of labor and a shift in the structure of social solidarity; and for Weber, the birth of the mean rational culture. Researchers have devoted entire careers to commenting upon and contrasting the texts produced by these authors, and it is not my aim in this book to pile more work upon that existing body, nor do I wish to pass judgment upon these three great thinkers. So eminent are their theories, in fact, that, although some elements of each have clearly been shown to be misguided, I, like others whose vocation it is to study social relationships, could easily adopt Weber's contention that charismatic figures are the switchmen of history,

Durkheim's normative foundation of social relations, or Marx's focus on conflict over tools of productions as the motor of history.

This said, one goal of my research is to contribute to the theoretical framework of studies of epochal transitions by developing a temporal concept of institutions that explains the concatenation of history. Indeed, by using a continuous time series, I am able to show that the historical process that produced the mercantile social organization resulted from the interaction of, on one level, people who were continuously entering into relationships with each other and, on the other, the institutions that contained the constantly renegotiated rules of their encounters. Mercantile oligarchy was born from the social rewiring of the feudal network that occurred during the thirteenth and fourteenth centuries as commercial institutional dynamics provided a set of rules to organize the new social organization. Weakly linked clustered hierarchies were replaced by a social structure that separated a group of capital holders (core) from the rest of the population (periphery).

I set out to examine the foundations of Renaissance mercantile social organization by modeling commercial ties in medieval Genoa. To achieve my goal, I built a data set that records thousands of tangible relationships spanning three centuries, which I bring to bear on my analysis of the historical dynamic that transformed the feudal world of men-of-arms into a society of merchants.

A large proportion of the Genoese participated directly in the expansion of medieval trade that has been labeled the "Commercial Revolution." However, most were not initially "merchants" in the strictest sense; rather, they were a variety of people who saw overseas trade as an opportunity for profit. Among them, the seafaring feudal elite naturally deployed its control over public offices and its skill in war to control the Mediterranean commercial networks. In the first two chapters of this book I showed that Genoa benefited from the multivalence of its commercial operators, who, unlike those involved in the preexisting trade network, could draw on the financial capital and the military support of a whole polity to take advantage of the opportunistic nature of long-distance trading.

Unsurprisingly, the equity partnerships that organized the long-distance partnerships of the period were not regulated by a price mechanism, but rather by stable custom agreements that mirrored the social flexibility and limited temporal commitment of contemporary commercial relations. However, as trade increased throughout the thirteenth century, the quantitative change produced a qualitative transformation. As such, the data analysis confirms two key revolutionary principles of medieval equity partnerships. First, commercial partnerships escaped the integrated feudal social system. As a result, economic relationships could be organized for the purposes of business alone, creating the potential for a segregated economic sphere. Second, simply through the pooling of resources, increasingly large amounts of capital could be accumulated, thus initiating the open-ended process of capital accumulation and thereby sowing the seeds of capitalism, a compulsive system that exerted force over individuals regardless of their intentions and wishes.

I have also shown that the limited incidence of economies of scale in the early part of the commercial revolution could not be the main cause underlying capital concentration dynamics. Instead, the cumulative nature of the increasingly large quantities of disposable funds held by some individuals created a self-reinforcing accumulative process that fostered the social separation that divided capital holders from others. This book demonstrates that this divisive form of selection was associated with the social dynamics of the community as a whole.

In fact, toward the end of the thirteenth century, as vertical political contention emerged and trade volume peaked, the elite combined their formal status with their new financial strength to reorganize their control of the city through the routinized form of economic activity that gave rise to the Genoese merchant class. Around this time, within the partner selection pattern that I identified for temporary equity partnerships, there was a concomitant emergence of intra-status ties in response to the loss of the aristocrats' monopoly over the economy and a rise of "merchants" as a distinct occupational category in Genoa. The commenda, the classic equity partnership framework, with its temporary commitment and its fixed – non–market driven – profit allocation, declined. Previously, commendae had provided the perfect instrument for forming the heterogeneous social pairings that characterized the medieval commercial revolution. However, they made little sense under the increasingly homogeneous and connected commercial network of the Renaissance.

From then on, an increasingly well-defined oligarchy began to rely on a commercial repertoire to ensure its domination. Indeed, the records show that credit and insurance contracts, two key commercial instruments used by routinized traders of the fourteenth and fifteenth centuries, did not result directly in an increase in trade; rather, they 1) facilitated further concentration of capital, 2) marked the rise of commercial occupational categories, and 3) cemented oligarchic control. Thus, while the commenda induced social changes, and so could be said to have contained the seeds of its own demise, credit-based institutions and forms of insurance provided a framework for consolidating the social architecture of the time and, as a result, lasted longer.

The analysis in Chapter 4 demonstrated that credit instruments thrived, providing a robust framework for social exchange among the mercantile class. As a result, they helped to solidify the social categories of the time, which were moving away from the dichotomic status-based division that had characterized feudal relationships until that point. Similarly, in Chapter 5, I showed that the insurance network was laced with a solidaristic attitude that enhanced the cohesion of the oligarchic mercantile network. At the same time, the numerical and cumulative nature of commercial ties grew to be a currency for social exchange that facilitated the integration of merchants into homogeneous communities through joint commercial activity.

A consideration of insurance was a fitting way to conclude the book. Indeed, the emergence of third-party insurance signals both a strengthening and a weakening of the elite network. On one hand, the insurance network of the time appears to have been almost like a "club" – as the lack of competition, the relative uniformity of prices, the constant size of maximum individual exposure, and the lack of profitability do not point to a competitive market. In addition, unlike modern insurance underwriters, who use the aggregation of risk exposure to dampen the randomness of hazards, the Renaissance insurers spread the risk among themselves. On the other hand, the decrease in the proportion of commercial patronage and the increase in the interchangeability of the participants anticipated and prepared for the more anonymous nature of modern social relationships and a new form of elite competition.

In the course of my study, I have been careful to describe precisely the institutional framework that organized the rules of commercial encounters while systematically examining relational data. While doing so, I have asserted the social nature of commercial exchange, and thus challenged two well-ingrained Western-centric models of economic development.

First, the demonstration that social dynamics and institutional "life cycles" were closely associated, coupled with a detailed historical reading, challenges economic theories that assume that history is driven by transaction cost optimization and, therefore, take social changes for granted. Consider North's contention that institutional dynamics in the West brought about economically efficient institutions that simply "performed" better in the context of demographic expansion (1973, 1990). Implicit in this theory is the idea that private property and markets regulated by price mechanisms are "superior." There have been numerous critiques of North's model, the most obvious criticism being that his notion of individual choice is ahistorical in that it assumes a rational pursuit of wealth that is independent of social context. To date, however, objections and alternative readings of the institutional history of the medieval period have rarely posed a challenge to North's theory because they have not been based on the systematic examination of empirical evidence. This is one of the contributions of my research. Not only do the details of my historical examination expose the empirical inconsistency of North's theory; more crucially, my algebraic measurements confirm that it was not economic optimization that drove the dynamics of medieval economic institutions but instead changes in the partner-selection pattern that reflected the transformation of the structure of social ties. This is not to say that the rise of commercial institutions did not have an independent effect on medieval actors; however, it must be realized that history involves the continuous mutual shaping of, on the one hand, the interacting actors who continuously weave and reweave social structure and, on the other, the overarching formal institutions that give shape to this movement.

Second, my examination of real relational data from Genoa during the period in question contradicts the position of historians who state that the business strategies of merchants and their commercial innovations played the key role in Europe's medieval economic surge.[1] In fact, my research demonstrates that those who participated in the medieval trade expansion were often multivalent operators who took advantage of the opportunistic nature of trade to fulfill their expansionist ambitions. Price differences in space and time – accentuated by monopolies and inelastic demand and supply conditions – were such that commercial surplus eventually surpassed the land-based assets that had up until then granted economic control to the feudal elite. In Genoa, it was only during a period of economic consolidation that routinized traders were able to refine their commercial techniques and develop a repertoire of business tools that cemented the oligarchic elite.

---

[1] One reason for this selective memory is that the notion of rationality and business technique both legitimize economic theories that encourage the autoregulation of markets and therefore limit the role of the public authorities to that of a guardian of free trade and private property.

The classic historical narrative of the European strategic entrepreneur has survived so long for two reasons. First, the dearth of commercial records for the twelveth and thirteenth centuries has facilitated the tacit acceptance of the view that Renaissance merchants like Datini (1335–1410) are representative of earlier centuries as well. Second, social scientists often forward a calculative and strategic theory of action, as they are imprisoned in the restricted notion of rationality adopted by most economists and rational choice proponents in general. According to such thinking, actors are not rational if they do not adopt a preference for a behavior because its economic outcome has been calculated to be optimal. In reality, however, medieval Genoese traders were rational in that they purposely pursued their interest in the context of their social network positions. Because of a lack of information, the multivalence of their objectives, the intrinsic opportunistic nature of medieval commerce, and the extremely long duration of each venture, it was very often not possible either to know what, if any, alternative choices were available or to evaluate the consequence of possible choices. The issue at hand is not simply that medieval European traders lacked the technical expertise to devise and implement commercial strategies. Also key here is the fact that the structure of commerce did not warrant or reward calculating business acumen as such.

Clear evidence that the medieval traders did not make business decisions on the basis of calculative parameters is revealed in my analysis of the partner-selection pattern associated with three types of agreement. In all three cases, the selection-process dynamic was dictated not by financial prerogatives but by the historical transformation of the structure of social ties – a transformation in which commerce played a major role.

Capitalism is a peculiar system in that it relies on a self-reinforcing mechanism whereby individuals work to accumulate wealth solely in order to further increase their capital. However, this empty outlook on life was not followed by the long-distance operators of the twelveth and thirteenth centuries. For them, material wealth derived from commerce was not an end per se. Rather, it was either a means intended to advance a variety of interests within the feudal organization of the city, or simply a by-product of military operations engaged in while hunting Muslim pirates or participating in the ongoing Mediterranean wars. However, while medieval trade had little to do with price markets or capitalism, the cumulative nature and commensurability of money provided for a metric that was altogether different from the preexisting system of exchange and set in motion a competitive system in which accumulation was not a choice but rather the only option. The skilful operators were those who forged social relationships in the context of the market in order to avoid the fatal isolation inherent in capitalism.

Among those, the well-traveled Genoese aristocracy was best positioned to understand the conditions of the new playing field as they abandoned the secular factionalism for oligarchic mercantile control.

Conversely, however, for the rest of the population, the rise of capitalism marked the dissolution of the social bonds that had hitherto ensured the cohesion of their communities.

# Appendix A

*Sample of Prices and Income (in £)*

| | | |
|---|---|---|
| 1150–1225 income | Wages of oarsman (per sailing season) | 3–5 |
| | Wages of captain (per sailing season) | 10–12 |
| | Salary of governor of colonial territories (per year) | 75 |
| 1150–1225 prices | Price of a knight's horse | 10–25 |
| | *Canna* (approx. 2.5 meters) of common cotton cloth (fustian) | 0.10–0.20 |
| | *Canna* (approx. 2.5 meters) of English wool cloth (Stanford) | 1.50–2.00 |
| | Food for an adult for a year | 2.5 |
| | Price of large galley | 150–200 |

| | | |
|---|---|---|
| 1226–1300 income | Annual wages for servants (women) | 2–4 (+ food) |
| | Annual wages for wool workers | 12–18 |
| | Salary for mercenary on horse (per campaign) | 50 |
| 1226–1300 prices | Price of common cotton cloth (*canna* = approx. 2.5 meters) | 0.15–0.20 |
| | Price of English wool cloth (*canna* = approx. 2.5 meters) | 1.50–3.00 |
| | Price of a mule | 8.00–12.00 |
| | Price of a slave | 4–12 |
| | Price of wholesale wine ( 95 liters) | 0.2–0.4 |

| 1301–75 income | Annual income of notaries | 35–70 |
| | Pay of crossbowmen (*balistierii*) (2 months) | 5.5 |
| | Annual wages of city's scribes | 50 |
| 1301–75 prices | Bag of North African wool (150 kg) | 8–10 |
| | Price of a cuirass (*corellus*) | 10–15 |
| | Annual rent for apartments (*stallius*) in town center | 4–6 |
| | Price of a slave | 10–18 |
| | Price of knives (per dozen) | 1 |

| 1376–1450 income | Annual wages for justice's consul | 250 |
| | Wages of sailors (sailing season) | 15–18 |
| | Annual wages of mathematic teachers | 60–150 |
| 1376–1450 prices | Price of red English cloth (*canna* = approx. 2.5 meters) | 10–12 |
| | Annual rent for one andiron and two hammers | 4.5 |
| | Price of nails (1,000) | 25 |
| | Value of cargo of largest ships | 100–150,000 |
| | Price of a crossbow | 1–1.5 |

# Appendix B

## Sample of Long-Distance Trade Participants' Occupations, 1154–1400

| | | | |
|---|---|---|---|
| *acimator* | shearer | *capsiarus* | chest maker |
| *afaitator* | tanner | *carpentator* | carpenter |
| *baiolus* | messenger | *carzatorius* | carder |
| *balistarius* | crossbowman | *cirurgie* | surgeon |
| *bambaxarius* | cotton weaver | *clavonerius* | locksmith |
| *bancherius* | banker | *clericus* | scribe |
| *barberius* | barber | *conciapellius* | tanner |
| *barcharolius* | boat maker | *coquarius* | baker |
| *bastaxius* | carrier | *cordonanerius* | shoemaker |
| *baticularius* | bottle maker | *coriarius* | tanner |
| *battitor* | flax breaker | *corrigiarius* | belt maker |
| *beccuniere* | tanner | *cultellarius* | cutler |
| *boterius* | shoemaker | *draperius* | draper |
| *calafatus* | caulker | *ervarius* | tanner |
| *calderlarius* | chaudronniers | *faber* | blacksmith |
| *calegarius* | stocking maker | *ferrarius* | blacksmith |
| *caligarius* | boot maker | *filator* | spinner |
| *calzolarius* | shoemaker | *formaiarus* | cheese maker |
| *campanarius* | bell ringer | *fornarius* | baker |
| *campsor* | money changer | *galeotius* | sailor |
| *canabaserius* | rope maker | *guanterius* | glove maker |
| *canavarius* | butler | *iudex* | judge |
| *canonicus* | canon | *lanerius* | wool worker |
| *canzelerius* | chancellor | *lardarolus* | larder |

*(continued)*

Translations are mine; note that spelling varied not only over time but also from notary to notary.

*(continued)*

| | | | |
|---|---|---|---|
| *macelarius* | butcher | *scriba* | scribe |
| *magisteraxie* | carpenter | *scudarius* | shield maker |
| *magistri scolarum* | schoolteacher | *selarius* | saddle maker |
| *marescalcus* | stable man | *servante* | servant |
| *marinarius* | sailor | *spatarius* | mat maker |
| *medicus* | physician | *speziarius* | druggist |
| *mercerius* | mercer | *stationarius* | sacristan |
| *molinarius* | miller | *tabernarius* | innkeeper |
| *mulatius* | muleteer | *tairius* | pulley maker |
| *murarius* | mason | *taliator* | tailor |
| *ortolanus* | gardener | *testor* | weaver |
| *osbergerius* | armorer | *tinctor* | dyer |
| *panetarius* | baker | *tinctor endigi* | dyer (blue) |
| *peliparius* | pelter | *tinctor vermilii* | dyer (red) |
| *pellarius* | tanner | *tonditor* | sheep shearer |
| *piscator* | fisherman | *tornator* | potter |
| *placerius* | clerk | *victurale* | carrier |
| *platarolius* | silver worker | *vogherius* | sailor |
| *sartor* | tailor | *zocularius* | clog maker |

# Appendix C

## Commenda Network Graphs

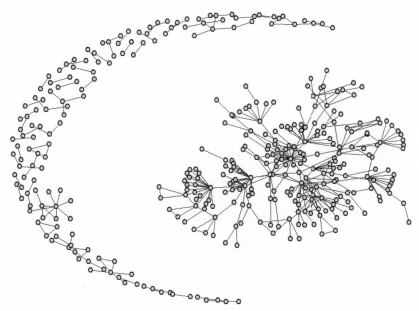

FIGURE C.I. Commenda network, 1154–64.

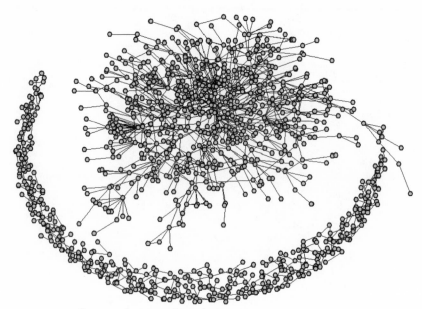

FIGURE C.2. Commenda network, 1182–97.

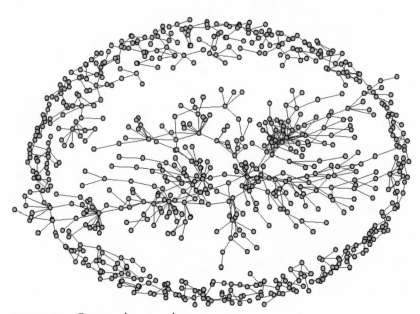

FIGURE C.3. Commenda network, 1215–39.

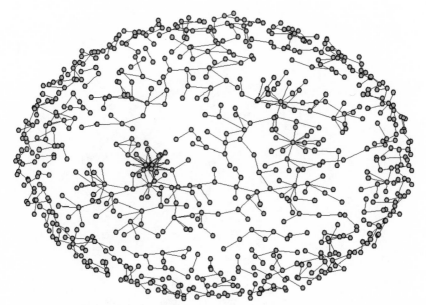

FIGURE C.4. Commenda network, 1245–68.

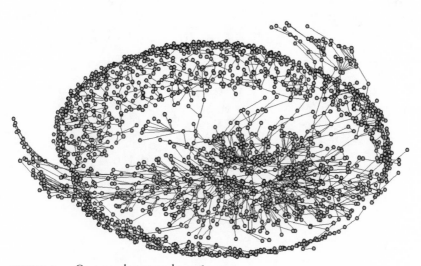

FIGURE C.5. Commenda network, 1269–95.

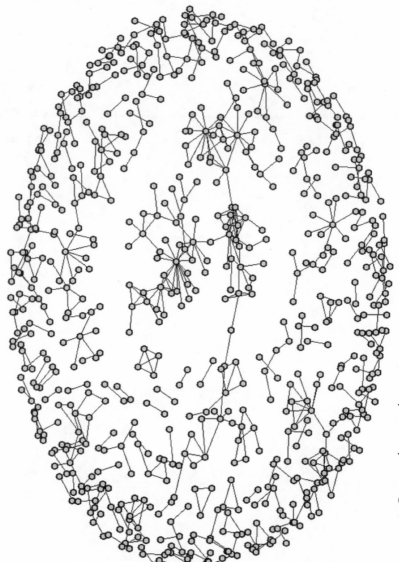

FIGURE C.6. Commenda network, 1296–1315.

# Appendix D

## *Nodal Degree Distributions of Commenda Networks, 1154–1315*

1154–64, n = 379

| Nodal degree | 1 | 2 | 3 | 4 | 5 | 6–7 | 8–9 | 10–13 | 14–19 | 20+ | Sum Nodal Degree |
|---|---|---|---|---|---|---|---|---|---|---|---|
| Frequency | 241 | 77 | 21 | 13 | 8 | 5 | 3 | 5 | 5 | 2 | 777 |

1182–97, n = 1073

| Nodal degree | 1 | 2 | 3 | 4 | 5 | 6–7 | 8–9 | 10–13 | 14–19 | 20+ | Sum Nodal Degree |
|---|---|---|---|---|---|---|---|---|---|---|---|
| Frequency | 578 | 229 | 94 | 63 | 30 | 39 | 21 | 11 | 5 | 5 | 2,462 |

1198–1215, n = 1,112

| Nodal degree | 1 | 2 | 3 | 4 | 5 | 6–7 | 8–9 | 10–13 | 14–19 | 20+ | Sum Nodal Degree |
|---|---|---|---|---|---|---|---|---|---|---|---|
| Frequency | 538 | 251 | 108 | 61 | 35 | 40 | 25 | 22 | 10 | 4 | 2,779 |

1216–39, n = 753

| Nodal degree | 1 | 2 | 3 | 4 | 5 | 6–7 | 8–9 | 10–13 | 14–19 | 20+ | Sum Nodal Degree |
|---|---|---|---|---|---|---|---|---|---|---|---|
| Frequency | 472 | 137 | 69 | 27 | 16 | 15 | 7 | 4 | 5 | 1 | 1,444 |

1245–68, n = 716

| Nodal degree | 1 | 2 | 3 | 4 | 5 | 6–7 | 8–9 | 10–13 | 14–19 | 20+ | Sum Nodal Degree |
|---|---|---|---|---|---|---|---|---|---|---|---|
| Frequency | 508 | 115 | 48 | 19 | 15 | 5 | 1 | 1 | 0 | 0 | 1,134 |

1269–95, n = 1,823

| Nodal degree | 1 | 2 | 3 | 4 | 5 | 6–7 | 8–9 | 10–13 | 14–19 | 20+ | Sum Nodal Degree |
|---|---|---|---|---|---|---|---|---|---|---|---|
| Frequency | 1,162 | 343 | 127 | 66 | 39 | 36 | 23 | 21 | 4 | 2 | 3,468 |

1296–1315, n = 723

| Nodal degree | 1 | 2 | 3 | 4 | 5 | 6–7 | 8–9 | 10–13 | 14–19 | 20+ | Sum Nodal Degree |
|---|---|---|---|---|---|---|---|---|---|---|---|
| Frequency | 414 | 175 | 66 | 23 | 16 | 19 | 4 | 4 | 2 | 0 | 1,366 |

# Appendix E

*List of Top Mercantile Nonaristocratic Families,*
*1375–1450*

| | | | |
|---|---|---|---|
| Adurnus | Bondinarius | Cassali | Faxanus |
| Albarus | Bonetus | Castilionus | Fornarius |
| Amicus | Bozzolus | Castro | Franchi |
| Anchona | Bracelis | Cavatorta | Gambarus |
| Andora | Branchaleonus | Cazanus | Ganducius |
| Archerius | Brazaforte | Ceraxia | Gavirotus |
| Ardimentus | Brignale | Cicerus | Ghisius |
| Bainonus | Calcinaria | Claparia | Goanus |
| Bargalius | Caligeparius | Clericus | Gradanus |
| Basadonus | Campanarius | Coronatus | Grassus |
| Becharius | Campofregossius | Corsus | Griffiotus |
| Bechignonus | Campora | Costa | Gropallus |
| Benedictus | Campus | Dernice | Groterius |
| Besognus | Cantellus | Dosius | Holedo |
| Bestagnus | Caparalia | Dragus | Illionus |
| Blancus | Carega | Drizacorne | Iudex |
| Boliochus | Carpina | Facius | Iustinianus |
| Bombel | Casanova | Fatimentus | Lasagna |

*(continued)*

I established the list by combining information about customs records of 1376–77 (Day 1963), the lists of the grand *consilio* of 1382 and 1396 and of the tax assessment of 1414 (Sieveking 1909, pp. 84–9). Establishing a list of the top commoner mercantile families is tricky. Criterion selection, spelling changes, and name absorption are among the pitfalls. However, by and large, the list (I kept the spellings as I found them in the document) constitutes a good approximation, and it should be used for gaining a sense of the occupational recruitment mechanism and not to try to corroborate specific historical details.

(*continued*)

| | | | |
|---|---|---|---|
| Leardus | Natonus | Porrus | Sermaneti |
| Levantus | Odericus | Premontorius | Spignanus |
| Longus | Oliverius | Recho | Stella |
| Marchus | Opizus | Rex | Symonotius |
| Marrufus | Paganus | Rodulffus | Tarigus |
| Marxacia | Palmairus | Rogoretus | Tomsus |
| Merlanus | Pasanus | Ruffoli | Tortorinus |
| Mignardus | Paterius | Sachus | Valletarius |
| Millanus | Pezagnus | Sancto Blaxius | Viali |
| Moanarius | Picacius | Sancto Systro | Vignosus |
| Monellia | Pichonus | Sanelli | Virmilia |
| Monleone | Pichus | Sarzanus | Voltagius |
| Montaldo | Pignatarius | Sauli | Zoalius |
| Monterubeus | Pinu | Scarampus | |
| Murchius | Pisanus | Semenza | |
| Murta | Podio | Senestrarus | |

# Appendix F

## *Partner Selection Probability Model*

This appendix describes the probability model and the test of the pairing selection of the insurance network's core.

*First step*: The calculation of each clan's probability distribution Pi (x) is a solution to the classic probability problem of getting a given allocation of colored tiles from repeated single draws from a bag full of colored tiles.[1] Obviously, the higher the number of tiles of a given color in the bag, the higher the probability that the color will be drawn. For the purpose of our test, imagine that each Genoese family is a color and that each of the tiles is an underwriting family tie in a given policy.[2] Thus the most active underwriting clans are more likely to be part of each family distribution of an insurance contact.

The "tiles-drawing probability" problem has a well-known mathematical solution. However, the theoretical solution is not easily operationable for such a large, diversified "bag" of underwriting as the one in our sample. Indeed, our bag contains 1,168 tiles (insurance ties) unequally distributed among 26 colors. Remember that for each clan, one needs to figure out the probability of having a given number of colors (families) for a given number of draws (number of policies contracted). This is why I decided to model the underwriting frequency distribution and to run Monte Carlo simulations to estimate each family's probability

---

[1] Note that I considered that each draw was an independent trial. In other words, I considered that the underwriting decision was independent of previous experience, which is a conservative assumption for the purposes of my demonstration.

[2] For each contract I coded all the intra-core family ties.

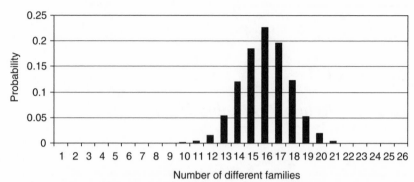

FIGURE F.1. Probability distribution of number of individual underwriting families for thirty insurance coverages.

of having the number of ties observed.[3] Thus, having entered the underwriting distribution by family for the whole insurance sample, I observed the frequency distribution of the number of different families in the underwriting pool for each merchant's family. For example, Figure F.1 reports the probability distribution of the number of different underwriting *alberghi* providing coverage for a fellow family when thirty different underwriting instances in the sample are counted. Thirty is the number of underwriting instances of the Pinnello *albergho,* which was, as such, tied to seventeen different *alberghi* in the data set. As the reader can see from Figure F.1, it looks like the probability of the Pinello being underwritten by exactly seventeen *alberghi* was a little less than 20%.

*Step 2.* Having repeated for each family the computation illustrated in step one and thus built twenty-six probability functions, I determined the "odds" y of a given family having entered into a number of underwriting ties equal or greater than the one counted from the data set.[4] Recall that

[3] I used the average value computed by two sets of 10,000 trials – and the corresponding error on pi (namely, $\{\sqrt{(\text{pi } (1 - \text{pi})/ \sqrt{N}\})}$.

[4] I defined $y_i = 1 - \{[\text{pi } (x_j \leq (c_i - 1)) + \text{pi } (x_j \leq c_i)]/2\}$, where $c_i$ denotes the observed cumulated frequency – that is, the number of families' insurance relationships for each i insured family To have an accurate measure of odds, we are looking for the proportion of the area under the curve of the distribution of odds $P_i (x_j)$ that is "left" of $c_i$. Since $P_i (x_j = c_i)$ is often large enough to skew the result, the linear interpolation ensures that a value of 0.5 indicates that the odds of having a lower number of underwriting families than that observed is equal to the odds of having a higher number, and thus that the number of underwriting alberghi observed is equal to the expected value given the probability distribution $P_i (x_i)$. Indeed, consider the hypothetical probability function $P(x)$ with $p(1) = 0.1, p(2) = 0.8, p(3) = 0.1$, and a merchant family underwritten by two fellow core *alberghi*. In this case, $P(x \geq 2) = 0.9$, which would indicate that the family is

TABLE F.I. *Insurance partner selection distribution*

| Policyholding[a] *Alberghi* | Number of Underwriting Instances | C = Number of Underwriting *Alberghi* | Odds Y |
|---|---|---|---|
| Calvo | 9 | 8 | 0.246 |
| Cattaneo | 76 | 19 | 0.833 |
| Centurioni | 33 | 15 | 0.157 |
| Cigala | 17 | 14 | 0.034 |
| Doria | 29 | 12 | 0.970 |
| Fornario | 72 | 23 | 0.108 |
| Fieschi | 3 | 3 | 0.416 |
| Franchi | 18 | 12 | 0.404 |
| Gentile | 34 | 18 | 0.157 |
| Giustiniani | 54 | 17 | 0.904 |
| Grillo | 51 | 21 | 0.121 |
| Grimaldi | 22 | 12 | 0.733 |
| Imperiale | 15 | 11 | 0.332 |
| Italiano | 26 | 13 | 0.766 |
| Lomellini | 27 | 15 | 0.396 |
| Mari | 16 | 12 | 0.230 |
| Maruffo | 11 | 10 | 0.094 |
| Negrono | 26 | 15 | 0.338 |
| Oliva | 22 | 14 | 0.282 |
| Pinello | 30 | 17 | 0.168 |
| Salvaigo | 12 | 6 | 0.986 |
| Spinola | 401 | 26 | 0.377 |
| Squarciafico | 60 | 19 | 0.712 |
| Usodimare | 11 | 8 | 0.614 |
| Vivaldi | 92 | 23 | 0.314 |

[a] The members of the Marini *albergho* are not sufficiently represented as policyholders in the sample to calculate meaningful odds.

the base line is randomly picked assuming the distribution of the pool of insurance underwriters. A value of 0.5 indicates that the odds of having a lower number of underwriting families than that observed is equal to the odds of having a higher number. In other words, the number of underwriting families is equal to the expected value given the probability

underwritten by a "low" number of *alberghi*. Equally misleading would be to use $P(x > 2) = 0.1$, which would indicate that the family is underwritten by a "high" number of *alberghi*. In reality, 2 is the expected value, and the odds $y = 0.5 = \{1 - [(01 + 0.9)/2]\}$ is the correct value to assess how (un)usual $c_i$ is: There is nothing "unusual" about our hypothetical merchant family being underwritten by members of two different *alberghi*. Note that $1 - \{[pi (x_j \leq (c_i - 1)) + pi (x_j \leq c_i)]/2\} = 1 - \{pi (x_j \leq (c_i - 1)) + (pi (x_j = c_i)/2)\}$.

distribution Pi (xi). In Table F.1, I provide a summary of key parameters of the insurance-ties distribution for the core network families to help the reader understand the procedure. In the second and third columns, I report the number of underwritings for each policyholder family and, in the next column, the number of different underwriting families. In the fourth column, I report the "odds" of getting a higher or equal value than that reported in column three. *Low* odds indicate that the policyholders were being insured by more than the expected number of families. For example, Table F.1 reports that merchants from the Fornario *albergho* were insured seventy-two times by members of twenty-three different *alberghi*. This is a high number of different counterparts, since the odds of having twenty-three or more different *alberghi* are only 0.108. On the other hand, *high* odds indicate that the observed number of underwriting *alberghi* is less than expected: The merchants of the Cattaneo *albergho* were insured seventy-six times by only nineteen different *alberghi*. This is a low number of counterparts because the odds of connecting with nineteen or more different insuring *alberghi* are 0.833.

*Step 3.* Looking at the value of odds (y), it is apparent that some *alberghi* had a higher diversity of counterparts than expected, while others had a lower diversity. Next, I determined whether the set of number Y of the odds y was different than the distribution of the odds of randomly picking a series of numbers uniformly distributed from 0 to 1.[5] I used the nonparametric Kolmogorov-Smirnov two-sample test for cumulative distributions and found that the cumulative distribution of odds of the number of underwriting *alberghi* S(y)[6] was statistically different[7] from the cumulative distribution of odds of a random sample of numbers of a uniform distribution (0,1) [denoted F(y)].[8] In Figure F.2, I report both cumulative distributions. It is clear from the graph that the surface of the odds of the observed frequencies (number of ties in sample) was lower that if randomly picked – in mathematical terms, $\int s(y)dy < \int f(y)dy$ – and thus that, as a whole, the odds of observing at least the

---

[5] The distribution of a random selection of numbers (from 1 to n) is a uniform distribution ($p(x) = 1/n$).

[6] S(y) is the empirical cumulative distribution function that specifies for each value of y the proportion of sample values less than or equal to y.

[7] ($p = 0.0695$); in other words, in 100 trials, if 25 numbers are picked at random from a uniform distribution (0,1), it is reasonable to expect that only about seven times the associated cumulative distribution will cut the sample cumulative distribution at $Dn = \max\{F(y)-Sn(y)\}$.

[8] F(y) is the cumulative distribution function of a random selection of numbers.

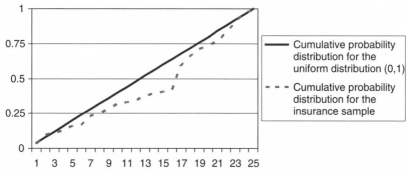

FIGURE F.2. Cumulative probability distribution for the insurance sample and for the uniform distribution (0,1).

number of ties per policyholding *albergho* were lower than would be expected had it been randomly allocated. Thus, I concluded that the data set indicates that insurance underwriting constituted a social mechanism that fostered more intra-elite family ties than a random pairing process would have suggested.

# Bibliography

## Primary Sources

Airaldi, Gabriella. 2002. *Gli annali di Caffaro: 1099–1163*. Genova: Fratelli Frilli.

Bach, Erik. 1955. "Oberto Scriba da Mercato 1182, 1183, 1184." In *La cité de Gênes au XIIème siècle*. Copenhagen: Gyldendalske boghandel.

Balard, Michel. Unpublished transcript of Genoese notarial records. References in Balard, Michel. 1978. *La Romanie Génoise: XIIème-début du XVème siècle*. Rome: École française de Rome.

Balletto, Laura. 1985. *Atti rogati a Ventimiglia da Giovanni di Amandolesio dal 1258 al 1264*. Bordighera: Istituto Internazionale di Studi Liguri.

Belgrano, Luigi (Ed.). 1868. *Il secondo registro della curia arcivescovile di Genova*. Genoa: Tipographia del istituto sordo-muti.

Belgrano, Luigi (Ed.). 1872. "Registrum Curiae Archiepiscolis Janua." *Atti della Società ligure di storia patria* 2. Genoa: Societa Ligura di Storia Patria.

Belgrano, Luigi, and Cesare Imperiale di Sant' Angelo. 1890–1929. "Annali genovesi di Caffaro e de'suoi continuatori dal 1174 al 1224." In *Annali genovesi di Caffaro e de'suoi continuatori*, vol. 2, edited by Luigi Belgrano and Cesare Imperiale di Sant' Angelo. Rome: Instituto sordo-muti.

Bratianu, George Ioan. 1929. *Recherches sur le commerce génois dans la mer Noire au XIIIe siècle*. Paris: P. Geuthner.

Chiaudano, Mario. 1925. *Contratti commerciali Genovesi del secolo XII, contributo alla Storia dell'accomendatio e della societas*. Turin: Fratelli bocca editori.

Chiaudano, Mario (Ed.). 1940. *Oberto Scriba de Mercato, 1186*. Turin: S. Lattes.

Chiaudano, Mario, and Mattia Moresco (Eds.). 1935. *Il cartolare di Giovanni Scriba*. Rome: S. Lattes.

Chiaudano, Mario, and R. M. della Rocca (Eds.). 1938. *Oberto Scriba de Mercato, 1190*. Turin: S. Lattes.

Chiaudano, Mario, and R. M. della Rocca (Eds.). 1940. *Oberto Scriba de Mercato, 1186*. Turin: S. Lattes.

Day, John. 1963. *Les douanes de Gênes, 1376–1377*. Paris: S.E.V.P.E.N.

Desimoni, Cornelio, and Luigi Belgrano (Eds.). 1854, 1857. *Liber Iurium Reipublicae Ianuensis*. Turin: August Taurinorum: Ex offisina Regina.

Doehaerd, Renée. 1941. *Les Relations commerciales entre Gênes, la Belgique et l'Outremont, d'après les archives notariales génoises aux XIIIème et XIVème siècles*: Brussels: Academica Belgica.

Doehaerd, Renée, and Charles Kerremans. 1952. *Les Relations commerciales entre Gênes, la Belgique et l'Outremont, d'après les archives notariales génoises, 1400–1440*. Brussels: Academica Belgica.

Eierman, Joyce E., Hilmar C. Krueger, and Robert L. Reynolds (Eds.). 1939. *Bonvillano*. Turin: S. Lattes.

Hall, Margaret, Hilmar C. Krueger, Renert G. Ruth, and Robert L. Reynolds (Eds.). 1938. *Guglielmo Cassinese*. Turin: S. Lattes.

Hall-Cole, Margaret, Hilmar C. Krueger, Ruth G. Renert, and Robert L. Reynolds (Eds.). 1939. *Giovanni di Guiberto*. Turin: S. Lattes.

Heers, Jacques. 1959. *Le livre de comptes de Giovanni Piccamiglio, homme d'affaires Génois, 1456–1459*. Paris: S.E.V.P.E.N.

Imperiale di Sant' Angelo, Cesare, and Genoa (Republic). 1936, 1938 and 1942. *Codice diplomatico della repubblica di Genova, I-III*. Rome: Tipografia del Senato.

Jarry, Eugene. 1896. *Documents diplomatiques et politiques. Les origines de la domination française à Gênes (1392–1402)*. Paris: A. Picard et fils.

Jehel, Georges. Unpublished transcripts of notarial records. Reference in Jehel, Georges. 1993. *Les Génois en Méditerranée occidentale (fin XIème – début XIVème siècle): ébauche d'une stratégie pour un empire*. Amiens: Centre d'histoire des sociétés Université de Picardie.

Krueger, Hilmar C., and Robert L. Reynolds (Eds.). 1951–53. *Lanfranco*. Genoa: Societa Ligure di Storia Patria.

Liagre-De Sturler, Leóne, and Archivio di Stato di Genova. 1969. *Les relations commerciales entre Gênes, la Belgique et l'Outremont, d'après les archives notariales génoises, 1320–1400*. Brussels, Rome: Institut historique belge de Rome Galerie Ravenstein 78, Academia Belgica.

Lopez, Robert S. 1953. "L'activitá economica di Genova nel Marzo 1253 secondo gli atti notarili del tempo." *ASLI* 54: 163–270.

Lopez, Robert S., Irving Woodworth, and Olivia Remie Constable. 2001. *Medieval trade in the Mediterranean world: Illustrative documents*. New York: Columbia University Press.

Mas Lattrie, (de), L. 1866. Traités de paix et de commerce concernant les relations des chrétiens avec les Arabes de l'Afrique septentrionale au Moyen Age. 2 vols. Paris: J. Baur.

Tucci, Raffaele di. 1933. *La nave e i contratti marittimi. La banca privata : studi sull'economia genovese del secolo decimosecondo*. Turin: Fratelli Bocca.

Tucci, Raffaele di. 1934. "Nuovi documenti e notizie sul genovese Antonio Malfante, il primo viaggiatore europeo nell' Africa occidentale, 1447." Bologne: Licinio Cappelli.

Tucci, Raffaele di. 1935. "Documenti inediti sulla spedizione e sulla mahona dei Genovesi a Ceuta 1234–37." *ASLI* 64: 273–342.

## Secondary Works2

Abulafia, David. 1977. *The two Italies: Economic relations between the Norman kingdom of Sicily and the northern communes*. Cambridge: Cambridge University Press.

Abu-Lughod, Janet L. 1989. *Before European hegemony*. Oxford: Oxford University Press.

Adler, Nathan M. 1906. *The Itinerary of Benjamin of Tuleda*. London: Adler.

Adler, Paul S. 2001. "Market, hierachy and trust: The knowledge economy and the future of capitalism." *Organizational Science* 12: 215–34.

Agosto, Aldo. 1981. "Nobili e popolari: L'origine del dogato." In *La Storia dei genovesi*. Genova: Atti del Covegno di studi sui certi dirigenti nelle istituzioni della repubblica di Genova; Genova: Centro internazionale sui certi dirigenti nelle istituzioni della repubblica di Genova.

Airaldi, Gabriella. 1986. "Genova e la Liguria nel medioevo." In *Communi e signorie nell'Italia settentrionale: il Piemonte e la Liguria*, edited by Anna Maria N. D. Patrone and Gabriella Airaldi. Genoa: Utet.

Airaldi, Gabriella. 1997. "The Genoese art of warfare." In *Across the mediterranean frontiers: Trade, politics and religions, 650–1450*, edited by Dionisius A Agius and Ian R. Netton. Turnhout: Brepols.

Airaldi, Gabriella. 2004. *Guerrieri e mercanti : storie del Medioevo genovese*. Racconigi (Cuneo): N. Aragno.

Angelos, Mark. 1994. "Women in Genoese commenda contracts, 1155–1216." *Journal of Medieval History* 20: 299–312.

Archer, Melanie. 1991. "Family enterprise in an industrial city: Strategies for the family organization of business in Detroit, 1880." *Social Science History* 15: 67–95.

Argenti, Philip P. 1958. *The occupation of Chios by the Genoese and their administration of the island, 1346–1566*. Cambridge: Cambridge University Press.

Ashtor, Eliyadu. 1969. *Histoire des prix et des salaires dans l'Orient médieval*. Paris: S.E.V.P.E.N.

Ashtor, Eliyadu. 1976. "Observations on Venetian trade in the Levant in the XIV century." *Journal of Economic History* 5: 533–86.

Ashtor, Eliyadu. 1986a. *East-West trade in the medieval Mediterranean*. Edited by Benjamin Z. Kedar. London: Variorum Reprints.

Ashtor, Eliyadu. 1986b. "Il ruolo del regno di Gerusalemme nel commercio di levante." In *I communi Italiani nel regno crociato di Gerusalemme: atti del colloqio "The Italian Commune in the crusading Kingdom of Jerusalem" (Jerusalem, May 28, 1984)*, edited by Gabriella Airaldi and B. Z. Kedar. Genoa: Universita di Genova.

Astuti, Guido. 1933. "Origini e svolgimento storico della commenda fino al secolo XIII." *Documenti e studi per la storia del commercio e del diritto commerciale Italiano* 3.

Bach, Erik. 1955. *La cité de Gênes au XIIème siècle*. Copenhagen: Gyldendalske Boghandel.

Balard, Michel. 1978. *La Romanie Génoise: XIIème-début du XVème siècle.* Rome: École française de Rome.

Balard, Michel. 1986. "Les transports maritimes Génois vers la terre sainte." In *I communi Italiani nel regno crociato di Gerusalemme: atti del colloqio "The Italian Commune in the crusading Kingdom of Jerusalem"(Jerusalem, May 28, 1984),* edited by Gabriella Airaldi and Benjamin Z. Kedar. Genoa: Universita di Genova.

Balard, Michel. 2001a. *Croisades et orient Latin (XIème-XIVème siècles).* Paris: Armand Colin.

Balard, Michel. 2001b. "Notes sur le commerce entre l'Italie et l'Egypte sous les Fatimides." In *Les Relations des pays d'Islam avec le monde Latin,* edited by Francoise Micheau. Marseille: Edition Jacques.

Balletto, Laura. 1983. *Genova nel Duecento: uomini nel porto e uomini sul mare.* Genoa: Università di Genova Istituto di medievistica.

Barkey, Karen, and Ronan Van Rossen. 1997. "Network of contention: Village and regional structure in the seventeenth century Ottoman empire." *American Journal of Sociology* 102: 1345–82.

Bautier, Robert-Henri. 1985. "Les marchands et banquiers de Plaisance dans l'economie internationale du XIIe au XVe siècles." In *Il "Registrum Magnum" del commune di Piacenza: Atti del covegno internazionale di studio (Piacenza, 1985).* Piacenza: Cassa di Risparmio di Piacenza.

Bearman, Peter. 1991. "Desertion as localism: Army unit and group norms in the U.S. civil war." *Social Force* 70: 321–42.

Bearman, Peter. 1993. *Relations into rhetorics: Local elite social structure in Norfolk England, 1540–1640.* New Brunswick, N.J.: Rutgers University Press.

Bearman, Peter, Robert Faris, and James Moody. 1999. "Blocking the future: New solutions for old problems in historical social science." *Social Science History* 23: 501–33.

Bearman, Peter, James Moody, and Katherine Stovel. 2004. "Chains of affection: The structure of adolescent romantic and sexual networks." *The American Journal of Sociology* 110 (1): 44–91.

Belgrano, Luigi. 1866. "L'interesse del denaro." *Archivio Storico Italiano* 2: 103–22.

Belshaw, Cyril S. 1965. *Traditional exchange and modern markets.* New Jersey: Prentice-Hall.

Belvederi, Raffaele. 1974. *Genova, la Liguria e l'oltremare tra Medioevo ed età moderna: studi e ricerche d'archivio.* Genoa: Fratelli Bozz.

Bensa, Enrico. 1897. *Histoire du contrat d'assurance au Moyen Age.* Paris: A. Fon Temoing.

Bertolotto, Gerolamo. 1896. "Nuova serie di documenti sulle relazioni di Genova coll'impero Bizantino." *ASLI* 28: 339–573.

Bezbakh, Pierre. 1983. *La société féodo-marchande.* Paris: Editions Anthropos.

Birdzell, Luther E., and Nathan Rosenberg. 1986. *How the West grew rich.* New York: Basic Books.

Birnbaum, Allan. 1952. "Numerical tabulation of the distribution of Kolmogorov's statistic for finite sample size." *American Statistical Association Journal* 47: 425–41.

Blau, Peter. 1964. *Exchange and power in social life.* New York: Wiley.

Bloch, Marc. 1953. *The historian's craft.* New York: Knopf.

Bloch, Marc. 1961. *Feudal society.* Chicago: Chicago University Press.

Bloch, Marc. 1964. "Le salaire et les fluctuations historiques." In *Mélanges Historiques.* Paris: S.E.V.P.E.N.

Blomquist, Thomas W. 1971. "Commercial associations in thiteenth-century Lucca." *Business History Reviews* 45: 157–78.

Blummenkrantz, Bernhard. 1960. *Juifs et Chrétiens dans le monde occidental 430–1096.* Paris: Mouton.

Boiteux, Louis A. 1962. "Contribution de l'assurance à l'histoire de l'économie en France." In *Les sources de l'histoire maritime en Europe, du Moyen Age au XVIIIème siècle; Actes du Quatrieme Colloque international d'histoire maritime, tenu à Paris du 20 au 23 mai 1959, présentés par Michel Mollat, avec la collaboration de Paul Adam, Marc Benoist et Marc Perrichet.* Paris: S.E.V.P.E.N.

Boiteux, Louis A. 1968. *La fortune de mer, le besoin de securité et les débuts de l'assurance maritime.* Paris: S.E.V.P.E.N.

Bonacich, Philipp. 1987. "Power and centrality: A family of measures." *American Journal of Sociology* 92: 1170–82.

Bonds, William Noonan. 1968. "Money and price in medieval Genoa (1155–1255)." Unpublished Ph.D. dissertation, University of Wisconsin at Madison.

Borgatti, Stephen, and Martin Everett. 1999. "Models of core/periphery structures." *Social Networks* 21: 375–95.

Boyd, John, William Fitzgerald, and Robert Beck. 2006. "Computing core/periphery structures and permutation tests for social relations data." *Social Networks* 28: 165–78.

Bragadin, Marco Antonio. 1955. *Histoire des républiques maritimes Italiennes: Venise, Amalfi, Pise, Gênes.* Paris: Payot.

Braudel, Fernand. 1949. *La Méditerranée et le monde Méditerranéen à l'époque de Philippe II.* Paris: A. Colin.

Braudel, Fernand. 1967. *Civilisation matérielle et capitalisme, XVème-XVIIIème siècles.* Paris: A. Colin.

Braudel, Fernand. 1992. *The wheels of commerce.* Berkeley: University of California Press.

Braudel, Fernand. 1995. *A history of civilizations.* London: Penguin.

Braudel, Fernand. 1996. *Autour de la Méditerranée.* Edition établie et présentée par Roselyne de Ayala et Paule Braudel. Paris: de Falois.

Brautein, Philippe. 1997. "Pour une histoire des élites urbaines: Vocabulaire, réalites et representation." In *Les Elites Urbaines au Moyen Age.* Rome: Publication de la Sorbonne.

Bullough, Vern. 1961. "Status and medieval medicine." *Journal of Health and Human Behavior* 2: 204–10.

Bullough, Vern. 1969. *The development of medicine as a profession: The contribution of the medieval university to modern medicine.* Basel and New York: S. Karger.

Buongiorno, Mario. 1973. *Il bilancio di uno stato medievale, Genova 1340–1529.* Genova: s.n.

Burt, Ronald S. 1992. *Structural holes: The social structure of competition.* Cambridge, Mass.: Harvard University Press.

Byrne, Eugene H. 1916. "Commercial contracts of the Genoese in the Syrian trade of the twelth century." *Quarterly Journal of Economics* 31: 128–70.

Byrne, Eugene H. 1918. "Easterners in Genoa." *American Oriental Society* 38: 176–87.

Byrne, Eugene H. 1920. "Genoese trade with Syria in the twelfth century." *American Historical Review* 25: 191–219.

Byrne, Eugene H. 1930. *Genoese shipping in the twelfth and thirteenth centuries.* Cambridge, Mass.: The Mediaeval Academy of America.

Cahen, Claude. 1965. "Quelques problèmes concernant l'expansion." In *L'occidente e l'islam nell'alto medioevo,* edited by Settimane di studio del centro Italiano di studi sull'alto medioevo. Spolleto: Presso la Sede del Centro.

Canale, Michel-Giuseppe. 1860. *Nuova istoria della repubblica di genova del suo commercio e della sua letteratura dalla origini all'anno 1797.* Firenze: Felice le Monnier.

Caro, Georg. 1895. *Genua und die Mächte am Mittelmeer 1257–1311: Ein Beitrag zur Gechichte des XIII. Jarhunderts.* Halle A.S.: M. Niemeyer.

Carruthers, Bruce G., and Wendy Espeland. 1991. "Accounting for rationality: Double entry bookkeeping and the rhetoric of economic rationality." *American Journal of Sociology* 91: 31–96.

Cattaneo Mallone di Novi, Cesare. 1987. *I "politici" del medioevo genovese (ricerche d'archivio): il Liber civilitatis del 1528.* Genoa: Copy-Lito.

Chandler, Tertius. 1987. *Four thousand years of urban growth and historical census.* Lewiston/Queenston: St David's University Press.

Chandler, Tertius, and Gerald Fox. 1974. *3000 years of urban growth.* London and New York: Academic Press.

Cipolla, Carlo. 1948. *I movimenti dei cambi in Italia dal secolo XIII al XV.* Pavia: A. Garzanti.

Cipolla, Carlo. 1993. *Before the industrial revolution.* London: Routledge.

Citarella, Armando O. 1968. "Patterns in medieval trade: The commerce of Amalfi before the crusades." *Journal of Economic History* 28: 531–55.

Citarella, Armando O. 1971. "A puzzling question concerning the relation between the Jewish communities of Christian Europe and those represented in the Geniza Documents." *Journal of the American Oriental Society* 91: 390–7.

Citarella, Armando O. 1993. "Merchants, markets and merchandise in southern Italy in the high Middle Ages." In *Settimane di studio del centro Italiano di studi sull' alto medioevo.* Spoleto: Presse la Sede dee Centro.

Clanchy, M. T. 1979. *From memory to written record.* London: Edward Arnold.

Claude, Dietrich. 1985. *Der Handel in westlichen Mittelmeer wahrend des Fruhmittelalters.* Akademie der Wissenshaft im Göttingen 144.

Coleman, James S. 1988. "Social capital in the creation of human capital." *American Journal of Sociology* 94: 95–120.

Contamine, Philippe. 1993. *L'économie médievale.* Paris: Armand Colin.

Costamagna, Giorgio. 1970. *Il notaio a Genova tra prestigio e potere.* Rome: Consiglio nazionale del notariato.

Dahl, Gunnar. 1998. *Trade, trust, and network: Commercial culture in late medieval Italy*. Lund, Sweden: Nordic Academic Press.

Danto, Arthur D. 1985. *Narration and knowledge*. New York: Columbia University Press.

Daston, Lorraine. 1988. *Classical probability in the enlightment*. Princeton, N.J.: Princeton University Press.

Day, Gerald W. 1988. *Genoa's response to Byzantium, 1155–1204: Commercial expansion and factionalism in a medieval city*. Urbana: University of Illinois Press.

Day, John. 1958. "I conti privati della famiglia Adorno (1402–1408)." *Miscellanea di Storia Ligure, Genoa* 9: 45–57.

Day, John. 1987. *The medieval market economy*. Oxford and New York: Blackwell.

de Roover, Raymond. 1953. *L'évolution de la lettre de change, XIV-XVIII èmes siècles*. Paris: S.E.V.P.E.N.

de Roover, Raymond. 1954. "New interpretation of the history of banking." *Journal of World History* 2: 1–43.

de Roover, Raymond. 1969. "The cambium maritimum contract according to the Genoese notarial records of the twelfth and thirteenth centuries." In *Economy, society and government in medieval City*, edited by David Herlihy, Roberto S. Lopez, and Vassily Slessarev. Kent, Ohio: Kent State University Press.

Del Treppo, Mario. 1957. "Assicurazioni e commercio a Barcellona nel 1428–1429." *Rivista Storica Italiana* 69: 508–41.

Del Treppo, Mario. 1972. *I mercanti catalani e l'espansione della corona d'Aragona nel secolo XV*. Napoli: Arte tip.

Del Treppo, Mario. 1994. *Sistema di rapporti ed elites economiche in Europa: secoli XII-XVII / a cura di Mario Del Treppo*. Pisa: GISEM; Napoli: Liguori.

Delort, Robert. 1966. "Précisions sur le commerce des esclaves à Gênes." *Mélanges d'archéologie et d'histoire de l'école Francaise de Rome* 7: 215–250.

Delumeau, Jean. 1985. "Exploitation d'un dossier d'assurances maritimes du XVIIème siècle." In *Ports, navires et négociants à Dunkerque*, edited by Christian Pfister-Langanay. Dunkerque: Centre National de la Recherche Scientifique.

Desrosières, Alain. 1993. *La politique des grands nombres: Histoire de la raison statistique*. Paris: Editions La Découverte.

Devisse, Jean. 1972. "Routes de commerce et échange en Afrique occidentale en relation avec la Méditerranée." *Revue d'Histoire Economique et Sociale* 50: 357–97.

Dewey, Alice G. 1962. *Peasant marketing in Java*. New York: Free Press of Glencoe.

Dobb, Maurice M. A. 1947. *Studies in the development of capitalism*. New York: International Publishers.

Doehaerd, Renée. 1938. "Les galères Gènoises dans la Manche et la mer Mer du Nord à la fin du XIIIème siècle et au début du XIVème siècle." *Bulletin de l'Insititut Historique Belge de Rome* 19: 5–76.

Doehaerd, Renée. 1949. "Chiffres d'assurances à Gênes en 1427–1428." *Revue Belge de Philologie et d'Histoire* 27: 736–56.

Doehaerd, Renée. 1976. "Féodalité et commerce XIème-XVème siècles." In *La noblesse au Moyen Age, XIème-XVème siècles*, edited by Philippe Contamine. Paris: Presse universitaire de France.

Doehaerd, Renée. 1978. *The early Middle Ages in the West: Economy and society*. Amsterdam: North-Holland.

Dotson, John E. 1994. "Safety regulations for galleys in mid-fourteenth century Genoa: Some thoughts on medieval risk management." *Journal of Medieval History* 20: 327–36.

Dubois, Henri. 1990. "Crédit et banque en France aux deux derniers siècles du Moyen Age." *ASLI* 31: 753–79.

Durkheim, Emile. 1915. *The elementary forms of religious life*. London: Allen Unwin.

Durkheim, Emile. 1964. *The division of labor in society*. New York: Glencoe.

Durkheim, Emile. 1979. *Suicide: A study in sociology*. New York: Free Press.

Edler-de Roover, Florence. 1934. *Glossary of medieval terms of business*. Cambridge: Mediaeval Academy of America.

Edler-de Roover, Florence. 1940. "The business records of an early Genoese notary, 1190–92." *Bulletin of the Business Historical Society* 14: 41–6.

Edler-de Roover, Florence. 1941. "Partnership account in the twelfth century Genoa." *Bulletin of the Business Historical Society* 15: 87–92.

Edler-de Roover, Florence. 1945. "Early examples of marine insurance." *Journal of Economic History* 5: 172–200.

Emery, Richard W. 1952. "The use of the surname in the study of medieval economic history." *Medievalia et Humanistica* 7: 43–50.

Emigh, Rebecca. 2002. "Numeracy or enumeration?" *Social Science History* 26: 653–98.

Epstein, Stephan R. 2000a. *Freedom and growth: The rise of states and markets in Europe, 1300–1750*. New York: Routledge.

Epstein, Stephan R. 2000b. "The rise and fall of Italian city-states." In *A comparative study of thirty city-state cultures*, edited by Mogens Hansen. Copenhagen: The Royal Danish Academy of Sciences and Letters.

Epstein, Steven A. 1984. *Wills and wealth in medieval Genoa, 1150–1250*. Cambridge, Mass.: Harvard University Press.

Epstein, Steven A. 1988. "Labour in thirteenth-century Genoa." In *Mediterranean cities: Historical perspectives*, edited by Irad Malkin and Robert L. Hohlfelder. London; Totowa, N.J.: Frank Cass.

Epstein, Steven A. 1991. *Wage labor and guilds in medieval Europe*. Chapel Hill and London: University of North Carolina Press.

Epstein, Steven A. 1994. "Secrecy and Genoese commercial practices." *Journal of Medieval History* 20: 313–25.

Epstein, Steven A. 1996. *Genoa and the Genoese, 958–1528*. Chapel Hill: University of North Carolina Press.

Erikson, Emily, and Peter Bearman. 2006. "Malfeasance and the foundations for global trade: The Structure of English trade in the East Indies, 1601–1833." *American Journal of Sociology* 112(1): 195–230.

Espeland, Wendy, and Michael Stevens. 1998. "Commensuration as a social process." *Annual Review of Sociology*: 313–43.

Espinas, Georges, and Henri, Pirenne. 1909. *Recueil de documents relatifs à l'histoire de l'industrie drapière en Flandre. p. 1, Des origines à l'époque bourguignonne T., 2, Deynze – Hulst*. Brussels: Comission Royale d'histoire.

Face, Richard. 1969. "Thirteenth century man of affairs, Symon de Gualterio." In *Economy, Society and Government in Medieval City*, edited by David Herlihy, Roberto S. Lopez, and Vsevolod Slessarev. Kent, Ohio: Kent State University Press.

Favier, Jean. 1998. *Gold and spices: The rise of commerce in the Middle Ages*. New York: Holmes & Meier.

Forcheri, Giovanni. 1974a. "La societa populi nelle costituzioni Genovesi del 1363 e del 1413." In *Ricerche di archivio e studi storici in onore di Giorgio Costamagna*. Rome: Centro di Ricerca Editore.

Forcheri, Giovanni. 1974b. *Navi e navigazione a Genova nel Trecento: il Liber Gazarie*. Genoa: s.n.

Formentini, Ubaldo. 1941. *Genova nel basso impero e nell' alto medioevo*. Milan: Garzani.

Fransson, Gustav. 1935. *Middle English surnames of occupation, 1100–1300, with an excursus on toponymical surnames*. Lund: C.W.K.Gleerup.

Freeman, Linton C. 1979. "Centrality in social networks: A conceptual clarification." *Social Networks* 1: 215–39.

Ganshof, Francois Louis. 1957. "Note sur le praeceptum negotiarorum de Louis le Pieux." In *Studi in onore di A. Sapori*. Milan: Instituto Editoriale Cisalpino.

Ganshof, Francois Louis. 1964. "A propos du tonlieu à l'époque carolingienne." In *L'occidente e l'Islam nell'alto medioevo*. Spoleto: Presso la Sede del Centro.

Geertz, Clifford. 1979. "Suq: The bazaar economy in Sefrou." In *Meaning and order in Marocaan society*, edited by C. Geertz, H. Geertz, and L. Rosen. New York: Cambridge University Press.

Gies, Joseph, and Frances Gies. 1972. *Merchants and moneymen: The commercial revolution, 1000–1500*. New York: Crowell.

Gil, Moshe. 2004. *Jews in Islamic countries in the Middle Ages*. Leiden and Boston: Brill.

Ginzburg, Carlo. 1980. *The cheese and the worms: The cosmos of a sixteenth-century miller*. Baltimore: Johns Hopkins University Press.

Gioffree, Domenico. 1966. "Il debito publico Genovese." *ASLI* 80.

Giordano, Maddalena, and Marco Pozza. 2000. *I trattati con Genova, 1136–1251*. Rome: Viella.

Glamman, Kristof. 1958. *Dutch-Asiatic Trade, 1620–1740*. Copenhagen and The Hague: Danish Science Press.

Gobel, Barbara. 1998. "Risk, uncertainity, and economic exchange." In *Kinship, network, and exchange*, edited by Thomas Sweitzer and Douglas White. Cambridge: Cambridge University Press.

Goitein, Shelomo. 1967. *A Mediterranean society: The Jewish communities of the Arab world as portrayed in the documents of the Cairo Geniza*. Berkeley: University of California Press.

Goldthwaite, R. 1993. *Wealth and the demand for art in Italy, 1300–1600.* Baltimore: Johns Hopkins University Press.

Goody, Jack. 1996. *East in the West.* Cambridge: Cambridge University Press.

Gorrini, Giacomo. 1931. "L'instruzione elementare in Genova e Liguria durante il Medioevo." *Giornale Storico e Letterario della Liguria* 1: 265–85.

Gould, Roger V. 1991. "Multiple networks and mobilization in the Paris Commune, 1871." *American Sociological Review* 56: 716–29.

Gould, Roger V. 1995. *Insurgent identities: Class, community, and protest in Paris from 1848 to the Commune.* Chicago: University of Chicago Press.

Gould, Roger V. 2003a. *Collision of wills: How ambiguity about social rank breeds conflict.* Chicago and London: University of Chicago Press.

Gould, Roger V. 2003b. "Uses of network tools in comparative historical research." In *Comparative historical analysis in the social sciences,* edited by James Mahoney and Dietrich Rueschemeyer. Cambridge: Cambridge University Press.

Gourdin, Philippe. 1995. "Présence Génoise en Méditerranée et en Europe du nord au milieu du XVème siècle: L'implantation des hommes d'affaires d'après un registre douanier de 1445." In *Coloniser au Moyen Age,* edited by Michel Balard and Alain Ducelier. Paris: A. Colin.

Gower, John C., and Pierre Legendre. 1986. "Metric and Eucledean properties of dissimilarity coefficients." *Journal of Classification* 3: 5–48.

Granovetter, Mark. 1985. "Economic action and social structure: The problem of embeddedness." *American Journal of Sociology* 91(3): 481–510.

Greif, Avner. 1989. "Reputation and coalition in medieval trade: Evidence on the Magrhibi trader." *Journal of Economic History* 49: 889–904.

Greif, Avner. 1994. "Cultural beliefs and the organization of society: A historical and theoretical reflection on collectivist and individualist societies." *Journal of Political Economy* 102: 912–50.

Greif, Avner. 1998. "Self-enforcing political systems and economic growth: Late Medieval Genoa." In *Analytic narratives,* edited by Robert H. Bates et al. Princeton, N.J.: Princeton University Press.

Greif, Avner. 2006. *Institutions and the path to the modern economy: Lessons from medieval trade.* Cambridge and New York: Cambridge University Press.

Grendi, Edoardo. 1974. "Capitazioni e nobilita a Genova." *Quaderni Storicici* 26: 403–44.

Grendi, Edoardo. 1987. *La repubblica aristocratica dei genovesi: politica, caritá e commercio fra Cinque e Seicento.* Bologna: Il Mulino.

Grierson, Philipp. 1959. "Commerce in the dark ages: A critique of the evidence." *Transactions of the Royal Historical Society,* 5th series 9: 123–40.

Groneuer, Hannelore. 1976. "Die Seeversicherung in Genua am Ausgang des 14. Jahrhunderts." In *Beitrage zur Wirtschafts-und-Sozialgeschichte des Mittelalters. Festschrift fur Herbert Helbig zum 65. Geburstag.* Vienna: Colonia.

Grossi Bianchi, Luciano, and Ennio Poleggi. 1979. *Una città portuale del Medioevo: Genova nei secoli X-XVI.* Genoa: Sagep.

Guseva, Alya, and Akos Rona-Tas. 2001. "Uncertainty, risk, and trust: Russian and American credit card markets compared." *American Sociological Review* 66: 623–46.

Hall-Cole, Margaret. 1935. "Early bankers in the genoese notarial records." *The Economic History Review* 6: 73–9.

Hall-Cole, Margaret. 1938. "The investment in wealth in thirteenth-century Genoa." *The Economic History Review* 8(2): 185–7.

Have, O. ten. 1986. *The history of accountancy*. Palo Alto, Calif.: Bay Books.

Havighurst, Alfred, P. 1958. *The Pirenne thesis, analysis, criticism and revision*. Boston: Heath.

Heers, Jacques. 1959a. "Le prix de l'assurance martime au Moyen Age." *Revue d'Histoire Economique et Sociale* 37: 6–19.

Heers, Jacques. 1959b. *Les livres de comptes de Giovanni Piccamiglio homme d'affaires Génois, 1456–59*. Paris: S.E.V.P.E.N.

Heers, Jacques. 1961. *Gênes au XVème siècle, activité économique et problèmes sociaux*. Paris: S.E.V.P.E.N.

Heers, Jacques. 1962. "Urbanisme et structure sociale à Gênes au Moyen Age." In *Studi in onore de A. Fanfani*. Milan: T.I.

Heers, Jacques. 1971. *Gênes au XVème siècle; civilisation méditerranéenne, grand capitalisme, et capitalisme populaire*. Paris: Flammarion.

Heers, Jacques. 1974. "The feudal economy and capitalism: Words, ideas and reality." *Journal of European Economic History* 3(3):609–674.

Heers, Jacques. 1977. *Family clans in the Middle Ages: A study of political and social structures in urban areas*. Amsterdam and New York: North-Holland.

Heers, Jacques. 1979. *Société et économie à Gênes, XIVème-XVème siècles*. London: Variorum Reprints.

Heers, Jacques. 1989. "Origines et structures des companies coloniales génoises (XIII-XVèmes siècle)." In *Etat et colonisation au Moyen Age et á la Renaissance*, edited by Michel Balard. Lyon: La Manufacture.

Herlihy, David. 1958. *Pisa in the early Renaissance: A study of urban growth*. New Haven, Conn.: Yale University Press.

Herlihy, David. 1967. *Medieval and renaissance Pistoia: The social history of an Italian Town, 1200–1450*. New Haven, Conn.: Yale University Press.

Herlihy, David. 1969. "Family solidarity in Medieval Italian history." In *Economy, Society, and Government in Medieval City*, edited by David Herlihy, Roberto S. Lopez, and Vassily Slessarev. Kent, Ohio: Kent State University Press.

Herlihy, David. 1990. *Opera mulebria: Women and work in medieval Europe*. Philadelphia: Temple University Press.

Heyd, Wiliem. 1886. *Histoire du commerce du levant au Moyen Age*. Paris: Société de l'Orient Latin.

Hobson, John M. 2004. *The eastern origins of Western civilization*. Cambridge: Cambridge University Press.

Hocquet, Jean-Claude. 1997. "Solidarités familiales et solidarités marchandes à Venise au XIVème siècle." In *Les élites urbaines au Moyen Age*, edited by XXVII ème congrès de la S. H. M. E. S. Paris: Publication de la Sorbonne.

Hoffman, Phillip T., Jean-Laurent Rosenthal, and Gilles Postel-Vinay. 2000. *Priceless markets: The political economy of credits in Paris 1660–1870*. Chicago: University of Chicago Press.

Holton, Robert J. 1985. *The transition from feudalism to capitalism*. New York: St. Martin's Press.

Hoover, Calvin B. 1926. "The sea loan in Genoa in the twelfth century." *The Quarterly Journal of Economics* 40 (3): 495–529.

Howell, Martha C. 1986. *Women, production, and patriarchy in late medieval cities.* Chicago: University of Chicago Press.

Hughes, Diane. 1975. "Urban growth and family structure in medieval Genoa." *Past and Present* 66: 3–28.

Hughes, Diane. 1977. "Kinsmen and neighbors in medieval Genoa." In *The Medieval City*, edited by Harry Miskimin, David Herlihy, and Abraham Udovitch. New Haven, Conn.: Yale University Press.

Hughes, Diane. 2004. "Domestic ideals and social behavior: Evidence from medieval Genoa." in *Medieval families*, edited by Carol Neel. Toronto: University of Toronto Press.

Hunt, Edwin S. 1994. *The Medieval super-companies: A study of the Peruzzi company of Florence.* Cambridge and New York: Cambridge University Press.

Hyde, John K. 1973. *Society and politics in Medieval Italy: The evolution of the civil life, 1000–1350.* New York: Macmillan.

Imperiale di Sant' Angelo, Cesare. 2004. *Caffaro e suoi tempi.* Genova: Fratelli Frili.

Ingram, Paul, and Arik Lifschitz. 2006. "Kinship in the shadow of the corporation: The interbuilder network in Clyde River shipbuilding, 1711–1990." *American Sociological Review*, 71: 334–52.

Jacoby, David. 2001. "Les Italiens en Egypte aux XIIème et XIIIème siècles: Du comptoir à la colonie?" In *Les Relations des pays d'Islam avec le monde Latin*, edited by Francoise Micheau. Marseille: Editions Jacques.

Jehel, Georges. 1975. "Le role des femmes et du milieu familiale à Gênes dans les activités commerciales au cours de la première moitié du XIIIème siècle." *Revue d'Histoire Economique et Sociale* 53: 193–205.

Jehel, Georges. 1993a. "Education, apprentissages, initiation au Moyen Age." In *Premier colloque international de Montpellier*, edited by Centre de recherche interdisciplinaire sur la societé et l'imaginaire au Moyen Age. *Crisma* 1: 174–90.

Jehel, Georges. 1993b. *Les Génois en Méditerranée occidentale (fin XIème – début XIVème siècle): ébauche d'une stratégie pour un empire.* Amiens: Centre d'histoire des sociétés Université de Picardie.

Jehel, Georges. 1994. "Le marché immobilier Génois XIIème-XIVème siècle." In *Villes et societés urbaines au Moyen Age.* Paris: Presses de l'Université de Paris-Sorbonne.

Jehel, Georges. 1995. "Expéditions navales ou croisade? L'activité militaro-diplomatique de Gênes dans l'Occident méditerranéen, Xème-XIVème." In *Coloniser au Moyen Age.* Paris: Colin.

Jehel, Georges. 1998. "Ad fortunam et risicum maris et gentium, ou la perception de l'univers marin au Moyen Age en Méditerranée." In *La Méditerranée médiévale, perception et représentation.* Sfax: Faculté des Lettres et Sciences humaines de l'Université de Sfax.

Jehel, Georges, and Simone Jehel (Eds.). 2000. *Les relations des pays d'islam avec le monde latin du Xème au milieu du XIIIème siècle, textes réunis et présentés par G. et S. Jehel.* Paris: Edition du Temps.

Kaeuper, Richard W. 1973. *Bankers to the crown: The Riccardi of Lucca and Edward I*. Princeton, N.J.: Princeton University Press.

Kedar, Benjamin Z. 1973. "Toponomic surnames and evidence of origin: Some medieval views." *Viator* 4: 123–30.

Kedar, Benjamin Z. 1976. *Merchants in crisis: Genoese and Venetian men of affairs and the fourteenth-century depression*. New Haven, Conn.: Yale University Press.

Kennedy, Hugh. 1985. "From polis to madina: Urban change in late antique and early Islamic Syria." *Past and Present* 106: 3–27.

Kent, Francis W. 1977. *Household and lineage in Renaissance Florence*. Princeton, N.J.: Princeton University Press.

Knight, Frank. 1921. *Risk, Uncertainty and profit*. Boston: Houghton Miffllin.

Kowalewski, David. 1991. "Core intervention and periphery revolution, 1821–1985." *American Journal of Sociology* 97: 70–95.

Krackhardt, David. 1990. "Assessing the political landscape: Structure, cognition, and power in organizations." *Administrative Sciences Quartely* 35: 342–69.

Krueger, Hilmar C. 1933. "Genoese trade with north west Africa." *Speculum* 8: 57–71.

Krueger, Hilmar C. 1962. "Genoese merchants, their associations and investments, 1155–1230." In *Studi in onore di A. Fanfani*. Milan: T.I.

Krueger, Hilmar C. 1985. *Navi e proprietà navale a Genova: seconda metà del sec. XII*. Genova: Società Ligure di Storia Patria.

Krueger, Hilmar C. 1993. "The Genoese traveling merchant in the 12th century." *Journal of European Economic History* 22(2):251–83.

Lachmann, Richard. 2000. *Capitalists in spite of themselves: Elite conflict and economic transitions in early modern Europe*. New York and Oxford: Oxford University Press.

Lachmann, Richard. 2003. "Elite self-interest and economic decline in early modern Europe." *American Sociological Review* 68: 346–72.

Landa, Janet T. 1994. *Trust, ethnicity, and identity: Beyond the new institutional economics of ethnic trading networks, contract law, and gift-exchange*. Ann Arbor: University of Michigan Press.

Lane, Frederic C. 1944a. *Andrea Barbarigo*. Baltimore: Johns Hopkins University Press.

Lane, Frederic C. 1944b. "Family partnership and joint venture in the Venitian republic." *Journal of Economic History* 4: 178–96.

Lane, Frederic C. 1963. "The economic meaning of the invention of the compass." *American Historical Review* 68: 605–17.

Lane, Frederic C. 1969. "Investment and usury." In *Social and economic foundations of the Italian Renaissance*, edited by Anthony Molho. New York: John Wiley & Sons.

Lane, Frederic C. 1973. *Venice: A maritime republic*. Baltimore: Johns Hopkins University Press.

Larner, John. 1980. *Italy in the age of Dante and Petrach, 1216–1380*. London and New York: Longman.

Laumann, Edward, and Frantz Pappi. 1976. *Networks of collective action: A perspective on community influence systems*. New York: Academic Press.

le Goff, Jacques. 1980. *Marchands et banquiers du Moyen Age*. Paris: Presses universitaires de France.

le Goff, Jacques. 1999. *Un autre Moyen Age*. Paris: Gallimard.

Le Roy Ladurie, Emmanuel. 1975. *Montaillou, village occitan de 1294 à 1324*. Paris: Gallimard.

Lebecq, Stéphane. 1983. *Marchands et navigateurs Frisons du haut Moyen Age*. Lille: Presses Universitaires de Lille.

Leifer, Eric. 1985. "Markets as mechanisms: Using role structure." *Social Forces* 64: 442–72.

Leifer, Eric. 1988. "Interaction preludes to role setting: Explanatory local action." *American Sociological Review* 53: 865–78.

Leoncini, Marieiia. 1966. "Maestri di scuola a Genova sulla fine del secolo XIV." In *Miscellanea di Storia Ligure in memoria di Georgio Falco*. Genoa: Feltrimelli.

Lestocquoy, Jacques. 1947. "The tenth century." *The Economic History Review* 17: 1–14.

Lestocquoy, Jacques. 1952. *Aux origines de la bourgeoisie: Les villes de Flandre et d'Italie sous le gouvernement des patricians (XIème-XVème siècles)*. Paris: Presse Universitaire de France.

Lewis, Archibald R. 1951. *Naval power and trade in the Mediterranean, A. D. 500–1100*. Princeton, N.J.: Princeton University Press.

Lieber, Alfred E. 1968. "Eastern business practices and medieval commerce." *The Economic History Review* 21: 230–43.

Lodolini, Armando. 1967. *Le Republiche del mare*. Rome: Biblioteca di Storia Patria.

Lombard, Maurice. 1947. "Les bases monétaires d'une suprématie économique. L'or musulman du VIIème et IXème siècles." *Annales, Economies-Societes-Civilisations* 2(2) : 143–60.

Lombard, Maurice. 1948. "Mahomet et Charlemagne, le probleme économique." *Annales, Economies-Societes-Civilisations* 3(2): 188–99.

Lombard, Maurice. 1972. *Espaces et réseaux du haut Moyen Age*. Paris: Mouton.

Lopez, Robert S. 1933. *Genova marinara nel duecento. Benedetto Zaccaria, ammiraglio e mercante*. Messina and Milano: G. Principato.

Lopez, Robert S. 1936. *Studi sull'economia genovese nel medio evo*. Turin: S. Lattes.

Lopez, Robert S. 1937. "Aux origines du capitalisme Génois." *Annales d'Histoire Eeconomique et sociale* 9: 429–54.

Lopez, Robert S. 1938. *Storia delle colonie genovesi nel Mediterraneo*. Bologna: Nicola Zanichelli.

Lopez, Robert S. 1942. "The life of the Genoese woolworkers as revealed in the thirteenth-century notarial records." *Bulletin of the Business Historical Society* 16: 101–5.

Lopez, Robert S. 1953. "An aristocracy of money in the early middle ages." *Speculum* 28: 1–43.

Lopez, Robert S. 1954. "Concerning surnames and places of origin." *Medievalia et Humanistica* 8: 6–16.

Lopez, Robert S. 1964. "Market expansion: The case of Genoa." *Journal of Economic History* 24(4): 445–64.

Lopez, Robert S. 1975. *Su e giù per la storia di Genova*. Genoa: Università di Genova. Istituto di paleografia e storia medievale.

Lopez, Robert S. 1979. "The dawn of medieval banking." In *The dawn of modern banking*. New Haven and London: Yale University Press.

Lopez, Robert S. and Harry Miskimin. 1962. "The economic depression of the Renaissance." *The Economic History Review* 14: 408–26.

Lot, Ferdinand. 1945. *Recherches sur la population et la superficie des cités remontant a la période gallo-romaine*. Paris: E. Champion.

Lunardi, Guiseppe. 1975. *Le monete della repubblica di Genova*. Genoa: Di Stetano.

Luzzatto, Gino. 1961a. *An economic history of Italy from the fall of the Roman empire to the beginning of the sixteenth century*. New York: Barnes & Noble.

Luzzatto, Gino. 1961b. *Storia economica di Venizia dall'XI al XVI secolo*. Venice: Centro Internationale delle Artie del Costume.

Manfroni, Camillo. 1899. *Storia della Marina*. Livourno: Academia Navale.

Mannucci, Francisco. 1910. "Delle societa Genovesi d'arti e mestieri durante il secolo XIII." *Giornale Storico e Letterario della Liguria* VI.

Markovsky, Barry, and Edward Lawler. 1994. "A new theory of social solidarity." In *Advances in group process*, edited by Barry Markovsky, J. O'Brien, and K. Heimer. Greenwich, Conn.: JAI Press.

Marsdsen, Peter V. 1981. "Models and methods for characterizing the structural parameters of groups." *Social Forces* 3: 1–27.

Marx, Karl. 1963. *The 18th Brumaire of Louis Bonaparte*. New York: International Publisher.

McCormick, Michael. 2001. *Origins of European economy*. Cambridge: Cambridge University Press.

McLean, G. A. 1938. *Insurance up through the ages*. Louisville, Ky.: Dunne Press.

McMillan, John, and Christopher Woodruff. 1999. "Interfirm relationships and informal credit in Vietnam." *The Quarterly Journal of Economics*: 1285–1320.

Melis, Federigo. 1950. *Storia della ragioneria*. Bologna: C. Zutti.

Melis, Federigo. 1965. *I primi secoli delle assicurazioni (secoli xiii-xiv)*. Rome: Istituto Nazionale delle Assiacrazioni.

Melis, Federigo. 1975. *Origini e sviluppi delle assicurazioni in Italia (secoli XIV-XVI)/ con introduzione di Bruno Dini*. Rome: Istituto nazionale delle assicurazioni.

Michaelsson, Karl. 1927. *Etudes sur les noms de personne Françaises d'après les rôles de taille Parisiens*. Uppsala: Almqvist & Wilsells Bobtryckeri.

Millett, Paul. 1983. "Maritime loans and the structure of credit in fourth-century Athens." In *Trade in the ancient economy*, edited by Peter Garney, Keith Hopkins, and C. R. Whittaker. London: Chatto & Windus.

Mintz, Beth, and Michael Schwartz. 1981. "Interlocking directorates and interest group formation." *American Sociological Review* 46: 851–68.

Mintz, Beth, and Michael Schwartz. 1985. *The power structure of American business*. Chicago: University of Chicago Press.

Miskimin, Harry A., David Herlihy, Abraham L. Udovitch, and Robert Sabatino Lopez. 1977. *The Medieval City*. New Haven, Conn.: Yale University Press.

Mizruchi, Mark. 1990. "Cohesion, structural equivalence, and similarity of behavior: An approach to the study of corporate political power." *Sociological Theory* 8: 16–32.

Molho, Anthony. 1971. *Florentine public finances in the early Renaissance, 1400–1433*. Cambridge, Mass.: Harvard University Press.

Moody, James, and Douglas White. 2003. "Structural cohesion and embeddedness: A hierarchical concept of social groups." *American Sociological Review* 68: 103–27.

Mundy, John H., and Peter Riesenberg. 1958. *The medieval town*. Princeton:Van Nostrand.

Murray, James M. 2005. *Bruges, cradle of capitalism, 1280–1390*. Cambridge: Cambridge University Press.

Musso, Gian Giacomo. 1975. *Navigazione e commercio genovese con il Levante nei documenti dell'Archivio di Stato di Genova (Secc. XIV-XV)*. Rome: s.n.

Nelson, Benjamin N. 1949. "Blancardo (the Jew?) of Genoa and the restitution of usury in medieval Italy." In *Studi in onore di Gino Luzzatto*. Milan: A. Giuffrée.

North, Douglass C. 1981. *Structure and change in economic history*. New York: Norton.

North, Douglass C. 1990. *Institutions, institutitonal change, and economic performance*. Cambridge and New York: Cambridge University Press.

North, Douglass C., and Paul Robert Thomas. 1973. *The rise of the western world*. Cambridge: Cambridge University Press.

Olivieri, Agostino. 1971. *Serie dei consoli del comune di Genova*. Bologna: Forni.

Origo, Iris. 1986. *The merchant of Prato, Francesco di Marco Datini, 1335–1410*. Boston: D. R. Godino.

Ortalli, Gherardo, and Dino Puncuh. 2001. *Genova, Venezia, il Levante nei secoli XII-XIV: atti del convegno internazionale di studi, Genova-Venezia, 10–14 marzo 2000*. Genoa, Venice: Società ligure di storia patria; Istituto veneto di scienze lettere ed arti.

Padgett, John. 1990. "Plea bargaining and prohibition in the federal courts: 1908-1934." *Law and society review* 24(2): 413–50.

Padgett, John. 2001. "Organizational genesis, identity and control: The transformation of banking in Renaissance Florence." In *Networks and markets*, edited by James E. Rauch and Alessandra Cassela. New York: Russell Sage.

Padgett, John, and Christofer Ansell. 1993. "Robust action and the rise of the Medici, 1400-1434." *American Journal of Sociology* 98(6): 1259–1319.

Padovan, Gino. 1941. "Capitale e lavoro nel commercio Veneziano dei secoli XI e XIIe." *Rivista di storia economica* 6: 51–65.

Pavoni, Romeo. 1983. "Signorie feudali tra Genova e Savona nei secoli XII e XIII." In *Atti del IV convegno sui ceti dirigenti della Repubblica di Genova*. Genova: Centro internazionale sui certe dirigenti nelle istituzioni della repubblica di Genova.

Pavoni, Romeo. 1988. "Aristocrazia e ceti dirigenti nel commune consolare." In *La storia dei genovesi, VIII vol. degli atti del convegno di studi sui certi dirigenti nelle istituzioni della repubblica di Genova, Genova 10–11–12.* Genova: Centro internazionale sui certe dirigenti nelle istituzioni della repubblica di Genova.

Pavoni, Romeo, and Università di Genova. Istituto di medievistica. 1992. *Liguria medievale.* Genoa: Ecig.

Petti Balbi, Giovanna. 1976. *Genova e Corsica nel Trecento.* Rome: Nella sede dell'istituto storico italiano per il medioevo.

Petti Balbi, Giovanna. 1980. "Apprendisti e artigiani a Genova nel 1257." *ASLI:* 137–70.

Petti Balbi, Giovanna. 1991. *Simon Boccanegra e la Genova dell '300.* Genoa: Marietti.

Petti Balbi, Giovanna. 1997. "Magnati e popolani in area Ligure." In *Magnati e popolani nell' Italia communale; Quindicesimo convegno di studi.* Pistoia: Centro Italiano Studi di Storia e d'Arte.

Pirenne, Henri. 1914. *Les périodes de l'histoire sociale du capitalisme.* Brussels: Hayez Imp. de l'Académie royale de Belgique.

Pirenne, Henri. 1938. "Marchands du palais et marchands d'abbayes." *Revue Historique* 183: 281–97.

Pirenne, Henri. 1939. "Villes, marchés et marchands au Moyen Age." in *Les villes et les institutions urbaines.* Paris-Brussels: Librairies Felix Alcan.

Pirenne, Henri. 1987. *Mahomet et Charlemagne: Byzance, Islam et Occident dans le haut Moyen Age.* Milan: Jaca Book.

Pistarino, Geo. 1978. "La donna d'affari a Genova del secolo XIII." In *Miscellanea di storia Italiana e Mediterranea per Nino Lamboglia.* Genoa: [s.n.].

Pistarino, Geo. 1986. "Genova e il vicino oriente nell'epoca del regno latino di Gerusalemme." In *Communi Italiani nel regno crociato di Gerusalemme: atti del colloqio "The Italian Commune in the crusading Kingdom of Jerusalem" (Jerusalem, May 28, 1984),* edited by Gabriella Airaldi and B. Z. Kedar. Genoa: Universita di Genoa.

Pistarino, Geo. 1992. *I segnori del mare.* Genoa: Civico Istituto Colombiano.

Pistarino, Geo. 1993. *La capitale del Mediterraneo: Genova nel Medioevo.* Bordighera: Istituto internazionale di studi liguri.

Plesner, Johan. 1934. *L'immigration de la campagne à la ville libre de Florence au XIIIème siècle.* Copenhagen: Gyldendal.

Polanyi, Karl. 1957. *Trade and market in the early empires: Economies in history and theory.* Glencoe, Ill.: Free Press.

Poldolny, Joel, and Karen Page. 1998. "Network forms of organization." *Annual Review of Sociology* 24: 57–76.

Poleggi, Emilio (Ed.). 1989. *Citta portuali del Mediterraneo: Storia e archeologia: Atti del covegno internazionale di Genova 1985.* Genoa. Sagep.

Poliakov, Leon. 1965. *Les juifs et le saint siége.* Paris: S.E.V.P.E.N.

Poovey, Mary. 1997. *A history of the modern fact.* Chicago: University of Chicago Press.

Postan, Michael M. 1927–28. "Credit in medieval trade." *Economic History Review* 1: 234–61.

Pounds, Norman J. 1974. *An economic history of medieval Europe.* London: Longman.

Powell, Walter. 1990. "Neither market nor hierarchy: Network forms of organization." In *Research in organizational behavior*, edited by L. Cummings and B. Staw. Greenwich, Conn.: JAI Press.

Powell, Walter W., and Paul J. Dimaggio. 1991. *The new institutionalism in organizational analysis*. Chicago: University of Chicago Press.

Pryor, John. 1977. "The origins of the commanda contract." *Speculum* 51(4): 5–37.

Pryor, John. 1983. "Mediterranean commerce in the Middle Ages: A voyage under contract of commanda." *Viator* 14: 133–94.

Pugh, Ralph. 1968. "Some medieval moneylenders." *Speculum* 43: 274–89.

Racine, Pierre. 1979. *Plaisance du Xème à la fin du XIIIème siècle: Essai d'histoire urbaine*. Lille: Université de Lille.

Raggio, Osvaldo. 1990. *Faide e parentele: lo stato genovese visto dalla Fontanabuona*. Turin: G. Einaudi.

Renouard, Yves. 1950. *Les hommes d'affaires Italiens au Moyen Age*. Paris: Armand Copin.

Reyerson, Kathryn L. 1986. "Women in business in medieval Montpellier." In *Women and work in preindustrial Europe*, edited by Barbara Hanawalt. Bloomington: Indianna University Press.

Reynolds, Robert L. 1929. "The market for northern textiles in Genoa, 1179–1200." *Revue Belge de Philologie et d'Histoire* 8: 831–851.

Reynolds, Robert. 1930. "Merchants of Arras and the overland trade with Genoa in the 12th century." *Revue Belge de Philologie et d'Histoire* 9: 493–533.

Reynolds, Robert. 1931. "Genoese trade in the late twelfth century, particularly in cloth from the fairs of champagne." *Journal of Economic and Business History* 3: 362–381.

Reynolds, Robert. 1938. "Gli studi americani sulla storia Genovese." *Giornale Storico e Letteraio della Liguria* 14: 1–24.

Reynolds, Robert. 1945. "In search of a business class in thirteenth-century Genoa." *The Journal of Economic History* Supp.(5): 1–19.

Robinson, Maxime. 1970. "Le marchand Musulman." In *Islam and the trade of Asia*, edited by D. S. Richards: Oxford: Bruno Cassirer; Philadelphia: University of Pennsylvania Press.

Rosenfeld, Rachel. 1992. "Job mobility and career processes." *Annual Review of Sociology* 18: 39–61.

Roth, Cecil. 1950. "Genoese Jews in the XIIth century." *Speculum* 25(2): 189–97.

Sabbe, Eric. 1934. "Quelques types de marchands des IXème et Xème siècles." *Revue Belge de Philologie et d'Histoire* 13: 176–87.

Sabbe, Eric. 1935. "L'importation des tissus orientaux en Europe occidentale au haut Moyen Age." *Revue Belge de Philologie et d'Histoire* 14: 811–48.

Sapori, Armando. 1952. *Le marchand Italien au Moyen Age; conférences et bibliographie*. Paris: A. Colin.

Savage-Smith, Emile. 1992. "Celestial mapping." In *History of cartography, II*, edited by J. Brian Harley and David Woodward. Chicago: University of Chicago Press.

Sayous, Andre, E. 1930. "La monnaie de Gênes aux XIIème et XIIIème siècles." *Annales, Economies-Societes-Civilisations* 2: 266–287.

Sayous, Andre, E. 1931. "Les mandats de Saint Louis sur son trésor et le mouvement international des capitaux pendant la VIIème croisade 1248–1254." *Revue Historique* 168: 254–304.

Sayous, Andre, E. 1936. "Les banquiers Génois de la fin du XIIème siècle." *Annales d'histoire economique et sociale* 8: 52–72.

Sayous, Andre, E. 1937. "Aristocratie et noblesse." *Annales, Economies-Societes-Civilisations* 46: 366–81.

Schaube, Adolf. 1906. *Handelsgeschichte der Romanischen Volker des Mittelmeergebiets bis zum Ende der Kreuzzuge.* Munchen: Oldenbourg.

Scorza, Angelo M. G. 1973. *Le famiglie nobili genovesi.* Bologna: A. Forni.

Sestan, Ernesto. 1960. "La citta comunale Italiana dei secoli XI-XIII nelle sue note caratteristiche rispetto al movimento comunale Europeo." In *Rapports du XI congrès international des sciences historiques.* Stockholm-Goteborg-Upsala: Almaquist & Wiksell.

Sieveking, Heinrich Johann. 1898. *Genueser Finanzwesen mit besonderer Berücksichtigung der Casa di S. Giorgio.* Freiburg i. B. etc.: J. C. B. Mohr.

Sieveking, Heinrich Johann. 1906. "Studio sulle finanze genovesi nel medioevo." *ASLSP* 35, vol. 2.

Sieveking, Heinrich Johann. 1909. "Aus Genueser Rechnungs-Steurbuchern." In *Sitzungberichte der Kais, Akademie der Wissenshaften in Wien.* Wien: Alfred Holder.

Simmel, Georg. 1971. *On individuality and social forms: Selected writings.* Chicago: University of Chicago Press.

Simon, Robert. 1989. *Meccan trade and Islam: Problems of origin and structure.* Budapest: Akademiai Kiado.

Slessarev, Vsevolod. 1967. "I cosidetti orientali nela Genoa del medioevo." *ASLI* 7: 39–85.

Slessarev, Vsevolod. 1969. "The pound value of Genoa's maritime trade in 1161." In *Economy, society and government in medieval City,* edited by David Herlihy, Roberto S. Lopez, and Vassily Slessarev. Kent, Ohio: Kent State University Press.

Slichter Van Bath, Bernard H. 1965. "The economic and social conditions in the Frisian districts from 900 to 1500." *AAG Bijdragen* 13: 97–133.

Sombart, Werner. 1902. *Der moderne Kapitalismus.* Leipzig: Duncker & Humblot.

Spufford, Peter. 1986. *Handbook of medieval exchange.* London: Bordell & Brewer.

Spufford, Peter. 2002. *Power and profit: The merchant in medieval Europe.* New York: Thames & Hudson.

Stark, David. 1996. "Recombinant property in east European capitalism." *American Journal of Sociology* 101: 993–1027.

Stark, David. 2001. "Ambiguous assets for uncertain environments: Heterarchy in postsocialist firms." In *The twenty-first century firm: Changing economic organization in international perspective,* edited by Paul J. Dimaggio. Princeton, N.J.: Princeton University Press.

Stefani, Guiseppe. 1958. *Insurance in Venice from the origins to the end of the serenissima.* Trieste: Assicurazioni generali di Trieste e Venezia.

Stiglitz, Joseph. 2000. "The contribution of the economics of information to twentieth century economics." *Quarterly Journal of Economics* 67: 76–90.

Stöckly, Doris. 1995. *Le systeme de l'incanto des galées du marché à Venise (fin XIIIème- milieu XVème siècle).* New York: E. J. Brill.

Surdich, Francesco. 1970. *Genova e Venezia fra Tre e Quattrocento.* Genova: Fratelli Bozzi.

Tabacco, Giovanni. 1989. *The struggle for power in medieval Italy: Structure of political life.* Cambridge and New York: Cambridge University Press.

Tenenti, Alberto. 1985. *Il prezzo del rischio: l'assicurazione mediterranea vista da Ragusa, 1563–1591.* Rome: Jouvence.

Thompson, Grahame. 2003. *Between hierarchies and markets: The logic and limits of network forms of organization.* New York: Oxford University Press.

Thrupp, Sylvia. 1948. *The merchant class of medieval London (1300–1500).* Chicago: The University of Chicago Press.

Thrupp, Sylvia. 1967. *Early medieval society.* New York: Appleton-Century-Crofts.

Tilly, Charles. 1964. *The Vendée.* Cambridge, Mass.: Harvard University Press.

Tilly, Charles. 1990. *Coercion, capital, and European states A.D. 990–1990.* Oxford: Basil Blackwell.

Tilly, Charles. 2005. *Trust and rule.* Cambridge: Cambridge University Press.

Tocqueville, Alexis de. 1952. *L'ancien régime et la revolution.* Paris: Gallimard.

Trennerry, Charles F. 1926. *The origin and early history of insurance.* London: P. S. King and Son Ltd.

Udovitch, Abraham. 1962. "At the origin of the western commanda: Muslim, Israel, Byzantium." *Speculum* 37: 198–207.

Udovitch, Abraham. 1970a. "Commercial technique in early medieval Islamic trade." In *Islam and the trade of Asia*, edited by D. S. Richards. Oxford: Bruno Cassier; Philadelphia: University of Pennsylvania Press.

Udovitch, Abraham. 1970b. *Partnership and profit in early medieval Islamic trade.* Princeton, N.J.: Princeton University Press.

Udovitch, Abraham. 1977. "Formalism and informalism in the social and economic institutions of the medieval Islamic world." In *Individualism and conformity in the classical Islam*, edited by S. Vryonis. Wiesbaden: Harrasòwitz.

Udovitch, Abraham. 1978. "Time, the sea and society, duration of commercial voyages on the southern shores of the Mediterraean during the high Middle Ages." In *Navigazione mediterranea nell' alto Medioevo, Settimane di studio del centro Italiano di studi sull' alto Medioevo 14–20 Avril 1977.* Spoleto: Presso La Sede del centro.

Udovitch, Abraham. 1979. "Bankers without banks: Commerce, banking, and society in the Islamic world of the Middle Ages." In *The dawn of modern banking.* New Haven and London: Yale University Press.

Usher, Abbott P. 1943. *The early history of deposit banking in Mediterranean Europe.* Cambridge, Mass.: Harvard University Press.

Uzzi, Brian. 1996. "The sources and consequences of embeddedness for the economic performance of organizations: The network effect." *American Sociological Review* 61: 674–98.

Vercauteren, Fernand. 1967. "The circulation of merchants in Western Europe from the 6th to the 10th century: Economic and cultural aspects." In *Early medieval society*, edited by Sylvia Thrupp. New York: Appleton-Century-Crofts.

Verlinden, Charles. 1955. *L'esclavage dans l'Europe médievale: Italie, colonies Italiennes du Levant, Levant Latin, Empire Byzantin.* Bruges: De Tempel.

Verlinden, Charles. 1974. "A propos de la place des juifs dans l'économie de l' Europe occidentale aux IXème et Xème siècles." In *Storiografia e storia. Studi in onore di Eugenio Dupre Theiseder.* Rome: Bulzoni.

Violante, Cinzio. 1974. *La societa milanese nell'eta precomunale.* Rome: Bari.

Vitale, Vito. 1949. "Vita e commercio nei notai Genovesi dei secoli XII e XIII." *ASLI* 72.

Vitale, Vito. 1951. *Il comune del podesta.* Milan: Riccardo Riccardi.

Vitale, Vito. 1955. *Breviario della storia di Genova; lineamenti storici ed orientamenti bibliografici.* Genoa: Societa Ligure di Storia Patria.

Wallerstein, Immanuel Maurice. 1976. *The modern world-system: Capitalist agriculture and the origins of the European world-economy in the sixteenth century.* New York: Academic Press.

Wasserman, Stanley, and Katherine Faust. 1994. *Social network analysis: Methods and applications.* Cambridge and New York: Cambridge University Press.

Weber, Max. 1978. *Economy and society.* Berkeley: University of California Press.

Westermann, William L. 1930. "Warehousing and trapezite banking in antiquity." *Journal of Economic and Business History* 3: 30–54.

White, Douglas, and Frank Harary. 2001. "The cohesiveness of blocks in social networks: Node connectivity and conditional density." *Sociological Methodology* 31: 305–59.

White, Harrison C. 1981. "Where do markets come from?" *The American Journal of Sociology* 87: 517–47.

White, Harrison C. 1985. "Agency as control." In *Principal and agents: The structure of business*, edited by J. W. Pratt and R. J. Zeckhauser. Boston: Harvard Business School Press.

White, Harrison C. 2002. *Markets from networks.* Princeton, N.J.: Princeton University Press.

White, Harrison C. 2008. *Identity and control: A structural theory of social action.* Princeton, N.J.: Princeton University Press.

White, Harrison C., Scott A. Boorman, and Ronald L. Breiger. 1976. "Social structure from multiple networks. I. Blockmodels of roles and positions." *The American Journal of Sociology* 81: 730–80.

Windolf, Paul, and Jurgen Beyer. 1996. "Co-operative capitalism: Corporate networks in Germany and Britain." *The British Journal of Sociology* 47: 205–31.

Wolff, Philippe. 1986. *Automne du Moyen Age ou printemps des temps nouveaux. L'économie Européenne aux XIVème et XVème siècles.* Paris: Aubier.

Woloch, Isser. 1994. *New regime: Transformation of the French civic order, 1789–1820s.* New York: W. W. Norton.

Yamey, Basil S. (Ed.). 1978. *The historical development of accounting: A selection of papers.* New York: Arno Press.

Young, Peyton H. 1998. *Individual strategy and social strucuture: An evolutionary theory of institutions.* Princeton, N.J.: Princeton University Press.

Zeliser, Viviana A. 1985. *Pricing the priceless child: The changing social value of children.* New York: Basic Books.

Zucker, Lynne, and Carolyn Rosenstien. 1981. "Taxonomies of institutional structure: Dual economy reconsidered." *American Sociological Review* 46(6): 869–84.

# Index